MW00335943

Praise for *Legacy*

"*Legacy of Darkness and Light* is not only fascinating and full of provocative insights but also a thoroughly enjoyable read. Michael Gellert's understanding of the importance of the god complex in the contemporary psyche and the world is presented in a very clear, down-to-earth, and convincing way. With his impressive erudition and unique perspective on facts we all know but don't interpret deeply enough, he conveys a real 'feel' for this complex and its manifestations. Most revolutionary is his radical approach to political and historical events as the collective acting out of a deeply rooted psychological complex. If you want to learn a new and timely way of looking at and thinking about the world around you, read this book."

—Gary Granger, Humanities Professor Emeritus,
Vanier College, Montreal

"Exploring the biblical God's impact on Western and Islamic civilization, this is a remarkable book. It shows how the Yahweh complex—named after the god of the Hebrew Bible or Old Testament—emerges in modern times in the lives of Sigmund Freud, Marilyn Monroe, the Beatles, the Rolling Stones, Bob Dylan, Winston Churchill, and many others. This fine book also helps us to recognize and live with our own Yahweh complex."

—David H. Rosen, MD, Author of *Transforming Depression*
and *The Tao of Jung*

"Gellert approaches his subject from a secular perspective, blending psychological analysis with cultural criticism, and his buoyant prose remains accessible even when discussing heady concepts . . . a compelling read. One comes away with the sense that while humans may be made in Yahweh's image, that isn't necessarily a good thing. A fascinating exploration of what the God of the Old Testament might tell us about ourselves."

—*Kirkus Reviews*

"This book is a powerful exposition of a dangerous complex that possesses many political leaders. I wish all aspiring politicians would read Michael Gellert's important book. It reveals the feet of clay of many people in positions of power."

—Lionel Corbett, MD, Professor of Psychology,
Pacifica Graduate Institute, and Author of
The God-Image: From Antiquity to Jung

"*Legacy of Darkness and Light* is an intense, serious, and sophisticated book. It is a stunning description of how the world works from a viewpoint you have probably never considered. It will reclassify your perceptions in a truly deepening way."

—Ann Walker, PhD, Book Review Editor, *Psychological Perspectives: A Journal of Global Consciousness Integrating Psyche, Soul, and Nature*

"In a powerful, fearless text about the human condition, Michael Gellert confronts us with sweeping views of history as well as up-close, personal encounters with our darkness. Through the prisms of our flawed selves, he shows how light can emerge, giving us a sense of individual significance and a capacity for the making of meaning. Together with his intense, ruthless insights, he offers compassionate illustrations of personhood in a process of becoming."

—Beverley Zabriskie, Jungian Analyst,
Jungian Psychoanalytic Association, New York

"Reading any book of Michael Gellert's will take precious moments of your life that you will never regret."

—Charles T. Zeltzer, PhD, Jungian Analyst and Alchemy Scholar

Praise for Earlier Books by Michael Gellert

Far From This Land: A Memoir about Evolution, Love, and the Afterlife

"Michael Gellert's wonderful new book is a fine testament to the power of illness to transform us. An illness itself is an altered state of consciousness. I greatly admire Michael's ability to use his own struggles to help and to heal others. This book is a delightful treat for all of us who are fascinated by the incredible healing powers of the unconscious mind."

—Raymond A. Moody, Jr., MD, PhD, Author of *Life After Life*, Research Pioneer who coined the term "near-death experience"

"A most unconventionally convincing story, so breathtaking that I had to periodically pause to come up for air."

—Barbara Brown Taylor, *New York Times*-Bestselling Author of *Holy Envy* and *Learning to Walk in the Dark*

"*Far From This Land* is one of the most profound and eloquent rebuttals of materialism to appear in this century. Psychoanalyst Michael Gellert's experience during brain surgery opened doors to the nature of consciousness foreshadowed in the works of Pierre Teilhard de Chardin and C. G. Jung. This book is a beautiful, towering accomplishment, and a powerful response to the challenges our species faces at this critical hinge of history."

—Larry Dossey, MD, Author of *One Mind: How Our Individual Mind Is Part of a Greater Consciousness and Why It Matters*

The Divine Mind: Exploring the Psychological History of God's Inner Journey
Winner of the Nautilus Book Award

"Michael Gellert reads God's inner journey from the pages of scripture—Jewish, Christian, and Muslim—into its continuation in three mystical traditions and on down to our own day. An engrossing account, enriched by Jungian psychology, that makes God's journey a persuasive metaphor for our own."

—Jack Miles, Pulitzer Prize–Winning Author of *God: A Biography*

"In this fascinating account, Michael Gellert applies depth psychology and trauma theory to Yahweh's inner journey from trauma to redemption, a journey that parallels the evolution of our consciousness as well. This creative, engaging book seems especially relevant to our time, when the Abrahamic religions and their patriarchal assumptions are so frequently in our daily news cycle—seeking transformation and redemption like the Yahwistic God himself."

—Donald Kalsched, Author of *The Inner World of Trauma* and
Trauma and the Soul

"Michael Gellert offers a road map that leads from the mind's myriad projections to the enigmatic soul and its own origin. Crossing some fascinating and at times painful terrain, he brings the reader into silent realms of contemplation, and concludes his book on a joyful, mystical note. It is an intriguing book, to put it mildly."

—Vraje Abramian, Translator of *Nobody, Son of Nobody: Poems of Sheikh Abu-Saeed Abil Kheir* and *Winds of Grace: Poetry, Stories and Teachings of Sufi Mystics and Saints*

America's Identity Crisis: The Death and Rebirth of the American Vision
(Originally published as *The Fate of America*)
Winner of the Nautilus Book Award

"Our nation leads the world in the race for ever-increasing technological capacity and excellence. Why is it we are not equally dominant in the race for spiritual excellence? This fascinating, insightful, psychological profile of the American psyche offers answers that both enlighten and stimulate."

—Governor Mario Cuomo, Author of *Why Lincoln Matters*

"A large-scale analysis of this country on a par with Tocqueville . . . an important book. It raises serious questions about our country, makes perceptive observations about our culture, and provokes us to look inside ourselves in a critical, yet constructive, way."

—Howard Zinn, Author of *A People's History of the United States*

"This is a book of profound and timely importance. Michael Gellert delineates the dilemma facing contemporary America with the insight of a scholar and the heart of a sage."

—Selwyn Mills, PhD, Author of *The Odd Couple Syndrome*

Modern Mysticism: Jung, Zen and the Still Good Hand of God

"A psychotherapist writes that rarest of works—a look at the wondrous and mysterious worlds of the unconscious mind, moving from the paranormal to the highest spiritual experience."

—Sophy Burnham, Author of *A Book of Angels*

"Gellert takes you with him, into the whale's belly and out! His experience in Calcutta is extraordinary—not to be wished for and not to be missed!"

—Diane Wolkstein, Author of *The First Love Stories*

"An innovative and important approach to psychic phenomena. Challenges the present-day psychological conception of projections in a refreshing and thought-provoking manner."

—Nathan Schwartz-Salant, Author of *The Borderline Personality* and *Narcissism and Character Transformation*

Legacy of Darkness and Light: Our Cultural Icons and Their God Complex

by Michael Gellert

ISBN 978-1-64663-973-1

Published by

◤ köehlerbooks™

3705 Shore Drive
Virginia Beach, VA 23455
800-435-4811
www.koehlerbooks.com

LEGACY OF
DARKNESS
AND LIGHT

Our Cultural Icons and
Their God Complex

MICHAEL GELLERT

VIRGINIA BEACH
CAPE CHARLES

In memory of Paul Babarik and Marshall McLuhan,
bold pioneers in the study of human community and culture

When there is a light in the darkness which comprehends the darkness, darkness no longer prevails. The longing of the darkness for light is fulfilled only when the light can no longer be rationally explained by the darkness. For the darkness has its own peculiar intellect and its own logic, which should be taken very seriously. Only the "light which the darkness comprehendeth not" [John 1:5] can illuminate the darkness. Everything that the darkness thinks, grasps, and comprehends by itself is dark; therefore it is illuminated only by what, to it, is unexpected, unwanted, and incomprehensible.

—*C. G. Jung*

The degree of character flexibility, the ability to open oneself to the outside world or to close oneself to it, depending on the situation, constitutes the difference between a reality-oriented and a neurotic character structure.

—*Wilhelm Reich*

The god that you most revere is the god that you see.

—*Patricia Berry*

CONTENTS

PROLOGUE

The God of Our Fathers

God is no saint, strange to say. There is much to object to in
him, and many attempts have been made to improve him.
Much that the Bible says about him is rarely preached from
the pulpit because, examined too closely, it becomes a scandal.
But if only some of the Bible is actively preached, none of
the Bible is quite denied. On the improbably unexpurgated
page, God remains as he has been: the original who was the
Faith of our Fathers and whose image is living still within us
as a difficult but dynamic secular ideal.

—Jack Miles

My father, Leslie, had a special wisdom. He had an ability to see into
the heart of many things, often dealing with them based on what
he felt in his own heart. On one occasion, when I was four years old, I
was feeling especially adventuresome. It was a Sunday morning, and on
Sunday mornings Leslie always took a long, hot bath while reading the
newspaper with a small support cushion under his neck.

I needed to urinate, and I could do so while he took his bath. The toilet
was right next to the bathtub, and as I stood facing it, a tantalizing thought
entered my mind. I said, "Dad, what would you do if I peed on you?"

Remaining absorbed in his paper and not even looking at me, he said,
"I don't believe you would do such a thing."

Pondering his disbelief, I said, "Do you dare me?"

Still fixated on his paper, he lackadaisically said, "You wouldn't dare."

And with that I turned my little fountain of youth upon him, laughing
and gleefully spraying his newspaper and hands with the precision of a
fireman putting out a fire. ("How bold one gets when one is sure of being

1

loved," a young Freud wrote his fiancée.) The paper went down suddenly into the water, and my daredevil attitude sprayed his hairy chest.

He bolted up and screamed at me in Hungarian, "I don't believe it! Are you crazy!?" An anger like I had never seen shot out from his eyes, and I realized I had done something terribly wrong. Frightened, I ran out of the bathroom and hid in my room for the rest of the morning. I do not remember the later events of the day, but I know that there were no consequences. Leslie never pursued the matter, and it was never mentioned or discussed.

Some forty years later, I was visiting my parents at their condo in Florida. Leslie and I were on lounge chairs, relaxing by the pool and enjoying the sun. I was reading a book, and he was, as usual, reading his paper. For some reason, my mind fell upon the old memory, now crusty from never having been spoken about and put to words.

"Dad," I said, "do you remember when I was a little kid and peed on you in the bathtub?"

He looked at me and said, "Of course I remember."

"How come you never did anything about it?"

Without missing a beat, he said, "Because I realized that the only punishment fitting for such a crime was to kill you, and because you were my only beloved son, I knew I couldn't do that, so I let the matter drop."

I can still hear the soft, deep timbre of his voice.

The Other Side of Something that Glitters

Leslie did not always exercise such control over his rage. I will never forget my first encounter with it in an unrestrained form. It was not too long after the event I described above. He came home one late afternoon in a huff, telling my mother that he had to miss going to synagogue. I can't remember anything else he said. I knew it wasn't a Friday-evening, welcome-the-Sabbath service, because I went to synagogue with him every Friday evening (waiting, with all the other kids, for that special moment to run up to the cantor after his blessing of the wine and get a little cup of it, a sweet wine for the occasion). Somehow, I knew I wasn't supposed to go on this particular visit to synagogue. Later I was able to piece together that he probably missed attending a Yizkor service at which he could recite the Mourner's Kaddish, the memorial prayer, on the anniversary of his father's death. He would do so in front of the unveiled scrolls of the Hebrew Bible—or, as it is commonly known, the Old Testament.

Leslie put his skull cap on his head and with prayer book in hand came into the living room where I was. He was going to conduct his own private prayer service, which, of course, I did not at the time understand. Now, this happened to coincide with the hour of one of my favorite events of the day. It was time for *The Howdy Doody Show!* I turned on the TV in great anticipation. Leslie brusquely told me to turn it off.

"But it's *The Howdy Doody Show*," I protested.

"Turn it off!" he said in a raised voice.

"No! I want to watch *Howdy Doody!*"

All of a sudden, Leslie lunged toward me and started beating me. My mind was spinning. The blows to my body and head came in rapid succession. My mother started screaming at him to stop. He was kicking me. She got in between his flailing arms and my little body, trying to protect me. I could sense her fear (probably as much for her own safety as for mine, and possibly for the safety of my brother, whom she may have been pregnant with at the time). The theme song from the show filled the air: "It's Howdy Doody time, it's Howdy Doody time." I tried to get away from him, but I caught a blow that sent me headlong into the television set. The set was typical of the 1950s, made with a wood box that had pointy corners. My temple went into one of the corners.

I vaguely recall the sensation of falling as I collided with the TV. I can remember nothing else, as if my mind buried the rest of the trauma to protect me. I imagine there must have been blood. I was not taken to the hospital, though I should have been. I should have been given stitches. An indented scar sat like a small crater in my temple for the next thirty years, until it finally faded in with the rest of my skin. But my memory of the event never faded. I knew even then that I'd always remember it.

In my adolescence, as I learned of Leslie's history as a prisoner who had been tortured by the Arrow Cross, the Hungarian Nazis, I came to understand his rage. At least, I came to understand it better. After all, there were many Holocaust survivors who managed to get through life without such explosions of violence. Only much later would I understand that something else was at work here that melded in with his war trauma.

The Stormy God Within Us: What This Book Is About

Who was this man who could be not only a loving father but also a monster—a monster who in his devotion to God almost became the devil? And moreover, who was this God who could permit this to happen and perhaps even condone it? Was it he who cast a spell on Leslie?

> His sneezings flash lightning
> And his eyes are like the glimmerings of dawn.
> Firebrands stream from his mouth;
> Fiery sparks escape.
> Out of his nostrils comes smoke
> As from a steaming, boiling cauldron.
> His breath ignites coals;
> Flames blaze from his mouth.
> Strength resides in his neck;
> Power leaps before him.
> The layers of his flesh stick together;
> He is as though cast hard; he does not totter.
> His heart is cast hard as a stone,
> Hard as the nether millstone.
> Divine beings are in dread as he rears up;
> As he crashes down, they cringe.

Thus did God speak to Job when he praised his most awesome creature, Leviathan, the monster of the sea. But it was not only God's beasts, Leviathan and Behemoth, who were monstrous. The dark side of God himself is revealed in stark terms throughout the Hebrew Bible, the one scripture that is mutually venerated by the three Abrahamic religions—Judaism, Christianity, and Islam. He often behaved in primitive ways, erupting in temper tantrums and meting out his wrath without moral consideration. His propensity toward evil on the largest scale was demonstrated by his apocalyptic flood—a final Apocalypse thereafter becoming a general feature of the Abrahamic belief system and a particular one intrinsic to the Yahweh complex.*

In addition to the near-total genocide of the deluge, Yahweh commanded the Israelites to commit numerous wholesale genocides in order to secure the Promised Land and to eliminate the threat of his chosen people being tempted by others who worshipped the rival gods of whom he was jealous. He was an explosive, brutal, and psychologically *young* God, and not the loving, equanimous, perfect being many today look to in their faith. As Freud caustically put it, he "was certainly a volcano-god. . . . an uncanny, bloodthirsty demon who walks by night and shuns the light of day." Yahweh's monsters, after all, were but symbolic, poetic ways to speak about his wild and dangerous nature.

This book is about the Abrahamic God's dark side and its impact

---

* As the term "evil" will appear in various contexts in this book, it may be helpful to provide a modern definition of it that is not circumscribed by theological language. What is evil? As journalist Lance Morrow writes, defining evil can be compared to defining pornography. Asked to define the latter in an obscenity case, US Supreme Court justice Potter Stewart said he couldn't define it, but he knew it when he saw it. For our purposes, I offer the following psychological definition that I use in my work as a psychotherapist (and here I use the psychological term "individuation" to signify personal development with an aim toward becoming the individual whom one is meant to become and whose identity is distinct from general, collective psychology): Evil is whatever we willfully or unconsciously do to stand in the way of another's individuation, well-being, or ability to thrive. At its worst, it is the active impulse to destroy their soul or psyche, the seat of their individuation, well-being, and ability to thrive. The fact that we may direct it against ourselves makes it no less evil. In either scenario, evil is the tyranny of anti-individuation.

on us. I wish to illustrate that this small but potentially deadly episode with my father was an expression of something that has been going on, in different forms, for a very long time. Many of our fathers have been instruments of God's dark side. That is because, psychologically speaking, they have lived under the roof of the same God. This God is himself a father to both them and their fathers, going all the way back to Abraham—the founding patriarch to whom the Abrahamic religions owe their origins—if not further. He is *the* Father, the one whom we address when we say, "Our Father who art in heaven." He is known as Yahweh (sometimes mispronounced as "Jehovah") in the Hebrew Bible, the Father in the New Testament, and Allah in the Qur'an.

What Leslie did to me was something that *happened to* him, that *seized* him. This is not to wash away his personal and moral responsibility for his action. Rather, this is to connect his action to a larger force that has come down to us through history. Rage like the kind he unfurled is built into the temperaments of Jews, Christians, and Muslims, just like it is built into the temperament of their mutually shared God, and these human and divine temperaments are related. It is true that peoples who have no connection to the Abrahamic religions are fully capable of rage, too, and often this is indistinguishable from Yahwistic rage.[*] It is also true that in the pantheons of other peoples, there are gods who, like Yahweh, blessed their wars and conquests. But there are significant differences that make Yahweh unique.

For one thing, he is not worshipped as one among other gods, balanced by them in their various roles; he is worshipped as the one and only God, who combines all roles. This endows him with an absolute authority and vitality heretofore unimagined. Though biblical scholars can trace the distinct, ancient Near Eastern gods who were merged together in the Israelite tradition to create Yahweh, this historicism does little to detract from the power that this new megapersonality held and still holds

---

* By the terms "Yahwistic" and "Yahwist," I do not mean, as biblical scholars do, the Jahwist or "J" author or school that, together with at least three other authors or schools, are believed to have written the Hebrew Bible. I use these terms in a psychological sense to signify the person who has a Yahweh complex or behaves like Yahweh.

over the many heirs of the Abrahamic heritage. The new whole was greater than the sum of its old parts.

On the ancient Near Eastern scene, Yahweh was a supergod who acted in ways and with purposes not yet witnessed. His unpredictable, stormy temperament consisted of more than merely the furies of nature or human nature projected onto him. His rage went well beyond the pale of other gods, too. His actions represented more than simply the Israelite version of the vengeful acts Greek gods inflicted against humans for their insults to them.

His wrath was filled with torment and deep resentment rooted in his being rejected by his creatures, and it struck with a personal sting yet with blind indifference. To this day, it is central to the divine mystery itself and is the raison d'être for the core religious attitude of all the Abrahamic traditions: in the Psalmist's words, "The fear of the Lord is the beginning of wisdom."

Of course, I would not say that the force that seized Leslie was literally the ancient Yahweh. Instead, he was gripped by the Yahweh complex—that is, a god complex that takes on the specific features of Yahweh. The idea of a god complex is not new in psychology. Someone with a god complex tends to be inflated, arrogantly believing that their abilities, knowledge, and opinions are infallible—even when the facts prove otherwise. Sometimes they believe they are specially privileged and permitted to do things others are not. This gives their self-delusion a narcissistic and sociopathic quality.

But with its distinct features, the Yahweh complex is a unique kind of god complex. It is modeled on the personality of Yahweh, a god whose role as creator quickly became overshadowed by that of a judge and warrior. In his judgments, he was frequently rigid and harsh, and in his punishments, petty and draconian (he was merciless with petty thieves, revealing how petty he himself could be). As a warrior, he was ruthless and savage. "The Lord is a man of war," the Hebrew Bible tells us. He was also emotionally needy and wounded, for which he compensated by demonstrating his power, as often against his chosen people as on their behalf. He was, again, not the exalted, omniscient, and perfect being many people today imagine God to be. Flawed in all-too-human ways, he was, as literary critic Northrop Frye observed, "not a theological god at all but an intensely human character as violent and unpredictable as King Lear."

Hence, the Yahweh complex doesn't always look like a god complex, and to the uninformed person's eye, it may appear merely as nasty human behavior. Or, among its more nuanced features that set it apart from other god complexes, it can make us gloomy and withdrawn, like Yahweh himself often was. Either way, it doesn't necessarily exude the inflation and pseudo-confidence that typify a god complex.

Like an inferiority, persecution, martyr, Napoleon, or other complex, the Yahweh complex has a life of its own, exerting its influence on us whether we like it or not and whether we are aware of it or not. The Yahweh complex does not make us *think* we are Yahweh the way, for example, a person with a messianic complex thinks that he or she has a special calling to help or save others at all costs. Rather, it makes us have the *attitudes*, *emotional style*, and *behaviors* of Yahweh, regardless of whether we recognize these as such. The Yahweh complex is Yahweh's personality within our own; it is, so to speak, Yahweh in us—an "inner other," a godlike force within our own psyches.

Unlike most other complexes, the Yahweh complex can operate collectively as well as individually, affecting sizable groups of people at the same time under the right circumstances. Jung might say that it is a collective and archetypal war-god complex similar to the Wotan complex that took hold of Nazi Germany and that was modeled upon the Teutonic or early-Germanic, tribal war-god Wotan, known in Scandinavia as Odin. Like the Wotan complex, the Yahweh complex has many functions in addition to war. Having traveled down to us through history via the collective psyche, it includes ingredients of both collective consciousness (that which we are all aware of) and the collective unconscious (that which we aren't). Though knowledge about Yahweh is accessible to us through our collective consciousness—through our scriptures and religious institutions—knowledge of our Yahweh complex largely escapes us as it inhabits the collective unconscious, a mysterious domain whose depth is difficult to fathom.*

It is important that we begin to understand how this complex, so prevalent and yet so overlooked, can influence us. Whether or not we still worship and think of God strictly according to our Abrahamic traditions, or for that matter even believe in him, the Yahweh complex can drive us to unconsciously act out the primitive attitudes, emotions, and behaviors that he typically demonstrates in the Hebrew Bible. If we fall into the grip of this complex, it can make us behave in the angry, controlling, power-driven way Yahweh often behaved. We will imitate his perfectionistic expectations, patriarchal authoritarianism, amorality, judgmental harshness, punitiveness, and drive to dominate others. In shaping our relationship to our own humanity as well as to others, the Yahweh complex can have detrimental effects on our culture, our organizations, and—when it possesses our leaders, as it often does—our public and international affairs. The Yahweh complex may well be the most influential complex of all.

A Brief History of the Biblical God

Our case studies will be mostly of various historical figures and cultural icons we are familiar with—rather than patients from my practice as a Jungian analyst—so that it may become evident how widespread the Yahweh complex is and how dark and dangerous it can be.** However, the fact that

---

* A definition of Jung's core concepts of the archetype and the collective unconscious may be called for here: to keep it simple, we can think of archetypes as instincts of the psyche. They developed in human evolution, as did all instincts, and hence act upon us forcefully. A war-god complex is archetypal because it behaves as an instinct does (in particular, the instinct for war). The collective unconscious is a layer of the mind that is below the individual's ego and personal unconscious. It is not unique to each of us the way the ego and personal unconscious are but is inherited and universally shared in common. It may be thought of as the psyche's storehouse of the archetypes.

** A word about my use of the terms "Jungian analyst" and "psychoanalyst": practitioners of the Freudian or neo-Freudian schools of psychology will be referred to as psychoanalysts, while practitioners of the Jungian school will be referred to as Jungian analysts, although some today refer to both simply as psychoanalysts or analysts.

the complex is so pervasive is not to suggest that it is responsible for all bad behavior. I rely on these diverse cases to illustrate specific kinds of behavior that fall under the rubric of this god complex, and at least in two instances (Marilyn Monroe and the Rolling Stones) to illustrate what is distinctly *not* the Yahweh complex but instead other god complexes interacting with it.

Because the following pages deal with a particular god complex, it is necessary to have some familiarity with the particular god upon whom it is modeled. Since this god is a complex one, it would be helpful to have at least a superficial knowledge of his complicated character so that we can distinguish the finer aspects of the complex as they emerge in the case studies. A few words about his origin and development are thus in order.

Bear in mind that what I will say here is only one interpretation of the story in the Hebrew Bible and only one view of God's nature as conveyed by that story. Much is inferred about him based not only on his declarations and actions but also on the feeling tone of the various, smaller books that comprise the Hebrew Bible. That feeling tone—whether the exaltation of the Book of Exodus, the sense of frustration and humiliation in the prophetic books, or the despair of the Book of Lamentations—hints at God's own feelings and emotional states *indirectly* and *by association*. If the people, or at least the authors, of the Hebrew Bible feel sad or deflated or abandoned, the chances are that God does too. Through his declarations and actions, as well as his silence and absence, he makes them feel the way he does. His wrath, however, operates differently. That erupts when nothing else motivates the people to give up their idols.

Scripture doesn't tell us much about what Yahweh was like before creation. Jack Miles, the acclaimed author of *God: A Biography*, notes his unique history of isolation, describing him as a "cosmic orphan." He was different than the Greek and other ancient gods: he had no parents or siblings. Other scholars add that he was lonely. He created the universe and humanity as a way to end his loneliness. In short, the biblical God knew nothing about relationships, about how to relate to others. His "onlyness" and complete otherness did not help him bridge his gap with the humanity whose devotion he so craved.

The Hebrew Bible is essentially the story of a lonely God seeking the fidelity of all of humanity at first and, when this failed to work, the Israelites in specific. It is the unfolding drama of a God who has claimed a particular people as his own, but a people who cannot keep their faithfulness to this one God above all the others who populated the ancient Near East. The more they resisted his overtures, the more angry and punitive he became. He complained loudly and frequently. "I the Lord thy God," he admitted, "am a jealous God visiting the iniquity of the fathers upon the children unto the third and fourth generation of them that hate me." He was not only a hurt and wounded God but also a vengeful and bullying one; not only saturnine but bitter.

For centuries he and his people went back and forth in an impassioned, approach-avoidance relationship: the people would reject him, and he would punish them; they would repent, and he'd forgive them. And the cycle would repeat, eventually culminating in Yahweh's orchestration of the Babylonian captivity, a punishment directly involving some ten thousand citizens but indirectly affecting all of them. As these ten thousand were mostly prominent members of society, including priests, professionals, craftsmen, and the wealthy, the Babylonian exile was an apocalyptic event on the same order as slavery in Egypt. This polar tension between God and his chosen people drives the story of the Hebrew Bible forward until its end when a truce, a new kind of covenant, is made between them and each redeems the other. (Miles shows how this victorious climax contrasts with the conclusion of the Old Testament, a Christian version of the original Hebrew Bible and an alteration that downplays that redemption so that, supposedly, Jesus could come and initiate it instead.)

In the course of all this, Yahweh's roles change, and his personality and character evolve. At first he is the *creator*. Together with Adam and Eve, he dwells in the Garden of Eden (the Bible portrays him strolling there in the afternoon breeze). When he exiles Adam and Eve from this garden for eating from the tree of the knowledge of good and evil, he goes into exile with them (or so the Talmud states) and similarly leaves behind *his* paradisaic condition. In other words, when Adam and Eve fell, *they took God down with them*. He now experiences the torment of his disappointment with humanity; hence comes Noah's flood. With his choice of Abraham, he decides to focus on a single people—rather than all of humanity—with whom to develop a special relationship.

With the Exodus from Egypt, the "House of Bondage," Yahweh leads his people out of slavery. (Why he allowed them to be enslaved in the first place is unclear. Perhaps it was a test of their faithfulness or part of his plan to save and impress them.) Establishing the 613 Mosaic laws as a way to organize their devotion to him, he becomes a *lawmaker*. He confines the people for forty years in the Sinai desert so that there can emerge a new, post-slavery generation without the habit of worshipping other gods. Then he leads them into Canaan, the "Promised Land," where many battles must be fought to wrest the land from its inhabitants. He becomes the Israelites' commander in chief, a *war god*. (Now come the genocides, over seventy-five of them if decimating single cities counts as separate episodes. Though, to be fair, it should be said that the practice of killing all the inhabitants of a city that refused to surrender to its conqueror was widespread in the ancient Near East.)

Generations later, he still cannot win humanity's adulation. His "stiff-necked" people (as he now calls them), including their kings, perpetually sin by worshipping other gods. Through his prophets he warns them of the impending destruction he will inflict upon them—namely, the Babylonian exile. His plan for vengeance is focused like a laser beam:

> Lo, I am bringing against you, O House of Israel,
> A nation from afar. . . .
> They will devour your harvest and food,
> They will devour your sons and daughters,
> They will devour your flocks and herds,
> They will devour your vines and fig trees.
> They will batter down with the sword
> The fortified towns on which you rely.

And his rage is overwhelming, not to mention grotesque in its extremes:

> Assuredly, parents shall eat their children in your midst, and children shall eat their parents. I will execute judgments against you, and I will scatter all your survivors in every direction. . . . One-third of you shall die of pestilence or perish in your midst by famine, one-third shall fall by the sword around you, and I will scatter one-third in every direction and will unsheathe the sword after them. I will vent all My anger and satisfy My fury upon them; and when I vent all My fury upon them, they shall know that I the Lord have spoken in My passion.

If you doubt that Yahweh delights in his fury, consider his own confession: "A sword, a sword is sharpened and also polished, sharpened for slaughter, polished to flash like lightning! . . . Ah! it is made like lightning, it is polished for slaughter."

Or if you doubt his capacity for sadistic humor and pleasure, here is perhaps the Hebrew Bible's most clear indication of it: "The hand of the Lord lay heavy upon the Ashdodites, and He wrought havoc among them: He struck Ashdod and its territory with hemorrhoids. . . . He struck the people of the city, young and old, so that hemorrhoids broke out among them."

In his plight, Yahweh compares himself to a husband whose wife has cheated on him (a new role in addition to creator, lawmaker, and war god). He becomes a jilted lover, and Israel, with her wayward idolatry, is likened to a whore. "I was brokenhearted through their faithless hearts which turned away from Me," he says. A haunting melancholy can be detected in his silence and absence in the latter part of the Hebrew Bible. This appears to have been triggered by his encounter with Job, who, Jung argues, compels him to reflect on his dark side—his immorality, lack of empathy, and cruel, capricious behaviors (such as wiping out Job's family in a contest with Satan to see how faithful Job is). He seems to undergo a period of retreat during which he examines himself and recognizes, as if for the first time, how dark his dark side actually is. As Jung said, "If Job gains knowledge of God, then God must also learn to know himself. . . . Whoever knows God has an effect on him. . . . The encounter with the creature changes the creator."

Yahweh already knew he had such a side; after all, he acknowledged to the prophet Isaiah, "I form the light, and create darkness: I make peace, and create evil: I the Lord do all these things." His was not a case of the right hand not knowing what the left one was doing but rather, as Jung explains, an antinomy or walking contradiction: each hand knew what the other was doing and didn't care. He simply didn't see how his dark side emotionally and morally violated the very same people whom he wanted to be worshipped by. Seeing this now woke him up. His melancholic retreat forced him to look at himself. This depression was of course an existential one rather than a clinical one, probably similar if not identical to the gloom or dark mood that often swallows people who suffer from a Yahweh complex.

At this point, an event occurs that further makes possible the transformation and victorious climax mentioned above (since melancholy alone doesn't necessarily have this effect): a sublime wisdom emerges as Yahweh *reconnects to his feminine side*. The Book of Proverbs personifies this wisdom as Chochmah, the Israelite version of Sophia, the Greek goddess of wisdom. The ability to compassionately relate to others in their suffering is very much a feminine feature as well as a wise one. (It is therefore no accident that in both the Hebrew Bible and the Old Testament, the books of Job and Proverbs are in close proximity to each other.) Having been there all along, Chochmah is as primordial as Yahweh is. Merely, he has forgotten and has become alienated from her as a result of his going from paradise into exile in the world. Reconnecting to her, he becomes a reintegrated God who no longer has to chase humanity to give him the sense of wholeness he can now find within himself. Such wisdom is a virtue that is also evident in those who have a positive Yahweh complex, a topic we'll turn to momentarily.

To recap: In the beginning, God goes into exile from the Garden of Eden with Adam and Eve and finds himself in deep emotional trouble.

Disillusioned with humanity and its rampant sinfulness, he unleashes the flood in an attempt to initiate a new beginning. Trying a different approach to win humanity's devotion, he selects Abraham and his descendants to be his special people. Soon comes the traumatic enslavement of his people in Egypt. The Exodus marks another new beginning. But the Israelites, too, sin by turning to idols, this eventually leading to the punishment of the Babylonian exile.

At around this time, Yahweh appears to undergo a quiet but profound transformation in response to his encounter with Job: he becomes more ethical and compassionate. He reconnects with his feminine side, the goddess Chochmah. She makes him whole again, and with his ethical development and his feminine side reintegrated, his relationship with his people also changes. Gone are his overbearing emotional needs, his anxiety and drive to be in control. Gone are his volatile outbursts, his bitterness from being unloved, and his testing and punitive behaviors. The people themselves now find him more attractive and approachable so that their idolatry naturally recedes. The Hebrew Bible ends on a note of victory and redemption. Not only does God redeem humanity, but humanity redeems God—a final and genuine new beginning.

All told, we can discern seven stages in Yahweh's evolution, all of them, as we shall see, featuring elements integral to the Yahweh complex:

1. His rejection, first by humanity and then by his chosen people →
2. The unleashing of his wrath in response to their rejection of him (e.g., the flood) →
3. His redemptive mission to earn their devotion (the Exodus and conquest of the Promised Land) →
4. The will to power and domination (i.e., his forcing them to worship him by threat of punishment) →
5. The mission's failure (his defeat due to their idolatry, leading to the Babylonian exile) →
6. The retreat into melancholy →
7. The emergence of wisdom (victory; true redemption)

The Dual Nature of the Biblical God

It is important to keep in mind that in exploring how Yahweh's dark side has shaped our own, we should not disregard his generous spirit and innate goodness. We must remember that he had a positive side as substantial as his dark one; otherwise, the principle of evil would have one-sidedly ruled the world. His positive side has also been a role model, not only for us but also for the positive Yahweh complex. As biblical scholar Richard Elliott Friedman points out, Yahweh's own description of his positive features is reiterated in one form or another in numerous passages in the Hebrew Bible: "Yahweh, Yahweh, merciful and gracious God, long-suffering and abundant in kindness and truth, keeping faithfulness for thousands, forgiving iniquity, transgression, and sin."

Friedman further reminds us that the text is replete with examples of Yahweh's compassion and mercy: he blessed Sarah (she was infertile and then she conceived); he consoled Hagar when Sarah coerced Abraham to send her and her son, Ishmael, into the wilderness; he spared Sodom from destruction; he did in the end spare Isaac from being sacrificed as originally required; he blessed Abraham by giving him descendants as numerous as the stars; he blessed Jacob in manifold ways, not least of all with visionary foresight; he protected Joseph during his difficult years in Egypt and set him high in the court of the pharaoh; through his prophet Moses he emancipated his enslaved people and, exercising paternal patience, guided and took care of them for forty years in the desert; he eventually forgave David for murdering his own soldier, Uriah, in a scheme to marry the latter's wife, Bathsheba, whom the king had impregnated; and he oversaw the end of the Babylonian exile and the people's return and restoration.

Moreover, Yahweh's basic intent in creating the world and its creatures was good-natured: "And God saw all that He had made, and found it very good." One can sense in the opening pages of Genesis that he wished abundance for humankind. And that is just the Hebrew Bible. The famous first sentence of the Qur'an is "In the Name of Allah, the Compassionate, the Merciful," and it is thereafter repeated at the beginning of all one hundred and fourteen "suras," or chapters, except one. In two suras he is identified as *al-Wadûd*, "the Loving One." We should therefore not give short shrift to the Abrahamic God's bright and good side.

It is *this* side of him that informs the positive Yahweh complex, giving the complex a more textured, dimensional quality. Like Yahweh himself, the complex can be not only dark but also bright. We can see it at work in key developments that followed on the heels of Yahweh's entrance onto the stage of history. He naturally had a huge impact on the lives of people in biblical times, and this in turn has continued down to our own times through both a negative *and* a positive Yahweh complex. The positive Yahweh complex has played a contributing role in civilization with regard to at least four great, lasting developments in addition to the obvious ones that we know as Judaism, Christianity, and Islam:

1. It helped provide a bedrock of ethics that has survived to this day and that has been the primary source of Western morality and a touchstone for Islamic ethics.

2. It helped introduce the idea of progress into a world that was formerly seen as eternally repeating the annual, nature-bound cycle of the seasons without anything new ever occurring.

3. It helped initiate, as a counterpart to ethics and the idea of progress, an advancement of consciousness, in particular the differentiation of the ego and superego, or of self-reflective thought and moral conscience.

4. It helped create a blueprint for democracy that some scholars believe was more influential in shaping American democracy than Greece and the Roman Republic. (Here it is important to distinguish between a blueprint for democracy and democracy itself: the reign of Yahweh was essentially authoritarian, though he did allow the Israelite tribes to organize themselves in a self-determining way.)

Deep-seated complexes of the collective unconscious are not one-sidedly bad. They usually serve a positive, adaptive, or innovative purpose as well; otherwise, they would not have endured as long as they have in the multimillennial evolution of the mind. The same features that made ancient Israel stand out in a most dazzling way compared to most other Near Eastern cultures at that time also characterize the positive Yahweh complex.

Thus, the Yahweh complex is Yahweh's legacy in both its shades and as such is as dichotomous as Yahweh's own dual nature. This book focuses more on the negative Yahweh complex because it's the source of many problems and is more difficult to identify as the ancient inheritance that it is, both in individual and collective experience. But again, this doesn't mean that the positive Yahweh complex should be overlooked or minimized. For this reason, we will take a closer look at the positive side of the complex in the book's final part.

Let us now turn to this legacy of darkness and light, to this Yahweh complex or phenomenon of Yahweh-within-us.

I

YAHWEH IN OUR SOULS

An archetypal force has no true care for its human
incarnation. A power beyond the ego demands
such immense service that we must bleed for it.

—*James Hillman*

1

How to Recognize the Yahweh Complex

> Don't live in the past, my brother says, get on with your life.
> How do I tell him that I am contained in my past (and my past
> is contained in me)? Can I explain to him that the past is not
> a place I revisit, but my present and future home? . . . . [The]
> past and the future and the moment are one.
>
> —*Barbara Grizzuti Harrison*

B y the end of the Hebrew Bible, God has retreated from the stage of
history. He is no longer visibly active in the affairs of the world. His
miraculous interventions cease, and he goes silent, as he also does again
at the close of the New Testament and Qur'an. But his lack of miraculous
interventions and his silence do not mean that he is altogether gone. He is
still here—again, in the form of the Yahweh complex dwelling within us.

The phenomenon of a dark god complex is part of our inheritance
from biblical times. Although both Yahweh and his people have a
redemptive experience at the conclusion of the Hebrew Bible, the
full range of his experience—and of *our* experience of him—has been
imprinted in our collective unconscious, available to us as an inherited
predisposition. Regardless of whatever redemption occurred, his pre-
redeemed, tormented, and wrathful spirit continues to live on in our
psyches, haunting us like a ghost from the past. Novelist Salman Rushdie
writes, "Now I know what a ghost is. Unfinished business, that's what."

It is our business as descendants of the Abrahamic traditions to
complete with each new generation *our part* in the mutual redemption of
God and humanity, just like it is the business of Christians in particular
to carry their own cross even though Jesus has already been crucified. It is

21

our fateful challenge to actively remember what happened in the Hebrew Bible and personally master for ourselves the difficulties that this history has left for us as part of its legacy. For our purposes, this simply means that we must master our Yahweh complex.

All this goes to say that even though Yahweh no longer manifests with spectacular displays of power as he once did, his psychology still exerts a powerful grip on us unconsciously. His personality has for many generations become incorporated into our own. However, he is not only within us; he is also interpersonally between us and collectively all around us. Hardly any sphere of activity is unaffected by the Yahweh complex. It is the invisible, psychological environment in which Jews, Christians, and Muslims live—so much so that we take it for granted and don't recognize it for what it is. As the saying goes, the fish is the last to know it's in water.

Jung grasped the principle underlying such phenomena as the Yahweh complex when he said, "The gods have become diseases." By this he meant that when the gods disappeared as external forces that humankind worshipped, they reappeared in our behavior as symptoms. When Pan, for example, was declared dead in the ancient Greek world, he resurfaced in the form of our panic attacks. (It is no accident that the root of the word "panic" is "pan.") The power of the religious imagination cannot be denied and dismissed, even if its gods are. And so, similarly, Yahweh disappeared from the stage of history, but he and his torment continue to brew in our Abrahamic psyches in the form of our attitudes, emotional style, and behaviors. The vacuum that he left at the center of this stage has been filled with the Yahweh complex, perhaps our chief disease since ancient times.

This chapter offers a portrait of the core features of the Yahweh complex. Not all of these can be observed all of the time, and in any given instance, there may be features that manifest strongly but are more rare. The Yahweh complex is as complicated and diverse as the god it is modeled upon. A good way to begin is with a brief overview of the nature of complexes, and specifically god complexes.

What Is a "Complex"?

Complexes are clusters or systems of emotionally charged ideas, impulses, and feelings that give rise to particular behaviors. Freud defined them as "circles of thoughts and interests of strong affective value." Certainly, they operate as closed systems with the same thoughts and emotions recurring persistently regardless of how irrational, destructive, or unhealthy these may be, and their most recognizable feature is their affect. They can flood us with their feeling states and moods. Probably the most famous complexes are the Freudian Oedipus complex and the Adlerian inferiority complex. Like all complexes, each of these has its own unique preoccupation and agenda.

Jung thought of complexes as autonomous subpersonalities within our overall personality. With a will of their own, they shape our perceptions and influence our actions. They are such prevalent psychic forces that he at one time called his school of psychology "complex psychology."

Freud and Adler assumed that complexes originate in the ego and are then repressed in the unconscious because they are unacceptable either to society or to our own self-esteem or both. Jung, however, believed that certain complexes, though having their origins in some historical experience, exist in the collective unconscious and are transmitted intergenerationally through it. They then become active and apparent when something in our conscious, current experience constellates or triggers them. Jung cautions us about looking for the deeper causes of individual pathology in the wrong places:

> A collective problem, if not recognized as such, always appears as a personal problem, and in individual cases may give the impression that something is out of order in the realm of the personal psyche. The personal sphere is indeed disturbed, but such disturbances need not be primary; they may well be secondary, the consequence of an insupportable change in the social atmosphere. The cause

of disturbance is, therefore, not to be sought in the personal surroundings, but rather in the collective situation. Psychotherapy has hitherto taken this matter far too little into account.

When a complex belongs to the collective unconscious, it can be constellated or triggered not only by individuals but by an entire society. Because members in a given society tend to share the same collective complexes and are especially susceptible to them, they may be triggered simply by the power of suggestion. The feeling states generated by these complexes are thus highly contagious and can have a triggering effect in their own right.

At worst, this can lead to the kind of mass movement that Jung describes as a "psychic epidemic." He observed a classical example of this in the case of Nazism. He explains that the German people developed an inferiority complex when they emerged from the Danube Valley in the Middle Ages and founded the beginnings of their nation. Because this took place long after the French and the English were well on their way to nationhood, the Germans were late in the acquisition of colonies and in the establishment of an empire.

When they did finally become a unified nation, "they looked around them and saw the British, the French, and others with rich colonies and all the equipment of grown-up nations, and they became jealous, resentful, like a younger brother whose older brothers have taken the lion's share of the inheritance." Later, when the Germans lost the First World War, they were humiliated by a punitive Versailles Treaty. They were also suffering under oppressive conditions of unemployment and poverty during the Depression. All this triggered their collective inferiority complex. Most saliently, it was triggered in Hitler's psyche, but being a collective complex, it didn't take much for him, with his histrionic flair and gifted power of suggestion, to ignite it in the psyches of the millions who became his followers. With the strike of a match, Nazism became a psychic epidemic, spreading like a wildfire.

We shall later discuss another factor that gave rise to the Third Reich, but this one sufficiently illustrates how inflammable and contagious collective complexes can be. Of course, it does not explain the evil of Hitler and the Third Reich, but merely one of its mechanisms.

As almost all peoples have at one time or another worshipped gods who gave order and meaning to their lives, the god complex is not only collectively shared by a particular people but is also universal. Embedded deep in our psyches, it is hidden from our everyday awareness until some event or situation triggers it—and even then, we may not be aware of it. There are potentially as many types of god complexes as there are gods. (I once treated a patient who described her father as having a Poseidon complex. The father was not especially verbal the way Yahweh was, but like Poseidon, the Greek god of the sea and of earthquakes, he made the earth shake with his raw, primitive, explosive affect.)

The Yahweh complex in particular is passed down to us from our Abrahamic collective unconscious—that is, from the layer of the collective psyche that is shared by all Jews, Christians, and Muslims. The god complex in general is then simply a larger and more universal classification that is not specific to a particular god like Yahweh and to a specific culture or civilization. It usually manifests with the more elemental characteristics of inflation and omnipotence. However, it can also unleash the same destruction that is typical to the many nature and war gods of almost all our world's religious traditions. This side of the god complex is universal, too, even if there is no signature of a particular god.

The god complex was first identified by psychoanalyst Ernest Jones in 1913. Among its chief characteristics, he noted, are megalomania (fantasies of omnipotence and omniscience) and, in states of insanity, overt identification with God; its close connection to the father, so much so that it may be regarded as a magnification of the father complex or one's fixation upon the father (the idea of God also being, to orthodox Freudians, a magnified, idealized, and projected form of the father); a colossal narcissism (its most typical feature) and a narcissistic exhibitionism or display of personal power; excessive modesty (rather than pronounced vanity) to compensate its strong primitive tendencies; a tendency toward aloofness and toward surrounding oneself in a cloud of mystery and privacy to convey that one is apart from other mortals (observable with nobility, celebrity, popes, business tycoons, and power brokers who prefer to be the "man behind the throne," directing affairs from above while being invisible to the crowd); judgmental harshness; atheism (naturally so because the person with a god complex cannot suffer the existence of any other god); an exaggerated desire—though rarely shown—to be loved, praised, or admired (an expression of the narcissism); and finally, fantasies of creating a vastly improved or altogether ideal world.

Jones acknowledges that the type of god complex will vary according to the particular god with whom one identifies, Christ being most common in the West. "With this Christ type there invariably goes also an anti-Semitic tendency, the two religions [Judaism and Christianity] being contrasted and the old Hebraic Jehovah being replaced by the young Christ." (In a later chapter we will examine how Jesus's modification of Yahweh's moral standards intensified the Yahweh complex but, aside from this significant factor, did not essentially change it. A Christ complex is today understood as a messianic or savior complex, while the Yahweh complex is more invested in dominating or controlling others than in saving them.)

Jones also grants that the god complex has a positive side: he cites Friedrich Nietzsche and Percy Shelley as two examples whose god complex was guided and controlled by higher values, giving us men who were genuinely godlike in their grandeur and sublimity. Although Jones does not conceive of the god complex as a universal inborn predisposition and an autonomous agent in the psyche with a personality of its own as Jung later does, he states that our unconscious identification of ourselves with God is "not at all rare" and occurs "here and there" with all of us.

Truly, we may add that as early as the Book of Genesis, there was already some sense of this: the serpent tempted Eve with the promise that if she ate the forbidden fruit, her eyes would open and she would be like God. Similarly, the Tower of Babel is a biblical story of the human aspiration to reach the heavens and be like God. It is a tale of our hubris. The citizens of Babel build a tower so high that God sees fit to confuse them by multiplying their languages so that they can no longer understand each other and complete their city. The Greek myth of Icarus imparts the same warning about our proclivity to fly too high. Icarus fashions wings made with wax, and when he flies too close to the sun (disregarding the instructions of his father, Daedalus), the wax melts, and he comes crashing to the ground.

What Is the "Yahweh Complex"?

By 1934, Jung was, along with Jungian analysts Erich Neumann and James Kirsch, already speaking about the Yahweh complex as a particular form of the god complex. Not much is known about his thoughts about it, at least at the present time, and his writings have not yet been fully published. We do know that all three psychologists appear to have thought of it as a distinctly Jewish complex rather than, as we are treating it here, a core Abrahamic complex common to Judaism, Christianity, and Islam. They also seem to have thought of it solely as a collective neurosis instead of an important cultural development with positive features as well as negative ones. I imagine they thought of it as a fixed set of symptoms rather than the recapitulation of a biblical narrative with discernible stages of development such as the seven outlined in the previous chapter.

What distinguishes the Yahweh complex from the generic god complex? When Jungian analyst Edward Edinger refers to "a kind of Yahweh complex," he uses the term in its broadest sense as an indication of inflation and the anger that stems from it. In fact, he could be discussing any god complex, as he himself insinuates when he then also refers to the Greek tradition:

We can identify a state of inflation whenever we see someone (including ourselves) living out an attribute of deity, i.e., whenever one is transcending proper human limits. Spells of anger are examples of inflated states. The attempt to force and coerce one's environment is the predominant motivation in anger. It is a kind of Yahweh complex. The urge to vengeance is also identification with deity. At such times one might recall the [biblical] injunction, "'Vengeance is mine,' saith the Lord," i.e., not yours. The whole body of Greek tragedy depicts the fatal consequences when man takes the vengeance of God into his own hands.

As Edinger points out, the primary features of the Yahweh complex, as with Yahweh himself, include anger, the will to power (the "attempt to force and coerce one's environment"), and vengeance (a targeted form of anger). Of these, the power drive is the most insidious. When we are under its spell, we want what we want and refuse to take no for an answer, even if we have to lord our will over others. We strive for power, using and abusing it so that we can get even more of it. The thrill of power compensates our feeling powerless and inferior.

But such a gambit for power is illegitimate. The strength and self-worth it provides come not from the power of our personhood or a desire to authentically serve others but from the pseudo-power of our one-upmanship and control over others. And that one-upmanship and control must always be maintained so that we can continue to function in the role of God. As we have discussed, Yahweh very likely was driven by the will to power to compensate feelings of powerlessness and inferiority due to his rejection and failure to gain his people's undivided devotion.

However, other gods have these primary features too—Zeus, Hera, and Nemesis, to mention only a few—and so does the god complex in general. What makes the Yahweh complex unique is that it has something extra: under its influence, we manifest *Yahweh's* attitudes, emotional style, and behaviors and not only those of other gods; or we express an ideology directly or indirectly derived from the Israelite tradition that worshipped him.

When expressed as an ideology, the Yahweh complex most typically consists of a religious zeal or fanatical striving for perfection, moral or otherwise. There is a visionary purpose, a drive for progress that surpasses the achievements of previous history. Yahweh introduced the notion of progress into a Near Eastern world that had no linear conception of history moving forward and changing the past. He was not merely a historical god; he was the god of history. The Yahweh complex seizes our ambition and propels it forward in service to some holy mission that represents redemption, whether religious *or* secular, personal or collective. When secular, redemption is translated into a sense that we are self-validated. We are, finally, worthy. This yearning for redemption is a distinct heirloom of the Israelite tradition. At any rate, there must be something specifically related to Yahweh (or, as the case may be, to Allah) to make the god complex Yahwistic.

To highlight the difference between a god complex in general and the Yahweh complex in particular, we can compare two film characters. There can be no doubt that there are many people in the world like them. The first character is Dr. Jed Hill, played by Alec Baldwin in *Malice*. Accused of medical malpractice that he in fact committed (he was drinking before an operation he performed unnecessarily), he is asked in a deposition if he has a god complex. He responds:

> The question is, "Do I have a god complex?" . . . which makes me wonder if this *lawyer* has any idea as to the kind of grades one has to receive in college to be accepted at a top medical school. Or if you have the vaguest clue as to how talented someone has to be to lead a surgical team. I have an MD from Harvard. I am board certified in cardiothoracic medicine and trauma surgery. I have been awarded citations from seven different medical boards in New England, and I am never, ever sick at sea. So I ask you: when someone goes into that chapel and they fall on their knees and they pray to God that their wife doesn't miscarry, or that their daughter doesn't bleed to death, or that their mother doesn't suffer acute neural trauma from postoperative shock, who do you think they're praying to? Now, go ahead and read your Bible, *Dennis*, and you go to your church and with any luck you might win the annual raffle, but if you're looking for God, he was in operating room number two on November 17, and he doesn't like to be second-guessed. You ask me if I have a god complex? Let me tell you something: *I am God.*

The second character is Terence Fletcher, played by J. K. Simmons in *Whiplash*. A brash instructor at an elite East Coast music conservatory, he is known for his intimidating teaching methods. The following occurs during a practice session of the jazz band:

FLETCHER: Stop! [The band comes to a halt.] Now, this one upsets me. We have an out-of-tune player. Before I go any further, does that player want to do the right thing and reveal himself? [Silence.] Okay. Maybe a bug flew in my ear. Bar 115. Five-six-and— [He cues the band to begin again and then seconds after they do, he stops them.] No, I guess my ears are clean because we most definitely have an out-of-tune player. Whoever it is, this is your last chance. [He paces back and forth, slowly.] Either you know you are out of tune, and are therefore deliberately sabotaging my band; or you do *not* know you're out of tune—which I'm afraid is even worse. . . . [The players are all terrified. He instructs the reed players to play, stops them, then instructs the trombone players, and stops them.] Ahhhh, he's here. [Silence. He focuses on Metz, an overweight trombonist.] Tell me it's not you, Elmer Fudd. [Metz is trembling and on the brink of tears.] It's okay. Play. [Metz plays, Fletcher stops him, leans in, and whispers:] Do you think you're out of tune? [Metz, terrified, looks down at the floor.] There's no fucking Mars bar down there. Look at me. Do you think you're out of tune?

METZ: Y-yes.

FLETCHER: [Shouting.] Then *why the FUCK didn't you say so!?!* [Silence.] I've been carrying your fat ass for too long, Metz. I will not let you cost us a competition because your mind's on a fucking Happy Meal and not on pitch. Stein, congratulations, you are now fourth-chair trombone. Metz—get the fuck out. [Still trembling and now in tears, Metz leaves. Once the door closes, Fletcher continues.] For the record, Metz was *not* out of tune. *You* were, Wallach. But Metz didn't know it. And that's bad enough. Alright, take ten.

Can you sense how different is the emotional tenor of the second character compared to the first? The inflated Dr. Hill is arrogant and contemptuous, to be sure, but he lacks the perfectionism, vindictiveness, and sadistic cruelty of Fletcher. The student is not performing the "right" way, so Fletcher feels entitled to annihilate him.

Think of the Israelite whose execution Yahweh ordered because he failed to observe the Sabbath properly by gathering wood (did he have a sick child at home whom he wished to warm up?), or, for that matter, the fifty thousand Israelites whom, not being sanctified priests, Yahweh slaughtered for merely looking into his ark. Ruthlessly Machiavellian, Fletcher manipulates the situation, setting up the student for a fall. He is like a cat playing with a mouse—or rather, like Yahweh toying with Job. With Fletcher there is a Yahwistic element of evil and venom that Hill does not quite have. Fletcher's abusive style of teaching has supposedly driven one student to his death. To the main character in the story he explains that he pushes his students beyond their limits in order for them to achieve greatness. This is his idea of redemption, his holy mission, and he is willing to destroy others in pursuit of it. *Thinking* he is God or like God, Hill has a garden-variety god complex, whereas Fletcher, *behaving* like the *biblical* God, has a full-blown Yahweh complex.

Specific Features of the Yahweh Complex

In an unpublished thesis entitled "The Yahweh Complex: A Case Study in Protestant Fundamentalism," Jungian analyst Randall Mishoe clinically focuses on certain ways this complex is our internalized counterpart to the god it is named after. He shows how the image of "Yahweh the Law-giver who is also judge and persecutor" is at the core of the complex, generating its potent effects on our psyches as if they were caused by Yahweh himself. He argues, as did Jung, that Yahweh suffered from a narcissistic personality disorder that is most apparent in the grandiosity of his perfectionism. The Yahweh complex leads to the same perfectionism and "splitting of instinct and spirit, male and female, good and evil," that characterizes Yahweh. This occurs because one side of any of these pairs is viewed as perfect in Yahweh's eyes, while the other side is cast off. Wholeness is sacrificed in service to perfection:

> The complex may shatter one's life with devastating splits in thought, feelings, and body, or with splits that separate each of these from the other. The result is a fragmentation that renders one powerless to attend to life's basic demands of establishing satisfactory relationships, finding fulfillment in work, and integrating experiences in such a way as to find meaning in life.

Yahweh's lofty ideal of perfectionism pits us against him and against it, and then when we naturally fail, it pits us and splits us against ourselves. We invariably come up short and polarized in our relationship to God, to ourselves, and to each other. In this way a "conflict of being torn into opposing halves occurs under the aegis of the Yahweh complex." Such perfectionism and splitting can lead to fundamentalism, as Jungian analyst Manisha Roy also illustrates in her treatment of Puritanism as a prominent American cultural or collective complex.

In addition to inflation, anger, the power drive, vengeance, perfectionism, splitting, and fundamentalist thinking, we may list the following as features of the person who is afflicted with a Yahweh complex (and again, not all of these manifest all the time and with all individuals): rage and combativeness; omnipotence; a history of trauma; criticalness and judgmental harshness; (wounded) pride, boasting (as in Yahweh's litany of his powers when confronted by Job), self-righteousness, contempt, feelings of superiority (compensating for an underlying insecurity), and arrogance; an intense desire to be admired and praised (also compensatory); lack of compassion (empathic failure); sternness and a legalistic, unforgiving attitude (as in Yahweh's demand for strict adherence to the Law); a preoccupation with morality *or* an altogether indifferent amorality; narcissistic vanity and entitlement (like Yahweh, one even feels entitled to be rageful and vengeful, as if this were a natural right); territoriality and imperial ambitions; an enemy-oriented heroism (a notion of heroism and greatness that needs an enemy in order to define itself); precalculated, Machiavellian manipulation of others; a patriarchal attitude and misogyny; hierarchal authoritarianism; bullying (verbal abuse, browbeating, or, as in Yahweh's case, intimidation through the threat of punishment); apocalyptic fever; disillusionment and melancholy (leading to a pessimistic, gloomy worldview and a bitter, saturnine disposition); a tendency toward paranoia; and cognitive distortions.

Of these features, the preoccupation with morality or an altogether indifferent amorality, paranoia, and cognitive distortions require some explanation.

Those with a Yahweh complex who are preoccupied with morality scrupulously practice the morals prescribed by Yahweh in the Mosaic Code or later modified by Jesus, whereas those who act without regard to moral imperatives exhibit Yahweh's own lack of morality. It would be a misunderstanding here to accuse Yahweh of being a hypocrite or like a bad parent who says to his children, "Do as I say, not as I do," as if his moral prescriptions for his people applied to him too. It was a given precondition that the Law was for the people and that he was beyond the Law, beyond recrimination. Again, he admitted as much in Isaiah when he said he was the source of good and evil, implying that his actions transcended them.

Nevertheless, from a modern standpoint, Yahweh's duplicity is inescapable, a duplicity that can similarly be observed, for example, with preachers who commit adultery, priests who molest children, or executives of charity organizations who engage in financial corruption. In their actions, they show their true Yahwistic colors. The only difference is that Yahweh was an antinomy, a simultaneous coexistence of good and evil. But we are not gods who can hold these side by side. We split them off from each other and become split ourselves, touting Mosaic ethics with our mouths while practicing Yahweh's lack of ethics with our deeds.

One might think that paranoia is not a common feature of god complexes. After all, what would a person who is confident in their status as a god be paranoid about? But in fact, the person with a god complex may be tormented by the same doubt that Jung says Yahweh suffered from: doubt in one's self-worth. Otherwise, why would the person need to be a god in the first place? What underlying inadequacy or insecurity does the god complex compensate for? Or possibly the person is afraid that others will envy his status and want to spoil it or rob it by bringing him down to mere mortality or by replacing him with themselves.

Stalin stands out as someone who had a god complex and was plagued by paranoia. He was obsessed with the belief that others were plotting against him. Of course, he had good reason to be fearful: he was a terrible tyrant. A Georgian by birth and not a Slavic Russian, he was educated at a Russified Orthodox Christian seminary and probably had, in particular, a Yahweh or Perun complex or some blend of the two (not unlike Putin, whom we shall discuss later). Perun was the pre-Christian Slavic god of thunder, lightning, and war. He was a brutal, detached, temperamental god whose attributes can be observed in the Russian leadership style (for example, he ruled over the world with great power and from his citadel high above it, an image resonant with the news photos and film clips of Soviet leaders on a high balcony, watching a parade of marching soldiers and missiles on trucks during the Cold War).

But the individual with a Yahweh complex can be especially prone to paranoia given Yahweh's own suspicious nature and paranoid streak. Job's friend Eliphaz the Temanite alludes to this aspect of Yahweh:

> If He cannot trust His own servants,
> And casts reproach on His angels,
> How much less those who dwell in houses of clay,
> Whose origin is dust,
> Who are crushed like the moth,
> Shattered between daybreak and evening,
> Perishing forever, unnoticed.

Yahweh's history of rejections and strong emotional investment in his plan for Israel further disposed him to a paranoid fear of being undermined.

Cognitive distortions, according to cognitive behavioral therapist David Burns, consist of exaggerated and irrational thought patterns that warp our perceptions of reality so that we see it myopically and negatively. Having them is like wearing a pair of dark sunglasses and not knowing it. Among other features, these distortions include all-or-nothing thinking (seeing things in black-and-white categories); filtering out the positive (dwelling exclusively on negative details); fortune-telling (anticipating that things will turn out badly and feeling convinced that one's prediction is an already-established fact); catastrophizing (magnifying the importance of things so that only the darkest scenario or possibilities prevail); emotional reasoning (assuming one's negative emotions necessarily reflect the way things really are: "I feel it, therefore it must be true"); "should" statements (thinking in terms of "shoulds" and "musts" that stem from disappointment and that aim to evoke shame and guilt in others); labeling and mislabeling (branding others in a fixed, negative, emotionally loaded way—for example, Yahweh's indictment of the Israelites as a "stubborn people"); and blaming (particularly in a one-sided way that lets oneself off the hook). All these cognitive distortions are common to both Yahweh and those gripped by the Yahweh complex.

In a word, if we want to understand the dark side of the Yahweh complex, all we have to do is look at the dark side of the Abrahamic God. When this complex overtakes us, his psychology becomes ours. It is, for the large part, an adolescent psychology, as the Hebrew Bible is very much the story of God's childhood and adolescence. Even his melancholic retreat has the quality of what psychoanalyst Erik Erikson calls the adolescent moratorium—that brooding, withdrawn phase that makes our teenage children so hard to understand and deal with. Yahweh begins to grow into adulthood with the return of wisdom; this phase corresponds to the positive Yahweh complex that sadly occurs less frequently than the negative Yahweh complex we are explicating here.

Any good inventory of Yahweh's features can provide a template or blueprint for this complex and its adolescent psychology, even if this is not its aim and is not proffered by a psychologist. Literary critic Harold Bloom's incisive *Jesus and Yahweh* notes the following traits of Yahweh: flamboyant; ironic irascibility; failure as a father (naturally, being an adolescent himself); endlessly surprising; with proclivities toward self-exile and wily evasiveness; uncannily menacing; has varied personalities (Bloom counts seven) and a puzzling character; bellicose; with complexities that are infinite, labyrinthine, and permanently inexplicable; capricious; a frightening ironist, particularly in his rhetorical questions; frequently given to hyperbole; the figure of excess or overthrow; an admonisher and not a teacher; inquisitive and turbulent; vengeful and murderous; an enigmatic God of alternating presence and absence; pugnacious; aggressive; indifferent to love and fear; a whirlwind that cannot be tamed; unbounded; requires endless praise, gratitude, and immense, unceasing love; mercurial; a quicksilver temperament upon which you absolutely cannot rely; alternating between impish mischief and moral terror; zealous; highly ambivalent; and perpetually and surprisingly anxious.

The person with a Yahweh complex can also manifest these features, all in varying degrees and some only in extreme cases. A list of the main features of the complex is presented in appendix I.

Some Preliminary Illustrations of the Yahweh Complex

The Yahweh complex emerges when one becomes identified with the Abrahamic God. The person may not *consciously* identify with him, but unconsciously, the behaviors of both are identical. In some fashion or another, the person behaves, talks, or thinks like Yahweh, regardless of their belief in his existence. Atheist and believer are equally susceptible to this complex.

It is remarkable how the Yahweh complex can seize us suddenly, appearing "out of nowhere," "out of the blue"—apt metaphors to describe phenomena that erupt from the unconscious without warning. Comedian Michael Richards, who played Kramer on *Seinfeld*, himself couldn't believe his behavior after performing one night in a Los Angeles comedy club. Responding to hecklers in the audience, he exploded in a racist rant that went viral on the internet. Interviewed days later on the *Late Show with David Letterman*, he said that he was "really busted up" over it. He explained, "I'm not a racist. That's what's so insane about this. And yet, it's said. It comes through. It fires out of me." Plainly, a part of himself he did not know had taken over that night.

This is how the Yahweh complex can operate: like a thief in the night, it robs us of our mind, our heart, our ethical sensibilities. Richards was conscientious enough to acknowledge that he needed to do personal work to "get to the force field of this hostility" (what an apt description of the Yahweh complex).

A similar thing happened to actor Will Smith at the Academy Awards when he slapped the emcee, comedian Chris Rock, for making a joke about his wife. Like Richards, he was gripped in a manner contrary to his usual demeanor. In an interview, Smith's mother said that she had never seen him "go off" like that. In four ways did Smith react as Yahweh would. Firstly, he was humorless and dour: he couldn't take a joke (his wife took it better than he did).

Secondly, he was inflated with wrath, acting out explosively and physically, like Yahweh often did when the chosen people behaved disgracefully. He would slap them down and physically punish them by sending epidemics, droughts, or poisonous serpents (all these did little to deter future transgressions).

Thirdly, Smith reached for the most sensational and shocking effect— to march on stage in the middle of Rock's presentation and attempt to shame him with a slap in the face with millions of viewers watching. The biblical God is famous for such public displays. No other Near Eastern god went as far as he did in trying to impress his people with dramatic events like drowning the Egyptian army in the Sea of Reeds or stopping the sun's movement across the sky during Joshua's battle against the Amorites.

Finally, Smith simply sounded like Yahweh: when he twice shouted, "Keep my wife's name out [of] your fucking mouth!" he might as well have said, à la one of the Ten Commandments, "Thou shalt not take the name of my wife in vain." (The actual commandment is "Thou shalt not take the name of the Lord thy God in vain.") The pumped-up, macho belligerence with which he delivered this decree made him appear, much like Yahweh, psychologically young and emotionally immature—these qualities perhaps accentuated since his language was foul compared to Yahweh's, which was always clean. To his credit, Smith quickly owned and apologized for his misdeed.

Such war-god complexes, if not precisely the Yahweh complex itself, are probably at work in episodes of road rage, too. "We are still as much possessed by autonomous psychic contents as if they were Olympians," Jung writes. It is for their sheer force and autonomy that in earlier times complexes were thought to be demons.

It is important to distinguish when otherwise common problems mask the Yahweh complex. Actor and director Mel Gibson offers a good example of how a dark, rageful Yahweh complex can lurk behind such problems. Born into a Traditionalist Catholic family, he was raised with fundamentalist and contrarian views. His father, Hutton Gibson, was a known Holocaust denier and conspiracy theorist. Like him, the younger Gibson tends to dismiss other traditions, even the Episcopalian tradition of his wife (he believes she will go to hell because she doesn't belong to the same faith as he does).

His 2004 film *The Passion of the Christ* sparked a fierce controversy over what many felt were its anti-Semitic imagery and overtones. His subsequent film, *Apocalypto*, is a story about the conquest and exilic captivity of one Mesoamerican people by another. Though it does not deal with the Jewish or Christian Apocalypse per se, its theme is intrinsically the same as the Apocalypse in the Hebrew Bible (except for the fact that the film's "apocalypto" was not orchestrated by God as a retribution for sin). Gibson was arrested in 2006 on a drunk-driving charge and, according to the police report, exploded into an angry tirade and spewed anti-Semitic remarks. In 2010 he was charged with domestic violence, and racist and sexist rants were recorded by his girlfriend and released on the internet.

However, in Gibson's case, religious intolerance, alcohol-related anger and aggression, domestic violence, racism, and sexism, serious as they all are, may have merely disguised the Yahweh complex that in all likelihood was their driving force. They may have been the symptoms of this problem rather than the problem itself. His behaviors were riddled with typical Yahwistic features: judgmental harshness, godlike inflation, a volatile temper, manipulative control of others, and, beyond question, a capacity to inspire: his 1995 epic, *Braveheart*, won Best Director and Best Picture at the Academy Awards and Best Director at the Golden Globe Awards. Similarly, his spectacular 2016 film, *Hacksaw Ridge*, is a moving testament to the bright as well as the dark side of God rising in men's souls in the midst of the hell of war. Gibson is an antinomy no less than the god he worships.

It is noteworthy that not all outbursts of the Yahweh complex are as extroverted and brutish as Richards's, Smith's, and Gibson's. The complex can be subtle and even genteel, its bullying not only the barroom-brawl or dockside kind. The feud between Søren Kierkegaard and Hans Christian Andersen illustrates this. Kierkegaard, a rationalist passionately dedicated to what has been described as an egocentric individualism, was Yahwistically moralistic, melancholic, and solemn (though he had a sharp wit). By contrast, the Romantic Andersen was, as his fairy tales show, intuitive, playful, and childlike—qualities more in the vein of Hermes or the Scandinavian trickster god Loki than Yahweh. Though his religious feeling was rooted in a liberal Christianity that spoke in a language of the heart and nature, he had a Yahwistic streak. Existential angst and bitterness were no strangers to either his writing or his personal life.

Contemporaneously competing as the two great Danish literary stylists of their time, Kierkegaard and Andersen were like oil and water, publicly slandering each other. Kierkegaard, a philosophical giant, bullied Andersen by proclaiming in a review of his charming but melancholic novel *Only a Fiddler* that he "completely lacks any philosophy of life." Andersen Yahwistically took revenge by parodying Kierkegaard as a theater hairdresser in his vaudeville play *A Comedy in the Open Air*, and then, some believe, he mocked him in his tale "The Snail and the Rosebush." The

Yahweh complex can strike us regardless of the level of our intelligence, education, and knowledge.

Bitterness is a serious problem because it in turn breeds contempt, not only for others but for the world and life itself. "Bitterness is like cancer. It eats upon the host," poet Maya Angelou said. Bitterness is what we are left with when we have failed to extract the wisdom from our suffering. A good but sad illustration of this is provided by Elvis Presley. His bitterness from feeling left behind by the "British invasion" of the Beatles and others is comparable to Yahweh's sense of marginalization and disillusionment from being repeatedly abandoned by his chosen people. Yet Yahweh at the end of the Hebrew Bible seems to have transformed his bitterness into wisdom. Elvis—a mere mortal, albeit a talented one—was unable to do this.

The Beatles visited him in 1965, a pleasant event according to their accounts (even though by other accounts Elvis did not seem too enthusiastic about meeting them). In 1970, feeling disempowered and by now unstable due to his abuse of prescription drugs, he took it upon himself to fight the drug culture that, ironically, he believed was ruining America's music and youth. He flew to Washington to initiate a meeting with President Nixon.

According to Nixon aide Egil "Bud" Krogh, "Presley indicated that he thought the Beatles had been a real force for [the] anti-American spirit." He wanted Nixon to make him a special agent for the Bureau of Narcotics and Dangerous Drugs (now the Drug Enforcement Administration) and to help in the war against drugs. (Nixon complied, and there were a number of occasions in which Presley used the phony badge Nixon had ordered to be made for him.) Given that both men were gripped by the Yahweh complex, each in their own way (Nixon will be discussed in a later chapter), they were less strange bedfellows than one might imagine.

Can women have a Yahweh complex, and if so, how does it manifest? The answer is yes, they can, and it manifests no differently, as Shakespeare's Lady Macbeth would surely confirm:

> Come, you spirits
> That tend on mortal thoughts, unsex me here,

And fill me from the crown to the toe top-full
Of direst cruelty! Make thick my blood;
Stop up the access and passage to remorse,
That no compunctious visitings of nature
Shake my fell purpose, nor keep peace between
The effect and it! Come to my woman's breasts,
And take my milk for gall.

Merely, we see more females with a Yahweh complex in modern times because women's liberation has given women more opportunities to develop and express psychological complexes. Women in leadership positions get an especially "bad rap" when their Yahweh complex emerges because neither men nor women accept a controlling and ill-tempered female boss as easily as they would accept such a male boss.

A good example of a woman with an aggressive Yahweh complex or Yahwistic "animus"—Jung's term for a woman's masculine side—is Martha Stewart. She has a delightful persona, but underneath, people who have known her or worked for her report, seethes a mercurial, hair-trigger temper and a domineering personality. She has the same problem that Job encountered with Yahweh: Yahweh's "white shadow," a dark side that everyone can see except the one who has it and who, moreover, believes they have no such blemishes. Stewart wasn't convicted for insider trading but for obstructing justice. Her attitude, like Yahweh's, was that she was above the law. "I have done nothing wrong," she insisted throughout the investigation and trial, even though the facts showed otherwise.

When a Negative Yahweh Complex Grips a Nation's Leader

Whereas fundamentalist beliefs like Gibson's—the Christian variety—are desirable by many because they keep one buoyant in facing life's challenges, their oppressive preoccupation with sin can also sink one into melancholy and even clinical depression. Calvin Coolidge was a competent president who would have been reelected easily for a second term had his performance in the White House not taken a dramatic turn when his son died unexpectedly. He fell into a deep depression, probably made worse by the fundamentalist leanings that had been inculcated into him from his Congregationalist upbringing. "I do not know why such a price was exacted for occupying the White House," he said.

Philosopher Michael Platt, in his review of Coolidge's autobiography, concludes that the president believed that God had punished him by taking his son. In particular, he believed he was punished for his pride and self-indulgence. Political scientist Robert Gilbert quotes an associate of Coolidge's: "He reveled in his success" and "would almost tiptoe around, touching things and half-smiling to himself." Gilbert adds that Coolidge saw his son's death as a punishment for enjoying the perks and pomp of the presidency. This belief in a wrathful, vindictive God who inflicts a living hell upon us for our supposed sins is a glaring example of the Yahweh complex operating diabolically within our souls. As Jung says, "A living God afflicts our reason like a sickness." More will later be said about fundamentalism—one of the more common manifestations of the Yahweh complex—and its related doctrine of original sin.

There is something to be said for the proclivity to become melancholic or depressed under the sway of the Yahweh complex. It can motivate us to work on the complex ("No pain, no gain," as the saying goes). However, the conundrum here for some is that melancholy or depression drains motivation and flattens emotions, so there can be a tendency to stay stuck in the complex. Nevertheless, melancholy or depression can be worked with and should be expressed and explored, for this forces us to turn inward and downward into our depths, where the unconscious resides and holds the possibility for rejuvenation and psychological rebirth.

Another requirement for the motivation to change is conscience. Regret, shame, or guilt over one's poor behavior due to their Yahweh complex is a motivating emotion. Without conscience, one cannot even recognize that their behavior is poor, much less that they have such a complex. Which brings us to Donald J. Trump. Blended into his general god complex is his distinct Yahweh complex: he both thinks of himself as if he were God *and* behaves like Yahweh. His inflation is self-evident in such publicized statements as "I am the chosen one" and his tweet "I'd like to remind everyone that I am the most Stable Genius, and if there was another Genius as Stable as me, they are FFFAKE [*sic*]."

As early as 2017 and in a letter to the editors of *The New York Times*, psychoanalyst Lance Dodes—at the time a psychiatry professor at Harvard Medical School—and a host of other mental health professionals warned about Trump's "grave emotional instability." Dodes later said that in Trump's mind, the millions who support him are "not just fans. From his standpoint they're worshippers. He sees himself in his delusional belief as a god, and the people who support him, worship him. He doesn't care about them, mind you, as we know. It's an entirely one-way street."

However, the contagion of the Yahweh complex is *not* a one-way street: as the assault on Capitol Hill showed, Trump's followers caught his Yahwistic outlook, sense of entitlement, and rage as if these were a virus as contractible as COVID-19. In their identification with and glorification of him, they became collectively gripped by the same complex that grips him. The above characterization of them as worshippers points to this cultlike aspect of his popularity. As journalist Mehdi Hasan commented, when a golden statue of Trump was displayed at the Conservative Political Action Conference in 2021, the Trump cult—again, consisting of millions—stooped to an idolatry similar to that in the biblical episode of the golden calf. Trump's supporters, including seasoned politicians as well as ordinary folk, behave as if they are in a hypnotic trance, a psychological state whose main catalyst is a suggestibility that, unchecked, can lead to insurrections like the kind Moses faced in that biblical episode and that descended upon Capitol Hill.

Trump's childhood history, like Yahweh's, predisposed him to developing a brittle, conflict-oriented character. As the son of a cold, hard-to-please, Yahwistic father (who drove Trump's older brother to alcoholism and an early death), Trump's way of surviving was to protect himself by standing up to him and by being equally detached. Like father, like son. Tony Schwartz, Trump's cowriter of *The Art of the Deal*, adds:

> Trump felt compelled to go to war with the world. It was a binary, zero-sum choice for him: You either dominated or you submitted. You either created and exploited fear, or you succumbed to it—as he thought his older brother had. This narrow, defensive outlook took hold at a very early age, and it never evolved. "When I look at myself in the first grade and I look at myself now," he told a recent biographer, "I'm basically the same." His development essentially ended in early childhood.

Trump enacted this defensive, Yahwistic outlook when he urged state governors to use force to subdue protesters following the death of George Floyd. He said, "You have to dominate. If you don't dominate, you're wasting your time. They're going to run over you. You're going to look like a bunch of jerks. You have to dominate."

Putting aside the influence of his father, Trump's own Yahwistic style includes rage (according to a number of his staff); bullying; blaming and scapegoating; paranoia (as observable in his conspiracy theories); vengefulness; vanity and boasting; an autocratic and imperial approach to leadership; emotional reasoning; pettiness ("Nobody does petty like the former president," political consultant Tim Miller said); apocalyptic rhetoric (North Korea "will be met with fire, fury, and frankly power, the likes of which this world has never seen before"); Machiavellian behaviors (such as threatening to hold back approved congressional funds to Ukraine in an attempt to manipulate that country's president to help him illicitly win the 2020 US presidential election); lawlessness (more on the scale of Yahweh's violations than Martha Stewart's, as he repeatedly demonstrated); a reckless, scorched-earth policy of dismantling the American government; and persistent and pernicious lying—the sign of an underlying inferiority complex that compels one to believe that they can't "win" without distorting the truth. (A scorched-earth policy is a Yahwistic feature inasmuch as Yahweh instructed the Israelites to raze everything to the ground when they vanquished entire populations in Canaan. Likewise, Yahweh's lies comprised scores of promises to the Israelites that he never kept. As Miles writes, "The failure of prophecy, a fact of massive importance in the history of Israelite and then of Jewish religion, is a personal failure in the life of God.")

Yet none of these characteristics surpass Trump's Yahweh-like lack of conscience and compassion. He had no qualms about abdicating his responsibility to vigorously lead the fight against COVID-19, his lackluster performance costing many their lives. Nor was he disturbed by his *own awareness* that he was violating his vows to protect the US Constitution when he tried to overthrow the government in the insurrection he mounted. (With regard to the latter, we learned from the January 6 committee hearings that he knew what he was doing and planned it ahead.) As for his lack of compassion, he showed little empathy for those who lost their lives due to the pandemic or for their grieving families. The same could be said for his deportation policy with its camps that separated children from their parents.

But is it enough to explain Trump's actions and policies as the consequences merely of what is *lacking* in him, as if a vacuum alone can be the source of these? As Jungian analyst Adolf Guggenbühl-Craig argues, the lacunae or "holes" in our psyches are a predominant feature of psychopathology, yet something must fill that void to make a person truly a dangerous sociopath. Something more forceful must be at work. This lands us on the doorstep of evil. If "evil" sounds too harsh or intangible a descriptor to assign to Trump, let us use perhaps the next best word to grasp that forceful something: "hatred."

Here is how the Czech president Václav Havel understood this principle independently of and well before the election of Trump: "Hatred is a diabolical attribute of a fallen angel: it is a state of the spirit that aspires to be God, that may even think it is God, and is tormented by the indications that it is not and cannot be." And here is how he describes the person who hates: "A serious face, a quickness to take offense, strong language, shouting, the inability to step outside himself and see his own foolishness." Trump is a typical hater.

Trump's god complex epitomized not only Yahweh's *Sturm und Drang* but also his lapses into malignant narcissism. Yahweh's self-preoccupation and capacity for wickedness are amply illustrated in the Book of Job and elsewhere. It is largely due to these same features that Bob Woodward surmised that Trump was not fit to be a president. Psychoanalyst Erich Fromm, who coined the term "malignant narcissism," conceived it as an extreme mix of narcissism, antisocial behavior (a polite term for sociopathy), aggression, and sadism. It is not only the "most severe pathology and the root of the most vicious destructiveness and inhumanity" but also the "quintessence of evil."

Insofar as American society is a democracy, Trump's antisocial tendency surfaced in his antidemocratic policies and actions—his attacks on the press, his overall lack of understanding of and respect for the Constitution, his efforts to undermine the legitimacy of the 2020 election (if not also the 2016 one), his incitement of insurrection (itself in turn incited by the war god within him, whom we are fortunate did not lead him and us into an actual war with another nation), and his general demagoguery. The latter naturally goes with what Fromm, among others, would underscore as his authoritarian personality or character.

Regarding Trump's sadism, journalist William Saletan writes that "in 2016, after winning his party's presidential nomination, he bragged for months about all the Republican candidates he had beaten. As president-elect, he toured the country, boasting about the emotional pain he had inflicted on Democrats and others who had stood in his way. . . . He savaged Hillary Clinton and her supporters, calling the election a 'slaughter.'" When his supporters invaded the Capitol fourteen days before his presidency ended, *The New York Times* reported that "the president had appeared to White House aides to be enjoying watching the scenes play out on television."

Trump seems to be developmentally arrested in the insecurities of what psychoanalyst Melanie Klein calls a paranoid-schizoid position—an inflexible, infantile condition in which the ego cannot discern good from bad and is not attuned with the real world. What made his serial lies most pathological was that with enough repetition of them, he eventually appeared to believe them. Even if he knew they weren't true, he believed that they were "right" because, in his view, they *should* be true. Because of the severity of his delusional cognitive distortions, he was unable to recognize his blind spots, as every great leader must. He thus could not learn from his mistakes. Like Coolidge's, his was a tragic presidency, but also a much darker one.

The Variability of the Yahweh Complex

There are naturally different degrees to which the Yahweh complex can affect people. Generally speaking, some act it out sometimes—when it periodically erupts or explodes—and others act it out practically all the time (like Trump). The latter kind, who are fortunately more rare, are completely possessed by the complex, swimming in it like a fish in the sea or a fetus in the womb. They don't "wake up" from it; that's how deeply entrenched it is in their psyches and how entangled they are with it. It is as if they have not yet been psychologically born as individuals with a distinct identity. Or if they were individuals once upon a time, they have for some reason or other surrendered their individuality to become this more archaic, brittle personality. Yahweh's character has integrally become their own.

Not surprisingly, those permanently engulfed in the complex can be more dangerous than the first kind, dispensing evil and death if they are also sociopathic. Most people with a Yahweh complex will go only so far in their Yahwistic actions, as they still have some sense of propriety even if they are unaware of the complex. Because Yahwistic sociopaths have neither awareness of their complex nor conscience about their actions, there is no limit to how destructive they can be. At their worst, they unconsciously imitate Yahweh at *his* worst—namely, when he was genocidal and apocalyptic.

Like most complexes, the Yahweh complex begins to form early in our development, when we are first getting a sense of ourselves in relation to the world around us. As with Yahweh himself in the story of Genesis (not to mention Adam and Eve), something goes awry in how we acclimate to the new world we are in. This could be a particular event or series of events, often of a traumatic nature, or it could consist of our adopting the emotional style of a parent, as in Trump's instance.

Another example: history tells us that *both* parents of Martin Luther had a Yahweh complex, so it is likely that his own was a case involving familial influence (as with Gibson, Coolidge, and Trump); here too the apple didn't fall far from the tree. Luther displayed his complex when he railed against the Jews for declining his invitation to convert to Protestantism. He vented his preoccupation with his sinfulness—and the self-loathing this precipitated—when in a melancholic episode he announced at the dinner table, "I am like ripe shit, and the world is a gigantic asshole. We probably will let go of each other soon."

Furthermore, and not to be underestimated, the culture can be a significant factor. In Luther's instance, medieval Christendom was steeped in Yahwistic values and psychology. Cultural historian Johan Huizinga writes:

> At the close of the Middle Ages, a sombre melancholy weighs on people's souls. Whether we read a chronicle, a poem, a sermon, a legal document even, the same impression of immense sadness is produced by them all. . . . In the fifteenth century, as in the epoch of romanticism, it was, so to say, bad form to praise the world and life openly. It was fashionable to see only its suffering and misery, to discover everywhere signs of decadence and of the near end—in short, to condemn the times or to despise them.

This cultural milieu of "immense sadness" cannot have been separate from the world as Luther knew it, and so it was also this (in addition to original sin) that he was implicitly referring to when he described himself and the world in scatological terms.

This said, neither trauma nor familial and cultural influence *cause* the Yahweh complex. Again, they constellate or trigger it, drawing it out of its latent condition in our Abrahamic collective unconscious. It is not only what Jungian analysts Joseph Henderson, Samuel Kimbles, and Thomas Singer would call a "cultural complex," but it is also a civilizational one. This über complex of Western and Islamic civilization infiltrates every corner of life just like the way Yahweh did in his time. Given that this complex is so ubiquitous, the question is not whether one is a Yahwist but rather *how much* a Yahwist one is.

The transformation we must undergo to work our way out of the Yahweh complex's grip can involve any number of the seven stages of Yahweh's evolution in the Hebrew Bible. Again, these are rejection → wrath → a redemptive mission → the will to power and domination → the mission's failure → melancholy → wisdom. Naturally, when we apply this to our own process of individuation or personal development, we should keep in mind that it is a loose psychological schema and not a fixed, rigid formula. The Yahweh complex usually does not de facto crystallize in a fashion that requires us to replay this entire progression from rejection and rage to wisdom simply because that was Yahweh's experience. Everyone has their own experience that tends to parallel only some portion of this trajectory, and one's portion may even begin at a later stage, bypassing the preceding stages. Such is the nature of a collective, archetypal complex: because it preexists the ego, it does not have to unfold sequentially from its beginning and can be constellated or triggered at any stage.

Everyone's experience, though archetypal, is indeed unique. The poet-musician Leonard Cohen, for example, spent almost the entirety of his adult life in a state of deep melancholy and Yahwistic pathos—"He's so distant," former lover Joni Mitchell complained—only for this to blossom into a quietly joyful wisdom in his senior years, a blooming that was also akin to Yahweh's. Much of Cohen's early work, though beautiful and captivating, is gloomy; yet not long before he died, he said, "I've taken a lot of Prozac, Paxil, Wellbutrin, Effexor, Ritalin, Focalin. I've also studied deeply in the philosophies and the religions [including five years of training in a Zen monastery], but cheerfulness kept breaking through." His later work, distinguished by such elevated, inspiring songs as "Hallelujah" and "If It Be Your Will," reflects this breakthrough. Perhaps both states of mind—melancholy and cheerfulness—are to be expected given Cohen's cryptic description of himself as the little Jew who authored the Bible.

As we shall see in the final part of the book, with some rare individuals the Yahweh complex can first manifest in the stage of wisdom. In that instance, it is a positive Yahweh complex, and such people are often called "old souls." However, the dark side of the complex does not disappear simply because the positive side is accentuated. Even old souls tend to experience both sides. Merely, they exhibit a capacity to identify more with the complex's positive features, or to more skillfully turn the negative Yahweh complex into a positive one through their conscientious efforts.

Nelson Mandela, originally labeled a terrorist, modeled Yahweh's mercy when Yahweh was at his best. He drew upon his Methodist upbringing to convince his nation that it would never be truly free unless the oppressed forgave their oppressors, for without forgiveness the oppressors would be forever chained to their crimes and sins. (Of course, this forgiveness would not be given for free; it had to be earned through the redemptive process of meeting with South Africa's Truth and Reconciliation Commission.) Mandela understood what Hannah Arendt meant when she said that "forgiveness is the only way to reverse the irreversible flow of history" and that it is consequently the "key to action and freedom." He knew that forgiveness or mercy is divine and the source of true power. One might argue that Mandela championed Yahweh's mercy more consistently and better than Yahweh himself.

When the complex manifests at an earlier stage, as it more typically does, one has to pay their dues and work toward wisdom through the subsequent stages, or through some other path that perhaps better suits their temperament or experience. Without effort, the individual rarely finds this wisdom that will release them from the complex's hold. Because one must struggle to psychologically separate out from the complex, it is unfortunately more common for people to stay trapped in it. Most of us don't like hard work, especially hard inner work that demands us to raise our awareness. Some folks remain fixated on the stage of wrath, others on the will to power, and yet others on defeat and melancholy. Instead of extracting wisdom from their suffering, they get stuck in bitterness or some other dark aspect of the complex.

How We Will Proceed

The rest of this book presents a variety of illustrations of how the Yahweh complex manifests in its various shades and stages. We will explore its eruption in our everyday lives and relationships. We will also look at Western history and culture and briefly discuss Islam. Our overall aim will be to make this complex more visible so that we can become more conscious of it. In that way, *we* will have the complex rather than *it* having *us*.

Increased awareness won't necessarily make the complex go away, but at least we will be able to develop a more enlightened and empowered relationship to it. Otherwise it will continue to exert its power upon us in unconscious and tyrannical ways. We may here wish to remain mindful that Yahweh's experience is the prototype of the complex: the conclusion of the Hebrew Bible consists of his victory in creating a renewed and more authentic relationship to his people and evidently to himself, to his own dark side. Such a victory is possible for us, too. Consciousness has an inherent capacity to change and evolve. We can learn not only from our own mistakes but also from the mistakes—and wisdom—of others. Their illustrations can foster our learning.

There are phenomena that we will *not* examine because they do not involve the Yahweh complex solely and are culturally wider occurrences, if not universal. However, they're worth mentioning here so that we are at least aware of their importance and that the Yahweh complex may be among their ingredients. They include patriarchy, with its dour effects on marriage, parenting, and the treatment of girls and women (which can be not only abusive but murderous, as studies in gendercide show); totalitarianism and modern, state-sanctioned genocide; nuclear proliferation; and climate change, deforestation, ocean pollution, and overpopulation, the latter four all contributing to the destruction of our planet and thousands of its species.

Regarding our ecological crisis, only a society under the influence of a dark god complex—Yahwistic *or* generic—would find it acceptable to turn the earth into a cesspool or garbage can for its waste. In particular, though, Yahweh's explicit attitude toward his creation has been internalized as Western society's own: in the very first chapter of the Hebrew Bible, he says to Adam and Eve, "Be fruitful and multiply, and fill the earth and subdue it; and have dominion over the fish of the sea and over the birds of the air and over every living thing that moves upon the earth." (How different Yahweh is from the nature deities of indigenous cultures and nature-oriented traditions like Taoism and Zen Buddhism.) Nevertheless, all of the above phenomena would exist worldwide even if the West's imitation of the biblical God, with his genocidal and scorched-earth policy in warfare, his penchant for apocalyptic measures, and his ecological bias, were taken out of the equation.

There are also phenomena that are driven by a kind of god complex, operating as if they were gods themselves and believed in as if they were supernatural forces. I am referring particularly to the modern gods of technology, materialism, capitalism, and progress. They run roughshod over ecological sobriety and are used as excuses to justify our negligence and abuse of the earth. These too exceed the scope of our inquiry.

No doubt, some of the following illustrations may seem dated as time goes on and as they are surpassed by even better ones. Nevertheless, insofar as they capture the Yahweh complex in action, they will remain resonant alongside whatever new examples history provides, and they can serve as good teaching aids, regardless of when the events they portray occurred. Particular events and situations may come and go, but the factors shaping them can endure long after they are forgotten, only to resurface in new events and situations. As William Faulkner said, "The past is never dead. It's not even past."

2

Master of the Universe: The Young Bill Gates

Bill Gates is an American success story. He's as American as apple pie.

—Don Hewitt

Financial empires are similar to geopolitical ones in this regard: both are built by ambitious people who are talented at seizing opportunities and taking control of resources—including people—in an effort to gain power and wealth. Bill Gates's empire is no exception, and without his empire-building appetite, the computer revolution that he ushered in would surely not have happened when it did or the way it did. The computer program I am using as I type this is Microsoft Word. Gates has made my research and writing a pleasure compared to the days of typewriters and long waits on the busy phone line of my local library's reference department. Almost everyone has benefited from the contributions of this genius. He created the software industry and changed the course of history. But as history shows, such talent and drive often go hand in hand with self-centeredness and its effects on others.

As author Wendy Goldman Rohm explains, in his role as a revolutionary innovator and corporate empire builder, Gates historically belongs to the same league as industrial barons like Rockefeller and Carnegie, some of whom were coldly strategic and cutthroat in their methods. Like Rockefeller, whose Standard Oil monopoly was broken into thirty-four independent companies by the US Supreme Court, Gates was bound to sooner or later have a run-in with the government for the same reason.

In 1998, the Department of Justice, eighteen states, and the District of Columbia filed *The United States v. Microsoft*. The particular issue at stake was Microsoft's bundling its Internet Explorer web browser software with Windows, thereby restricting the market for competing web browsers and virtually winning the "browser wars." As Gates expressed at various times, he believed that since he created the market and demand for his products, he should have exclusive access to it; he called this a "natural monopoly." Whether he meant that it was his God-given right to completely dominate the market or that monopolies were natural by-products of social evolution, or both, is unclear. In any case, he was advocating laissez-faire, a completely unrestrained free market.

The US government intervened on the grounds that his business practices were anticompetitive and predatory. Although many would have liked more comprehensive sanctions, a settlement was reached in which Microsoft was required to share its application programming interfaces with third-party companies. Curiously, two forces exercising power in a godlike way collided here—the monopoly and the government attempting to break it. (All governments exercise power in this way. It is no accident that Thomas Hobbes called his classic treatise on statecraft, with its advocacy for a strong government that unites people in a social contract and under the authority of an absolute sovereign, *Leviathan*—the biblical and divine monster of the sea.) The government here was acting in service to the public interest and, ultimately, democracy.

For Gates's part, we may say that his monopolizing, as is the case with monopolizing in general, was a financial analog to monotheism. His belief that his products should be the sole ones available on the market was a kind of monotheism in the same way that Yahweh's demand that Israel worship only him—or risk widespread destruction and death—was a kind of monopoly. Both were forms of monomania, psychiatry's term in the nineteenth century for a singular obsession or pathological preoccupation in an otherwise sound mind.

Gates's ethical standards naturally trickled down to his company. The judge presiding over the above legal case observed that "Microsoft is a company with an institutional disdain for both the truth and for rules of law that lesser entities must respect. It is also a company whose senior management is not averse to offering specious testimony to support spurious defenses to claims of its wrongdoing." The first sentence here reminds us of Yahweh's violations of his laws while demanding that others obey them, and the second, his bombastic defense of himself to Job.

Gates's emotional and interpersonal style was, certainly in his younger days, distinctly Yahwistic too, and thus in sync with a young god like Yahweh. Whether consciously or not, he saw himself as an entitled master of the universe. Microsoft co-founder Paul Allen portrays Gates in his memoir as a tough, abusive taskmaster, pushing people to work as hard as they could by browbeating and yelling at them. (Needless to say, Gates was himself bullied as a child.) Videotapes of staff meetings show a young Gates behaving in a mean-spirited, condescending fashion. A know-it-all, he relied on personal verbal attacks—interrupting his managers' presentations with comments like "That's the stupidest thing I ever heard"—and quarreled for hours until the other was exhausted. On some days, Allen said in a *60 Minutes* interview, working with Gates was "like being in hell."

In 1982, Allen developed cancer. Feeling already miserable and marginalized, he passed by Gates's office one night during this period and overheard him talking with Steve Ballmer, who was hired to help run the company. "They were basically talking about how they were planning to dilute my share down to almost nothing, and it was a really shocking and disheartening moment for me." He was in the middle of radiation therapy. He had been friends with Gates since high school. Episodes like this might suggest that Gates has a cold heart or no heart at all.

We shouldn't be too surprised by Gates's monopolizing, disdain for truth and the law, autocratic management style, and lack of compassion. Again, he was no worse than his predecessors, the industrial barons of America—or, for that matter, others who are more contemporary. Steve Jobs and Elon Musk can similarly be described as masters of the universe, infected with a god complex and driven by the will to power. This is not unusual, as empires, corporate and otherwise, are not built by reasonable, staid people but rather by radical innovators or revolutionaries on a mission of progress, or at least what they think is progress. With both positive and negative effects, they forge ahead and take us with them.

Musk, for instance, has been accused of whitewashing more than one death in connection to his self-driving Teslas, yet he still insists that if airplanes have an autopilot capacity, so should cars. Indeed, cars may one day be safely self-driving, but at the present level of our technology, is it wise to allow them on our roads and highways? Here we see the dark and bright sides of the god complex seamlessly interwoven.

All this said, in a bold second act, Gates has demonstrated an impressive turnabout using his resources as one the wealthiest people in the world. Gradually shifting out of his role as chairman of Microsoft and finally stepping down in 2014, he has been engaged in philanthropy. The Bill & Melinda Gates Foundation has helped the poor and disadvantaged all over the world with successful health and agriculture programs. Gates was also active during the COVID-19 pandemic, contributing $1.75 billion to fight it. Much of this funded the production and procurement of crucial medical supplies and included a substantial sum that went to Gavi, a global organization providing vaccines to children in the poorest countries.

Gates's initiatives to spur private- and public-sector investment in clean energy research and development, and also his own investments of $2 billion by 2021, aim to enhance the global effort to reduce carbon emissions to zero by 2050. His book *How to Avoid a Climate Disaster: The Solutions We Have and the Breakthroughs We Need* is a highly readable yet serious account of what he has learned about climate change and some of the strategies available to prevent a global catastrophe (of course, there are differing views about these). He writes with a sense of urgency but remains optimistic. He is not prone to apocalyptic thinking or Yahwistic gloom about the end of the world. The man who built and managed a corporate empire is applying his analytical skills to better understand and deal with the world's most pressing problem.

As an active and full-time philanthropist, Gates doesn't just hand over the money and trust someone or some organization to spend it well. Participating directly, he undertakes extensive research to become an expert in the fields to which he is contributing. He travels all over the world in his charitable and research pursuits.

To what can we attribute this dramatic transformation? While it is true that a number of wealthy industrialists have contributed to philanthropic causes, this development is quite striking in Gates's instance, given how *mis*anthropic he was as a younger man. Certainly, such a radical change is not beyond the scope of the Yahweh complex. Evidently, a negative Yahweh complex can flip or evolve into a positive one depending on the individual's capacity to change and grow. As Yahweh also experiences a change of heart in the later books of the Hebrew Bible, this evolution is naturally part of the trajectory of the Yahweh complex. Yahweh eventually outgrew his adolescent psychology, and so did Gates. Both were afflicted with the impatience and hypercriticism of youth, and both matured.

3

Eliot Spitzer's Fall

It is impossible to calculate the moral mischief, if I may so express it, that mental lying has produced in society. When a man has so far corrupted and prostituted the chastity of his mind, as to subscribe his professional belief to things he does not believe, he has prepared himself for the commission of every other crime.

—*Thomas Paine*

The story of Eliot Spitzer illustrates how the dark side of the Yahweh complex can destroy a person's life, undermining the seemingly divine calling of its positive side. Eliot Spitzer, governor of the state of New York from 2007 to 2008—barely fifteen months—was on a path that could have led to the US presidency. Arguably, he could have been America's first Jewish president, its Benjamin Disraeli or Léon Blum. He was brilliant, bold, and impassioned with a drive to fight wrongdoing in society and government. He was a stalwart champion of justice.

In particular, Spitzer's story reveals how the Yahweh complex impairs our judgment and takes prisoner our free will. In this way does it split our dark side off from our ethical side so that the former breaks loose and is acted out in ways not unlike Yahweh's own acting out. Spitzer built his reputation as a New York State attorney general crusading against corporate corruption. During his tenure, he also arrested and prosecuted sixteen people operating a prostitution ring out of Staten Island. It thus came as a shock to his constituents when in 2008 he resigned as the state's governor after having been himself exposed as the patron of a high-profile prostitution service. Putting aside for the sake of argument questions about the morality of prostitution, Spitzer's unquestionable ethical lapse was that he, like Yahweh, enforced the law with others while regarding himself above it.

Spitzer's interpersonal style was power driven and Yahwistic and his emotional intelligence young. He had an explosive temper and was known for bullying and for his threats of revenge. Jack Welch, former chairman and CEO of General Electric, recounted an incident at the 2004 Democratic National Convention. At the time, Spitzer was investigating Kenneth Langone, former director of the New York Stock Exchange. "We were having an amiable chat," Welch recalled. "Then—boom—he flipped his lid. He snapped. He started sticking his finger in my chest and said, 'You can tell your friend Langone that I'm gonna put a stake through his heart!'"

In an op-ed piece in *The Wall Street Journal* in 2005, former Goldman Sachs chairman John Whitehead criticized Spitzer for being too aggressive. Whitehead later reported that Spitzer subsequently called him and threatened him: "I will be coming after you. You will pay the price. . . . You will pay dearly for what you have done." Spitzer denied this. As governor, Spitzer boasted to a state legislator, "I'm a fucking steamroller." His combative modus operandi endeared him to his opponents about as much as Yahweh was liked by Israel's enemies.

As Spitzer acknowledged in the documentary film *Client 9: The Rise and Fall of Eliot Spitzer*, his downfall was a tragedy of Greek proportions. Perhaps he was here alluding to Oedipus Rex, who set in motion his own demise by unwittingly killing his father and marrying his mother, and who gouged out his eyes as a form of penance. But unlike Oedipus, Spitzer did not appear willing to pay the price for insight—namely, an examined life. His responses to the interviewer blatantly showed his blind spot, how he was a mystery to himself, a man unconscious of his own inner dynamics. Asked how he explains his behavior, he seemed clueless. Though he possessed an intellect that was finely honed—he was a sharp prosecuting attorney and an astute observer of political and socioeconomic ills—he lacked curiosity about himself.

Were Spitzer to have more fully appreciated that the compulsive force that sabotaged him was a part of himself, he might not have so lightly sloughed off responsibility for understanding himself, insinuating that what happened to him was some mystery of fate. As Jung says, "When an inner situation is not made conscious, it happens outside, as fate. That is to say, when the individual remains undivided and does not become conscious of his inner opposite, the world must perforce act out the conflict and be torn into opposing halves." Spitzer's hypocritical behavior was a function of his unconsciousness. His problem was not only his dark side or his Yahweh complex but also his being undivided from it. It left him no choice but to fall victim to it.

In 2013, Spitzer unsuccessfully ran for the office of New York City comptroller. "Five years later," he said, "I think I can ask for forgiveness. . . . I am asking for an opportunity to come back and serve." Surely he deserved forgiveness as any of us do when we have made a mistake. But during the campaign, Stephen Colbert on his show asked him, "Shouldn't the job of comptroller go to someone who has shown a modicum of self-comptrol?" Instead of seizing the opportunity to explain what he had learned about himself in those five years in order to not repeat such behavior, Spitzer answered, laughing, "Yes, you are right." To Colbert's follow-up question, "Why should the people trust you?" he answered, "Based on the totality of a record."

Of course, an ability to laugh at oneself and an overall impressive record are assets, and privacy is, after all, a basic human right. Nevertheless, his answers raised further questions: had he earned the voters' forgiveness and trust with his self-examination and the wisdom this might have given him, and if not, could he have realistically expected them to give him a second chance?

4

Schopenhauer's Gloom

So long as you do not know
This dying and coming to life again,
You are but a gloomy guest
On this dark Earth.

—Goethe

It seems as if everyone affected by a Yahweh complex emanates, to some degree or another, existential gloom. As shall be discussed when we turn to Churchill, Lincoln, and Dylan, even those with a positive Yahweh complex can be at the same time terribly susceptible to Yahweh's dark, gloomy moods sprouting out of their collective unconscious. How much more would a confirmed atheist, misanthrope, and recluse like the great philosopher Arthur Schopenhauer be prone to them? In this matter he even trumped Nietzsche. Though the latter was keenly inspired by Schopenhauer and in crucial ways suffered more than him, he remained, in his own words, a "tragic optimist."

Schopenhauer ran as fast and as far away from religious faith as he could, only to fall right into the arms of Yahweh. He incarnated the spirit of Yahweh as he existed in his melancholic period, though unlike Yahweh, he did not mine his melancholy so as to arrive at some spiritual awakening or wisdom. Bitter he was not. Rather, he had a morbid outlook. His existential pessimism perhaps surpassed even that of Ecclesiastes. "Life," he said, "is *a disappointment, nay, a cheat.* . . . Would not a man rather have so much sympathy with the coming generation as to spare it the burden of existence?" It is true that his teaching that life consists of suffering is close to the Buddhism he admired, but with one significant difference: the Zen masters, representing at least one school of Buddhism, also found great joy in life, and their souls were light due to their liberation from their emotional *attachment* to suffering, if not from the suffering itself.

Schopenhauer, by contrast, seemed burdened by gloom. This was evident not only in his writings but also in his personal life: he was a true loner—never married, involved in any social club or institution, or known intimately by the people whose acquaintance he made. He was a cold and contemptuous man. In restaurants he required two tables, one for himself and the other next to it unseated in order to assure that no one interrupted his privacy with small talk. In one infamous episode, an argument with his landlady, he pushed her down a staircase. The court mandated that he pay her restitution for the rest of her life. He felt no remorse. When she died twenty years later, he wrote in his diary, "*Obit anus, abit onus*" ("The old woman dies, the burden is lifted"). His only true love, aside from philosophy, was his poodles.

One wonders if Schopenhauer's philosophic genius might have provided him some way to better manage his Yahweh complex. His notion of the "world as idea" parallels our hypothesis that our religious imagination, and in particular the god who sits on its throne, shapes our experience of the world. "The world is my idea," he said, meaning that how we perceive the world is determined by the instrument that perceives it—namely, our minds. This is a thoroughly rational, Kantian position that frees us from our impression that the world is as it appears.

On the irrational, unconscious level of his temperament, however, Schopenhauer was a hostage to Yahweh. He almost admits as much, again in his own words: "The sole thing that reconciles me to the Old Testament is the story of the Fall. In my eyes, it is the only metaphysical truth in that book, even though it appears in the form of an allegory. There seems to me no better explanation of our existence than that it is the result of some false step, some sin of which we are paying the penalty."

Original sin, as we shall discuss, is a Christian innovation, not a Jewish one. Nonetheless, it is a doctrine about Yahweh's punitiveness. Schopenhauer proved that one does not have to believe in Yahweh in order to live in his universe.

II

YAHWEH IN OUR RELATIONSHIPS

The striving for personal power is a disastrous delusion and poisons man's living together. Whoever desires the human community must renounce the striving for power over others.

—Alfred Adler

5

Was Freud Truly a "Godless Jew"?

If God did not exist, it would be necessary to invent him.

—*Voltaire*

The question posed by the title of this chapter revolves around Freud's own widely quoted description of himself as a "godless Jew." By this term, he meant that he was not only an atheist but also the member of a long lineage of people whose belief in a particular god he had been disabused of. The question then is had he been truly disabused of this belief?

My argument here is that the specific *content* of the belief may have been jettisoned, but his underlying, unconscious predisposition as displayed in his attitudes, emotional style, and behaviors suggests that the belief had merely morphed into another form and that its essence remained the same. He may have dropped Yahweh from his load of ancient belongings, but he was now under the yoke of his modern Yahweh complex and hence not a godless Jew at all.

Let's take a look at how this complex manifested, and especially how it affected his personal relationships. The sources I will draw upon for my argument will be *The Freud/Jung Letters* and Jung's autobiography, *Memories, Dreams, Reflections*. With both sources there can be little doubt that what Jung observed about Freud, his mentor, was filtered through Jung's perception and that other students of Freud might have had different impressions (and certainly, most did). The subjectivity of every individual's psyche is an objective fact.

The Relational Dynamics

A good place to begin is with the arrangement of their relationship. Freud was Jung's mentor from 1906 to 1913. In 1906, Freud was fifty years old and Jung was thirty. Freud resided in Vienna and Jung in Zurich. They met in person periodically, the first time in Vienna in 1907. On their first meeting, they "talked virtually without a pause for thirteen hours" until two in the morning. They also traveled together to America to lecture at Clark University in 1909. Nevertheless, most of their relationship was conducted through their correspondence.

Jung's attitude to Freud in the early stage of their relationship was deferential and idealized. "I rejoice every day in *your* riches and live from the crumbs that fall from the rich man's table," he wrote to Freud in 1907. He regarded him as a father figure and as the "first man of real importance" he had encountered. In a letter later in the same year, Jung admits that he had, with "boundless admiration," a "religious" crush on him. Exactly what he meant by this is unclear, but we can assume that he saw Freud as a kind of prophet bringing to humanity news of a new world: the realm of the unconscious mind. He may also have seen him as a personal redeemer. Of course, this role would have involved more than the typical guidance and initiation a young man would seek from a wise elder.

Jung further confesses, with some disgust and shame, that his veneration of Freud was undeniably erotic and rooted in his boyhood trauma of sexual assault by a man he once worshipped. In other words, it featured what Freud would have called a "repetition compulsion," the psyche's way of working out a trauma by repeating it until it is, by virtue of some insight, resolution, or mastery, no longer a compulsion. Jung's attraction to Freud was charged not only with eros or sexual libido but also with the psyche's instinctual urge to heal itself. Freud was a redeemer to Jung inasmuch as he compelled Jung to repeat and heal the traumatic violation he had suffered as a boy. We can imagine how far Freud had to fall to become simply a mortal in Jung's eyes, given how high the latter had raised him.

On Freud's part, he hoped that Jung, the son of a Protestant pastor, would bring the burgeoning discipline of psychoanalysis, the so-called "Jewish science," to the world at large. He reportedly told his Jewish collaborators, "[Jung] will save us." It has been well documented that Freud was fascinated by Moses even in childhood and later saw psychoanalysis as an important movement that he spearheaded in much the same way Moses led his people out of slavery and gave them a revolutionary code to live by: the Mosaic Law. This reveals Freud's own religious character, influencing him whether he believed in God or not. He was on a mission.

For him to then choose Jung as a savior to widely establish and carry on the tradition of psychoanalysis—essentially making him Moses's Joshua or Jesus's Paul—shows that he put his faith in Jung as much as Jung put his in Freud. Each needed the other in specifically religious ways. It is important to appreciate this dynamic in order to understand the backdrop of their relationship. How did their relationship devolve from this mutually beneficial arrangement—not to mention from the fondness each had for the other—to the bitter antagonism that eventually enveloped them?

After the Honeymoon

By 1911, Freud's Yahweh complex had surfaced in the form of fanatical zeal and an intolerance of ideas that he felt were incompatible with his. He had taken on both a religious language and the armor of dogma to protect psychoanalysis from Alfred Adler's diverging views on the primarily sexual nature of libido: "I now feel that I must avenge the offended goddess Libido, and I mean to be more careful from now on that heresy does not occupy too much space in the *Zentralblatt* [a journal established for the advancement of psychoanalysis and of which Jung became the editor]." Adler's association with Freud would not last much longer. Wilhelm Stekel, who supported Adler's views, would go with him.

Freud tolerated Jung's growing interest in astrology only because

Jung presented it as subject matter appropriate for psychoanalytic examination (similar to the approach of Sándor Ferenczi, another of Freud's collaborators with an interest in parapsychological phenomena). Jung treated astrology as "indispensable for a proper understanding of mythology" and as "knowledge that has been intuitively projected into the heavens." He described the signs of the zodiac as "character pictures, in other words libido symbols which depict the typical qualities of the libido at a given moment." Probably he was being shrewd in how he pitched this to Freud. (Later, Freud would explore the possibilities of parapsychology himself, especially telepathy.)

By 1912 we see more clearly the beginnings of Jung's own divergence from Freud's theories. Jung acknowledged this with respect and good humor: "Of course I have opinions which are not yours about the ultimate truths of psychoanalysis. . . . I would never have sided with you in the first place had not heresy run in my blood." But Freud holds together the opposition between them admirably, admitting he is defensive about Jung's decreased frequency of correspondence. We also see on Freud's part the seeds of "privation," as he calls it. He misses Jung and appears hurt by him, yet he frames this in a friendly, accommodating way, even if with some criticism:

> The indestructible foundation of our personal relationship is our involvement in psychoanalysis; but on this foundation it seemed tempting to build something finer though more labile, a reciprocal intimate friendship. Shouldn't we go on building? . . . Still, if you think you want greater freedom from me, what can I do but give up my feeling of urgency about our relationship, occupy my unemployed libido elsewhere, and bide my time until you discover that you can tolerate greater intimacy? When that happens, you will find me willing. During the transition to this attitude of reserve, I have complained very quietly. You would have thought me insincere if I had not reacted at all. . . . Rest assured of my [affection] and continue to think of me in friendship, even if you do not write often.

We thus see that Freud felt genuine warmth for Jung. By contrast, Jung was rather distant and cool, focusing in his next letter on others in their professional community.

My own hunch about what was brewing inside Jung and manifesting by way of his less frequent letters was his increasing recognition that he needed to become his own man. He knew, unconsciously if not consciously, that he would need to develop his own ideas apart from Freud's, and that he might not be able to do this under Freud's watchful eye. Barely three months after the above exchange, Freud visited Switzerland without meeting Jung, which Jung interpreted as Freud's displeasure at Jung's own recent development of the libido theory. Jung commented, "The parallel with Adler is a bitter pill; I swallow it without a murmur. Evidently this is my fate."

It turned out that Freud's choice to not visit Zurich was motivated by other and more ordinary circumstances, and his initial reaction to Jung's ideas on the libido theory were tentative and vague. He assured Jung that "there is no reason to suppose that this scientific difference will detract from our personal relations. I can recall that there were profounder differences between us at the beginning of our relationship." Nevertheless, it seems as if Jung anticipated what was to come, what he might have to do to extricate himself from Freud's grip on him—this in order to become a great thinker and pioneer in his own right. It is difficult to rise to one's calling with a famous father figure looking over one's shoulder. Evidently, this calling *was* his fate, only announced prematurely.

As Freud's other collaborators observed at this time, Freud was distressed by the "defections" of Adler and Stekel, and they were disturbed to hear from him that now "his relations with Jung were beginning to be strained." Though Jung wrote him that he had no intention to "follow Adler's recipe for overcoming the father. . . . That cap doesn't fit," their relations continued to deteriorate. Jung must have been painfully aware that Freud had to be obeyed in a monotheistic way and that he had little tolerance for dissension (indeed, after Freud's falling-out with Jung, the innovative Sándor Ferenczi too would become Freud's scapegoat—an appropriate term given its association with Yahweh's demand to be singularly worshipped by goat sacrifice.

In the period leading up to the final break between Freud and Jung, their letters became noticeably more formal, detached, and businesslike (by now Jung was the editor of the *Zentralblatt*, which required them to communicate with each other). In one exchange, Freud accused Jung of making a slip of the tongue, or pen (what came to be known as a Freudian slip). Without delving into the complexity of the German language, suffice it to say that it had to do with Jung's ambivalent allegiance to him. This accusation clearly triggered Jung, who, while acknowledging this ambivalence in his reply, harshly criticized Freud for neurotically infantilizing his pupils by reducing them to patients and children who "blushingly admit" their neurotic flaws so that Freud could "remain on top as the father, sitting pretty." True or not, this portrays Freud as a patriarch in general and a Yahwistic father in particular. We might, however, wish to take Jung's chastening words with a grain of salt. He seems Yahwistically inflated himself: "I am not in the least neurotic—touch wood!" he boasts in the same letter. Even if this were true, his self-description is hardly modest.

Freud responded with dignity and substance, regretting that Jung took his comment about the slip "out of all proportion to the occasion." Yet this exchange was the straw that broke the camel's back, and Freud terminated their personal relations while maintaining their professional one. The final dissolution of all relations was in sight and, one might conclude, unavoidable. The problem came down to basic arithmetic:

1 activated Yahweh complex + 1 activated Yahweh complex =
0 relationships

In Retrospect

Years later, as an older man completing his autobiography, Jung gave a considered assessment of the nature of Freud's preoccupation with sexuality—pinpointing it not exactly as an expression of the Yahweh complex but definitely driven as if it were:

I can still recall vividly how Freud said to me, "My dear Jung, promise me never to abandon the sexual theory. That is the most essential thing of all. You see, we must make a dogma of it, an unshakable bulwark." He said that to me with great emotion, in the tone of a father saying, "And promise me this one thing, my dear son: that you will go to church every Sunday." In some astonishment I asked him, "A bulwark—against what?" To which he replied, "Against the black tide of mud"—and here he hesitated for a moment, then added—"of occultism". . . . [by which he seemed to mean] virtually everything that philosophy and religion, including the rising contemporary science of parapsychology, had learned about the psyche.

And here emerges Jung's crucial insight—namely, that Freud was gripped by Yahweh's *spirit* and *psychology* if not his theistic image:

> One thing was clear: Freud, who had always made much of his irreligiosity, had now constructed a dogma; or rather, in the place of a jealous God whom he had lost, he had substituted another compelling image, that of sexuality. It was no less insistent, exacting, domineering, threatening, and morally ambivalent than the original one. . . . The numinosity, that is, the psychological qualities of the two rationally incommensurable opposites—Yahweh and sexuality—remained the same. The name alone had changed, and with it, of course, the point of view: the lost god had now to be sought below, not above.

Jung furthermore reveals how Freud was at the mercy of one of Yahweh's darker qualities: his bitterness stemming from his dividedness within and against himself (and to this we may add the bitterness Freud and Yahweh both felt from betrayal by the very ones they cherished):

> There was one characteristic of [Freud's] that preoccupied me above all: his bitterness. It had struck me at our first encounter; but it

remained inexplicable to me until I was able to see it in connection with his attitude toward sexuality. . . . Basically, he wanted to teach—or so at least it seemed to me—that, regarded from within, sexuality included spirituality and had an intrinsic meaning. But his concretistic [biological] terminology was too narrow to express this idea. He gave me the impression that at bottom he was working against his own goal and against himself; and there is, after all, no harsher bitterness than that of a person who is his own worst enemy. . . . For that reason I see him as a tragic figure.

I am reminded here of something D. H. Lawrence said: "It is a fearful thing to fall into the hands of the living God. But it is a much more fearful thing to fall out of them."

6

The Marriage of Marilyn Monroe and Joe DiMaggio

The most exciting attractions are between two opposites that
never meet.

—*Andy Warhol*

B ased on what we know about her, Marilyn Monroe did not exude
a Yahweh complex. But she gravitated toward men who did—or at
least, two men who did: Lee Strasberg and Joe DiMaggio. John Kennedy,
in spite of growing up in an Irish Catholic family with a patriarchal
mindset, did not exhibit an overpowering Yahweh complex. Also, to this
day it is still speculative whether he had a relationship with Monroe, as
is the case with Robert Kennedy (this has been rumored, too), so we
could put both brothers aside for our purposes. As for playwright Arthur
Miller, her third husband, he was, if anything, an anti-Yahwist with his
staunch refusal to comply with the demands of Senator Joseph McCarthy's
judgmental and punitive Un-American Activities Committee.

About Strasberg, Monroe's acting coach who famously taught method
acting at the Actors Studio, she said: "I think probably he changed my
life more than any other human being that I've met." Theirs was not a
romantic or sexual relationship but one between a student and her teacher.
In an almost psychotherapeutic way, he helped her deal with her imposter
syndrome, her persistent, "secret feeling that [she was] really a fake." The
film director Elia Kazan, who had an affair with Monroe and also studied
with Strasberg, writes about him:

> He carried with him the aura of a prophet, a magician, a witch doctor,
> a psychoanalyst, and a feared father of a Jewish home. . . . He was the
> force that held the thirty-odd members of the theatre together, made

them "permanent." He did this not only by his superior knowledge but by the threat of his anger. . . . No one questioned his dominance— he spoke holy writ—his leading role in that summer's activities, and his right to all power. To win his favor became everyone's goal. His explosions of temper maintained the discipline of this camp of high-strung people. I came to believe that without their fear of this man, the group would fly apart, everyone going in different directions instead of to where he was pointing. . . . I was afraid of him too. Even as I admired him. . . . He knew what was needed, and he was fired up by his mission and its importance.

There was nothing overtly abusive about Strasberg's Yahwistic emotional and teaching style, as long as it didn't violate the boundaries and personhood of others; many even liked it. Of course, one can say the same thing about a cult leader.

The second Yahwistic man Monroe gravitated toward was her second husband, baseball legend Joe DiMaggio (her first marriage, arranged for legal purposes when she was sixteen, lasted four years). Nicknamed "Joltin' Joe" and the "Yankee Clipper"—the latter likening his speed to a clipper sailing ship—and a three-time winner of baseball's Most Valuable Player Award, DiMaggio was as admired in the world of professional sports as Monroe was in the world of entertainment. Despite outer differences, underneath they were very much alike, Monroe wrote in her memoir, *My Story*. In particular, they shared a desire for a stable home and children. But there was more. "They had one big thing in common," a documentary explained. "Each was an enormous figure created by the hero machine, and inside that vast personage lived a small person, fearful to be seen. In their loneliness, they might have been brother and sister. Joe insisted they be husband and wife."

From the very beginning of their marriage in 1954, DiMaggio was prone to jealousy, and not only of other men whom Monroe was surrounded by but of women too. He wanted her to give up her career and be a stay-at-home wife. But Monroe was unable to assuage his fears of losing her, and her career decisions didn't help. During their honeymoon in Japan, the US Army asked her to go to Korea to entertain the troops stationed there as part of the UN occupation force. She accepted the invitation, returning afterward to Japan to reunite with an understandably displeased DiMaggio. Monroe let him know how much she had basked in the attention received from the troops, her first live audience. To the soldiers themselves she said, "I'll always remember my honeymoon in Korea—with the 45th Division."

However, the events that ended their marriage revolved around DiMaggio's reaction to Monroe's famous scene in *The Seven Year Itch*, in which she stood over a subway grate with the air blowing up her skirt. To promote interest in the film, the studio had arranged for the media to be present while the scene was being shot. DiMaggio was on the set, embarrassed and irate as he watched her skirt blow up and down while a crowd of spectators cheered. They argued about this in the days that followed until finally, she told friends, DiMaggio beat her, though she added that it was not without cause, as if such behavior could be condoned. Tearfully, she publicly announced the end of her marriage, and to the court she cited his mental cruelty as the cause. They were married for less than a year.

But their story didn't end there. Shortly after Monroe announced her separation from DiMaggio, he wrote to her in a letter: "I love you and want to be with you. . . . There is nothing I would like better than to restore your confidence in me. . . . My heart split even wider seeing you cry in front of all those people." Seven years later, after Monroe's marriage to Miller failed, she and DiMaggio would reconcile. When one of her psychiatrists had her committed to the Payne Whitney Psychiatric Clinic in New York for treatment for anxiety, depression, and drug addiction, it was DiMaggio whom she called to secure her release, and he showed up in person to get her.

To help her rest and recuperate, he took her to the Yankees' Florida training camp where he was a batting coach. They remained good friends until she died, and there was speculation that they would remarry. DiMaggio arranged for roses to be delivered thrice weekly to her crypt for the next twenty years. He reportedly suffered terrible guilt for what he felt was his role in destroying their marriage and contributing to her demise. He never talked about her publicly or otherwise exploited their relationship. He never remarried.

The War Between Gods

The marriage of Aphrodite and Yahweh has the makings of a marriage made in hell, and Marilyn Monroe and Joe DiMaggio's was exactly this kind of marriage. In the form of archetypal complexes, these were the gods ruling their fates, both as individuals and as a couple. It was not their fault that they had a stormy, difficult relationship. Theirs were characterological differences, built into their temperaments and inherited from the collective unconscious where the gods reside. They did not consciously choose their temperaments; these were psychologically predetermined dispositions.

We will later see that while the ego is not responsible for having such a temperament or predisposition, it is responsible for how it responds to and manages it. Monroe and DiMaggio were not psychologically oriented any more than the cultural milieu was at that time, so they unfortunately were unable to benefit from what modern psychology has to offer regarding archetypal complexes. We know little about how Monroe's psychiatrists dealt with her Aphrodite complex, or if they dealt with it at all, but evidently neither Monroe nor DiMaggio had much insight into what compelled them to make the choices and to behave in the ways they did. If they had had the psychological tools to navigate their turbulent relationship, they might have had a fighting chance.

As it stood, the fight was between the two of them rather than with the complexes within themselves. Their marriage might have been forged in true love just as much as the marriage of any two people *without* such complexes, but loving someone does not automatically mean we can live with them. The marriage may be made in heaven or hell, but either way, it must be lived on earth. When we marry and live with someone possessed by an archetypal complex, we also marry and live with their complex.

A marriage powered by the Aphrodite and Yahweh complexes is essentially the marriage of erotic love and beauty with the features of Yahweh—not an easy combination since their purposes are so opposite from each other. Aphrodite glorifies the bliss of love and beauty, whereas Yahweh is very much concerned with power itself. As Jung said, "Where love reigns, there is no will to power; and where the will to power is paramount, love is lacking. The one is but the shadow of the other." Both complexes can be either positive or negative or some blend of the two. Both can make their human subjects seem larger than life or miserable because their grandeur cannot be integrated into everyday life.

Jungian analyst Arlene Diane Landau tells us the following about what the dark side of Aphrodite looks like when someone has fallen into her grip:

> The shadow side of Aphrodite manifests when a woman is completely identified with Aphrodite's powers, when other archetypal qualities of the feminine are unimportant to her. The tragedies that result from this are the subject of numerous well-known novels and films and [are] exemplified in the lives of certain actresses and other celebrities. . . . The dark side of the pursuit of beauty is especially apparent with aging, when the Aphrodite woman must become something other than a source of beauty or dwindle to a bitter and lonely end. Those whose lives have been wounded by the shadow side of Aphrodite—or those who do not have enough of Aphrodite's joy in their personal makeup—may find understanding and rebirth through the consciousness gained in real-life exploration of an ideal that has ballooned into a distortion. In these times, when the idolization of Aphrodite—and the tragedy that ensues—are perhaps more widespread than ever, the crucial key for women is consciousness.

If we believe the stereotyped image of Monroe, she was an Aphrodite woman gripped by an Aphrodite complex. We might even say that she could have benefited from cultivating some Yahwistic strength, if not power, to give ballast to her unstable temperament and diaphanous ego. We might conclude that her need for such strength is what attracted her to men like Strasberg and DiMaggio. However, it is likely that this perception of her as unstable and needy has been exaggerated by the media and that she was in fact much more solid and self-empowered than she has been given credit for. After all, she engineered her rise to fame and took control of her career with self-confidence and skill. This at least is the viewpoint of the documentary *Reframed: Marilyn Monroe.*

Nevertheless, it is also likely that the Aphrodite complex took a heavy toll on her while at the same time providing her with a key to her success, the key here being how to use her natural beauty and appeal. This made her the object of other people's desires and projections. Even a mind as discerning as Arthur Miller's fell under the sway of her goddess qualities: when he first met her, he later wrote, "the shock of her body's motion sped through [him]."

A less archetypal and more historical key to Monroe's use of her beauty and appeal was her casual attitude toward sex. As is often the case, the historical may have triggered the archetypal; her personal history may have constellated the Aphrodite complex. Biographer Charles Casillo writes that Monroe had multiple episodes of sexual abuse beginning at age eight. Journalist Karina Longworth adds that "so many of the things that made Marilyn 'Marilyn'—the actual or implied easiness, the childlike voice and perspective, the lifelong search for male protectors—all of these things were, in fact, textbook long-term symptoms of child abuse."

Sexually abused children often develop a precocious and promiscuous sexuality. Although Monroe's sexual history does not blatantly feature these characteristics, there may have been a similar loosening or unmooring of her sexual mores due to her underlying trauma. Our archetypal complexes often have some connection with early trauma. DiMaggio did not have a traumatic childhood per se, but nonetheless, it was a difficult one. He was the eighth of nine children born to Sicilian immigrants and to a critical father who would tell him he was "good for nothing."

Not surprisingly, the godlike dimension of Monroe and DiMaggio's relationship was explosive. They had great sexual chemistry that bonded them together instinctually and emotionally. DiMaggio told his friend Rock Positano, "When we got together in the bedroom, it was like the gods were fighting; there were thunderclouds and lightning above us." In his plainspoken manner, DiMaggio has here described the numinous but conflicted quality of their mutual attraction: *the gods were fighting*.

As discussed above, the gods fought outside the bedroom, too. DiMaggio insisted upon having *all* of Monroe's attention and dedication, just like Yahweh did with his chosen people—his bride, as he called them. Similar to Yahweh, he was jealous, controlling, moody, self-preoccupied, critical, punitive, and violently rageful. Much like Yahweh did with his creatures, he blamed all this on Monroe, at least initially. Instead of examining his own role in their discord, he claimed she brought out the worst in him.

DiMaggio's Yahweh complex continued to plague him well after Monroe's death. According to a number of biographers, he was a gloomy loner with bitter hatreds "more defined than likes." He had an estranged relationship with a son (from a previous marriage) who struggled with substance abuse and homelessness and died at the age of fifty-seven. Obsessed with money, DiMaggio was alleged to have ties with the Mafia. (We shall later look at the relationship between the Mafia and the Yahweh complex.) To his friend Morris Engelberg he admitted, "I don't trust anyone. No exceptions." Known to end relationships for some slight transgression, there was a "core of hollowness to his life, a self-imposed emptiness." His few friends were expected to obey his rules, of which one was "Never wear the wrong-color outfit."

For her part, Monroe's extroverted, "hammed-up" goddess behaviors, which she was able to turn on and off at will, fueled DiMaggio's hypersensitivity and insecurity. Arguably, Monroe had a streak of the Yahweh complex herself, except that she acted hers *in*, not *out:* her inner critic regularly bludgeoned and alienated her. In a letter to Strasberg, she wrote, "I still am lost. I mean I can't get myself together. . . . My will is weak but I can't stand anything. I sound crazy but I think I'm going crazy. . . . I feel like I'm not existing in the human race at all."

Even more telling is a nightmare she recorded when she was married to Miller, in which Strasberg is operating on her with the assistance of her psychoanalyst, Margaret Hohenberg ("Dr. H"):

> [Her body is opened up and there is] absolutely nothing there—Strasberg is deeply disappointed but more even—academically amazed that he had made such a mistake. He thought there was going to be so much—more than he had ever dreamed possible . . . instead there was absolutely nothing—devoid of every human living feeling thing—the only thing that came out was so finely cut sawdust—like out of a raggedy ann doll—and the sawdust spills all over the floor & table and Dr. H is puzzled because suddenly she realizes that this is a new type [of] case. The patient . . . existing of complete emptiness. Strasberg's dreams & hopes for theater are fallen. Dr. H's dreams and hopes for a permanent psychiatric cure [are] given up—Arthur is disappointed—let down.

We can feel only sorrow and compassion for both Monroe and DiMaggio. They understood neither their own needs nor each other's. Human suffering is immense but made immeasurably more immense by our failure to understand ourselves. Although we, in our totality, are not identical to our complexes, when we identify with them, blindly serving them, they take us over and reduce us to a primitive, childish condition. Or a neurotic one. As Freud said, neurosis is the "result of a kind of ignorance, a not-knowing of mental processes which should be known." When we don't know our own mental processes, including our complexes, we are at their mercy. The Aphrodite complex is not as prevalent or cruel as the Yahweh complex, but would we want to be at the mercy of either of them?

7

The Breakup of the Beatles

Now Yahweh came down to see the city and the tower that
man had built. "So they are all a single people with a single
language!" Yahweh said. "This is only the beginning of what
they will do! There will be nothing too hard for them to do.
Come, let us go down and confound their language so that
they can no longer understand one another's speech." Yahweh
scattered them from there over the face of the whole earth,
and they stopped building the city. That is why it was called
"Babel" [meaning in Hebrew, "to confound"].

—*Genesis 11:5–9*

Was the dissolution of the Beatles the result of a divisive Yahweh
complex that settled upon the group, imbuing them with mistrust
and souring their relationships to each other? In the film *Let It Be*, one
could sense the Yahwistic friction and melancholic heaviness in the studio.
Paul would later describe this film as a documentary that shows how a
band breaks up, and George would refer to this period as the Beatles'
"winter of discontent." Like with the Hebrew Bible's end-stage Books of
Lamentations and Ecclesiastes, something was gone, leaving a flatness or
deadness in its place.

The Beatles' producer, George Martin, explained that the
disillusionment and bickering that had begun in the recording sessions
of *The White Album* had by the time of the *Let It Be* album intensified (this
in spite of the many loving feelings and humorous, joyful moments the
Beatles still shared together, as revealed in Peter Jackson's documentary,
The Beatles: Get Back). In order to organize things, Paul became bossy,
which the other Beatles resented. John would "waft off" with Yoko. George

didn't attend some sessions at all, even quitting the band for a few days. On the surface, exchanges like the following resemble the squabbles of any family:

> *Paul:* You always get annoyed when I say that. I'm trying to help you, but I always hear myself annoying you. . . . I'm not trying to *get* you. . . .
>
> *George:* Okay, I don't mind. I'll play whatever you want me to play, or I won't play at all if you don't want me to play. Whatever it is that will please you, I'll do it.

Yet it is precisely in their resemblance to typical family squabbles that such exchanges display a Yahwistic dynamic: a power conflict infuses the communication with elements of control and resentment, and a mutual feeling of not being heard and respected prevails. It was to this that George was speaking when he later said that the Beatles' relationships with each other became "very unhealthy and unhappy." John confirmed this: "The whole pressure of [making the film] finally got to us. Like people do when they're together, they start picking on each other. 'It's because of *you*—you got the tambourine wrong—that my whole life is a misery.' It became petty. But the manifestations were on each other because we were the only ones we had."

Bossiness, pickiness, pettiness, blaming others, a miserable disposition—are these not among the traits of Yahweh?

Partisanship, cliques, emotional splitting, projection, and paranoia—all Yahwistic traits—permeated the collective psyche of the group as well. Ringo illustrates how the entire band became enveloped by the Yahweh complex in what psychoanalysts, among others, understand as an "intersubjective field." This is a merging or connecting together of a number of individuals' psyches, usually on an unconscious level and often in a manner that confuses the inside with the outside. (Jung frequently referred to philosopher and anthropologist Lucien Lévy-Bruhl's related concept of this, pronounced in French as "*participation mystique.*") Note how the biblical archetype of judgment, even of oneself, is flying around like a bird in the sky but within each of the four members:

> I quit the band in '67, on *The White Album,* because I was in some emotional state where I honestly felt that I wasn't playing well. For some reason I felt I just wasn't playing good and *those* three were really close. And I thought, "Well, I've got to deal with this anyways." So I went over to John's—he was staying with Yoko in my apartment—and I said, "Look, man, I've got to say I feel I'm not playing really good and *you* three are really close." And he goes, "I thought it was *you* three." And I went to Paul's and knocked on his door and I said the same thing. I said, "And you three are really close." [He said,] "I thought it was *you* three." And I'm going on holiday, I'm off, and I went to Sardinia. When I got back—they said, "C'mon back, we love you"—George had decorated the whole studio with flowers, and that was a beautiful moment for me.

To "play well" means to truly *play.* However, unlike the flute-playing Krishna or the rotund Laughing Buddha, Yahweh was not a playful god.

Family Dynamics and the Assuaging Alchemical Agent of Water

The likelihood that all four musicians had been gripped by a dark complex is further supported by the fact that on both *The White Album* and *Let It Be*, the introduction of an outside musician changed the dynamic and broke the spell, at least temporarily. In a sense, the outsider played the role of a family therapist: his mere presence had a calming and sobering effect. George explains:

> It's interesting to see how people behave nicely when you bring a guest in, because they don't really want everybody to know that

they're so bitchy, and this happened back in *The White Album* when I brought Eric Clapton in to play on my "My Guitar Gently Weeps." Suddenly everybody's on their best behavior. So [while recording *Let It Be*] I put a message out to find if Billy [Preston] was in town, and told him to come in to [the studio on] Savile Row, which he did. Straightaway it just became a hundred percent improvement in the vibe in the room and everybody was happy also to have somebody else playing in the band.

George Martin adds: "Billy Preston was a great help. . . . He was an amiable fellow, too, very nice. He was a kind of emollient, if you like. He helped to lubricate the friction that had been there."

Martin's choice of the words "emollient" and "lubricate" is very telling: when the ego gets gripped by a complex and stuck in some situation or on some viewpoint, it becomes rigid and fixated upon the emotions evoked. In connection to this, Jung noted that one's readiness for inner transformation is often announced by dreams of water, for these indicate that the ego is becoming more fluid, more open to change. The alchemists, who projected psychological processes into concrete matter, practiced this dissolution of dense psychic states in a procedure they aptly called *solutio*. We may say that the outside musicians helped dissolve tensions by altering the bad chemistry not only between the Beatles but also between the Beatles and the Yahweh complex that had hijacked their creative process. Of course, much more would have been needed to make this more than a temporary change. Complexes have their own fluidity, returning again and again like a tide coming in, waterlogging us and sweeping us away in their current unless we learn how to swim against it.

And surely, the Beatles' Yahweh complex did return not long after they broke up. Yahweh's disgust with his people in the Hebrew Bible's prophetic period could easily be detected as the archetypal backdrop of John's diatribe against Paul in his haunting song "How Do You Sleep?" on his second solo album, *Imagine*. John wrote this attack on Paul's character in retaliation to what Paul later admitted was his "little dig at John and Yoko" in his song

"Too Many People" on *his* second solo album, *Ram*—as if it were necessary to also attack the other's spouse. However, what was said between one Beatle and another is less important here than what it meant: in publicly airing their grievances in this way, they weaponized their art, turning it into warfare aimed at hurting and damaging each other.

When the Yahweh complex gets hold of us with its anger and hostility, considerations such as modesty and self-restraint go out the window. In George's song "Sue Me, Sue You Blues" on his third solo album, *Living in the Material World*, we can hear his despair as he sings of the ex-Beatles' bitter legal battles with each other. This was less a complaint than a dirge. With their lawsuits, the creative and collaborative spirit that the Beatles once shared had deteriorated into passive-aggressive Yahwistic legalism, an approach to things we shall discuss in greater depth later. And as one of their final songs almost prophetically anticipated, boy, they carried that weight for a long time.

But at least for a short while between *Let It Be* and the above vitriol, the Beatles would, under Martin's Merlin-like guidance, reunite as a harmonious group, and the magic would return. They would consummate their legacy and gift to the world with their masterful swan song, *Abbey Road*, knowing beforehand that this album would be their last. They exited the stage like Yahweh exited from history: disillusioned, perhaps, but nonetheless victorious in spirit. Their concluding message, also gentle and glorious, was that at the end of the day, the love we get is measured by the love we give. (If only Yahweh had realized this; if only we would!) Their joy and goodness account for their undying durability, so it seems, generation after generation.

8

The Rolling Stones' Relationship to Yahweh

One of my views about people is that what we've done to
socialize ourselves is to put around ourselves this little hard
shell which is our civilized entities, but beneath that is the
covered wildness, which is what I call fury. Not only in a bad
way—it's the fury that changes the world, the fury that creates
great art and passionate love. It's ecstasy as much as rage.

—*Salman Rushdie*

The constellation of the Yahweh complex as a mutually shared
experience among the Beatles was different than the more typical
kind that nearly terminated the Rolling Stones. That kind, as Keith Richards
reveals in his autobiography, *Life*, more or less gripped Mick Jagger alone,
and was plainly observed and onerous to the other band members. Richards
diagnosed Jagger's god complex as a familiar rock 'n' roll syndrome:

> The immediate problem was that Mick had developed an overriding
> desire to control everything. As far as he was concerned, it was
> Mick Jagger and *them*. That was the attitude that we all got. It
> didn't matter how much he tried, he couldn't stop appearing, to
> himself at least, as numero uno. . . . Oh dear me, after all these
> years, the swollen head's arrived. He'd gotten to where it wouldn't
> fit through the doorway. The band, including myself, were now
> basically hirelings. . . . Mick got very big ideas. All lead singers do.
> It's a known affliction called LVS, lead vocalist syndrome.

One episode Richards relates with boyish glee and charm nevertheless
ended violently. One night in Amsterdam, Jagger and Richards went out,

Jagger having borrowed Richards's wedding jacket. Returning to the hotel where the band was staying, Jagger called up Charlie Watts, the band's drummer, at five in the morning, demanding to see him:

> "Where's my drummer?" No answer. He puts the phone down. Mick and I were still sitting there, pretty pissed—give Mick a couple of glasses, he's gone—when, about twenty minutes later, there was a knock at the door. There was Charlie Watts, Savile Row suit, perfectly dressed, tie, shaved, the whole fucking bit. I could smell the cologne! I opened the door and he didn't even look at me, he walked straight past me, got hold of Mick and said, "Never call me your drummer again." Then he hauled him up by the lapels of my jacket and gave him a right hook. Mick fell back onto a silver platter of smoked salmon on the table and began to slide toward the open window and the canal below it. And I was thinking, this is a good one, and then I realized it was my wedding jacket. And I grabbed hold of it and caught Mick just before he slid into the Amsterdam canal.

Although it was the lead singer who was afflicted by the Yahweh complex ("Thou shalt have no other gods in the band before me"), clearly the rest of the band was infected by the complex's toxicity and, in the above instance, infected in an explosive yet methodical, Yahweh-like way. (Arriving well dressed and clean shaven, Watts came prepared with a single purpose, like Yahweh gunning for Moses one night in the desert wilderness, aiming to kill him for not circumcising one of his sons. Had not his wife intervened, Moses would have died prematurely.)

"Once you release that acid," Richards concludes, "it begins to corrode." Richards's own public criticism of Jagger is proof of that, and not of the noble magnanimity and trustworthiness by which Ralph Waldo Emerson defines "friendship." Do we really need to know the details of Mick's drinking limit and visit to the hors d'oeuvres table (or, for that matter, the size of his penis and testicles, which Richards also unabashedly comments on)? Caught in a polarizing dynamic and Yahwistic vengefulness and one-upmanship, Richards had his own shadow that he did not see. There is enough of the psyche's dark side to go around for all of us. So yes, perhaps we really *do* need to know those juicy Mick details, if not to satisfy our McDonald's appetites, then to remind us that even gods succumb to their weaknesses and reap the consequences of that. A more grounded Jagger was reported to have later acknowledged his folly with good humor, and Richards apologized to him for publicly exposing it.

A Negative Relationship Is Still a Relationship

In the final analysis, the constellation of the Yahweh complex with the Rolling Stones was, at least in regard to their interpersonal dynamics, only *somewhat* different than it was with the Beatles. But the Rolling Stones had—and at the time of this writing still have—a relationship to Yahweh that is their distinct trademark, going well beyond interpersonal dynamics.

One may wonder if Yahweh was somehow at play in the Altamont concert tragedy in 1969. Four people died, three accidentally and one by homicide. Regarding the homicide, a young Black man was killed by a member of the Hells Angels in a scuffle occurring just feet from the stage. (It was later determined in a court trial that this member was acting in self-defense.) There are differing reports on exactly what arrangement the Rolling Stones' management had made with the Hells Angels, and admittedly, they were not the only band in the concert that agreed to this arrangement; but the general consensus is that they were to provide some form of stage protection. The documentary film *Gimme Shelter* shows that the Rolling Stones themselves were distressed by what happened. One commentator notes that they in fact "didn't know what kind of people they were dealing with." Still, what could they and the other bands have been thinking by recruiting an organization with a name like Hells Angels?

Coincidentally, or perhaps not, the band had played "Sympathy for the Devil" shortly before the killing occurred. A fight (not the one involving the killing) had broken out in the crowd, and Jagger interrupted the song.

Appealing to the audience to calm down, he said, "Something very funny happens when we start that number." That "something" was, to begin with, the contagion effect of the dark or primitive side of the psyche. In a crowd, this can be easily ignited, as can be observed in soccer-match riots. Add to this feverish state a song about evil—performed to the stirring, syncopated rhythm of a samba, no less—and all that this activates in the psyche, and anything can happen (though Rolling Stones member Bill Wyman said that this "was just one of many songs where there was fighting going on").

Accordingly, cultural critics called the Altamont concert the end of the Woodstock dream. An FBI agent's disclosure in 2008 revealed that its haunting effects trailed the band even years later. Angry that Jagger had blamed the Hells Angels for what happened at Altamont, a group of its members attempted to assassinate him in 1975 by using a boat to reach the back garden of his holiday home in Long Island (thus avoiding the security in front). The plot was foiled by a storm in which all the men were thrown overboard.

An album with a title like *Their Satanic Majesties Request* and a song like "Sympathy for the Devil" speak pointedly to the Rolling Stones' antipathetic, oppositional relationship to Yahweh, itself something of a Yahwistic negation of the biblical God. We should remember here that the Hebrew Bible depicts the devil not only as the instrument of Yahweh but as *interchangeable* with him: on at least one occasion, the same action was attributed to both.

The Rolling Stones' sympathy, of course, is sardonic: they are not championing evil but rather challenging it. In their recognition of a side of God that also exists within us and is exercised through us, they follow the tradition of such high art as Dante's *Divine Comedy* and Goethe's *Faust*, both of which similarly illustrate the soul's intimate encounter and relationship with evil. "Sympathy for the Devil" is expressly theatrical as Jagger assumes the persona of Lucifer and links him to some of history's worst crimes, insinuating that he is, as the New Testament proclaims, the prince or ruler of this world. The song's lyrics strike at the mystery of his evil, at the purpose of his trickery.

Finally, as the original bad boys of rock 'n' roll, the Rolling Stones' celebration of the senses—sometimes to an extreme—came as a reaction to the repressive Victorian Age that immediately preceded the modern era. More significantly, it represented a Dionysian revolt against the Yahwistic values of Western culture. As will be discussed later, Christianity has made an enemy of the instinctual, bodily side of our existence, associating it with the devil. No one will ever turn Jagger into a saint, he defiantly boasts on *Bridges to Babylon*, an album whose title connotes the band's connection to a place that in Christianity symbolizes sensuality, luxury, and sin. He cites Paul, Augustine, and John the Baptist—three of Christianity's greatest saints—as standard-bearers he has no wish to imitate.

The group's music and lyrics reveal a religious attitude in this regard, even if an unconventional one: Dionysus, the Greek god of fertility, wine, ecstasy, and ritually induced madness, has a very different temperament than that of Yahweh or the New Testament's Father. The Rolling Stones are in blessed service to a Dionysus complex. Ecstasy is the only thing they desire, they sing on *Steel Wheels* in their nostalgic "Slipping Away." Do they not capture our own nostalgia for a paradise lost or buried under the heap of our civilization's conquest over the instincts and nature? Is it not Jagger's raw sexuality that has incited so many—men as well as women— to project onto him this same but often dissociated part of themselves? For sixty years the Rolling Stones have been reminding us of our earthy, instinctual roots. If "Sympathy for the Devil" is their thundering ode to God's dark side, then "Heaven," also fittingly named, is their crowning paean to the sacredness of the sensual life.

III

YAHWEH IN OUR MIDST

Evil is an imitation of God—of God's inscrutable, peremptory, mysteriously smiting self. . . . Evil is not an abstraction or principle, but is, rather, the world's narrative energy. Evil makes the world go round; goes round the world.

—*Lance Morrow*

9

The Bully and the Prince

We hurt those to whom we need to make our power perceptible, for pain is a much more sensitive means to that end than pleasure: pain always asks for the cause, while pleasure is inclined to stop with itself and not look back.

—Friedrich Nietzsche

When I was ten I committed a reprehensible act that demonstrates how easily one can become an instrument of the Yahweh complex. On our walk to school, I cajoled my five-year-old brother, George—or Georgie, as he was called then—into coming with me to a local gas station restroom on the pretense that there were candies waiting for us. Behind closed doors, I angrily listed a number of things I was cross with him for. I was incensed by his disrespect toward me and tattling and other typical sibling-rivalry behaviors. *He broke my Law.* Feeling justified in punishing him, I then beat him up, careful to not leave any marks that could incriminate me with our parents. I threatened that if he told on me, I would beat him even worse. I made sure that his tears flowed before I decided that there had been enough retribution.

With Yahwistic brutality, I exerted my will to power. I was here a bully, gripped by my rage as well as meting it out. Unlike my father's eruption, however, mine was planned in advance and meticulously executed—evidence that this was not merely a learned behavior based on an earlier incident. The fact that it was premeditated and methodical, therefore quite Machiavellian, made it even more diabolical than Leslie's wrath because it was volitional; it was consciously willed. Even then I realized that my aim was not primarily to hurt George or provide myself with sadistic pleasure or revenge, angry as I was at him; it was to instill fear in him so that episodes like this would not need to be repeated in the future. I myself did not want to make this a regular pattern. I wanted to dominate his spirit once and for all.

Much later, when we were adults, George told me that even as a child, he sensed that what I did to him was a repetition of how Leslie treated me, a kick-the-cat syndrome expressing his brutal experiences in the war. Probably this was true, but only up to a point. Leslie and I had both been gripped by the same dark side of the Yahweh complex. Children and adolescents are especially susceptible to such dark impulses of the psyche due to the undeveloped and labile nature of their egos. They get assaulted by them in their raw, unfiltered forms and do not yet have a sufficient superego or moral conscience to be able to deal with them in an authentic, self-empowered way.

However, such explanations speak only to *personal* history or the lack of personal development. We all know how survivors of war can be terribly tormented, and how children can be terribly cruel. The issue is, rather, how twisted and cruel we *all* can be. No one who has been even briefly possessed by a *transpersonal* war-god complex has walked away smelling like a rose, and we are all, under the right conditions and at any age, susceptible to such seizures. As the Roman playwright Terentius said, "Nothing human is alien to me"—nor nothing divine, as the case may also be.

Bullying is the evil product of a god complex: one person inflatedly feels the right to abuse another. It may appear as if the bully acts with no consideration of the harm done, but in fact, most bullying occurs with special consideration of the harm done, which makes it especially cruel and evil. Its effects can be devastating. Elliot Rodger, a twenty-two-year-old man, wrote the following about his experience of being bullied in high school:

> Alfred and Brice apparently told everyone how weird I was at Pinecrest, and people in my own grade started to tease me. They found out that I didn't like being called a skateboarder, and it was true. Because I failed to become good at skateboarding, I developed a hatred for the sport, and whenever someone called me a skateboarder, it reminded me of my failure and I got very

angry. The whole school started calling me it just to anger me, along with other insulting names. They teased me because I was scared of girls, calling me names like "faggot." People also liked to steal my belongings and run away in an attempt to get me to chase after them. And I did chase after them in a furious rage, but I was so little and weak that they thought it was comical. I hated everyone at that school so much. It got to a point where I had to wait in a quiet corner for the hallways to clear before I could walk to class. I also took long routes around the school to avoid bullies. My parents began to consider not letting me continue there after Ninth Grade.

Even if bullying does not express the Yahweh complex in particular, it can trigger it in the victim. In extreme cases, its evil can generate a much greater evil, an archetypal or transpersonal evil that altogether defies human understanding. The Yahweh complex can be a diabolical force with a mind and will of its own. In 2014, Rodger went on a shooting spree in Isla Vista, California, killing seven people—including himself—and wounding thirteen others. His manifesto, from which the above account was taken, reveals how his Yahweh-like history of rejection continued into his college years and drove him over the edge. Similar to Yahweh and to other disillusioned youths involved in shooting sprees, Rodger was what is known as an "injustice collector": he kept an account of all the incidents in which he had been spurned. In his fantasies of revenge and his use of biblical language, we can almost hear Yahweh forecasting his apocalyptic punishments:

> It was only when I first moved to Santa Barbara that I started considering the possibility of having to carry out a violent act of revenge, as the final solution to dealing with all of the injustices I've had to face at the hands of women and society. I came up with a name for this after I saw all of the good looking young couples walking around my college and in the town of Isla Vista. I named it the Day of Retribution. It would be a day in which I exact my

ultimate retribution and revenge on all of the hedonistic scum who enjoyed lives of pleasure that they don't deserve. If I can't have it, I will destroy it. I will destroy all women because I can never have them. I will make them all suffer for rejecting me. I will arm myself with deadly weapons and wage a war against *all women and the men they are attracted to*. And I will slaughter them like the animals they are. If they won't accept me among them, then they are my enemies. They showed me no mercy, and in turn I will show them no mercy. The prospect will be so sweet, and justice will ultimately be served. . . . Only then would I have all the power. They treated me like an insignificant little mouse, but on the Day of Retribution, I would be a God to them.

In the United States, there has been in the years immediately preceding this writing a dramatic increase in shooting sprees, the causes of which are not altogether clear. We attribute this psychic and social epidemic to mental illness, to lack of gun control, and to the copycat effect, all undoubtedly key factors. However, a dark war-god complex coupled with, on the part of the shooters, a history of having been bullied or themselves bullying also appears to be a strong factor.

Eric Harris and Dylan Klebold, who carried out the Columbine High School massacre in 1999, were victims of bullying too, although some authorities claim that Harris was more often a perpetrator than a victim. That he was under the sway of a god complex is clear: he wrote "Ich bin Got"—"I am God"—in his school planner and the yearbooks of several friends. Who would be the god with whom he identified unconsciously (that is, based on his collective unconscious)? Most likely Yahweh. Yahweh was not only a god of retribution, massacring thousands of his own people at a time, but a bully who coerced his people into worshipping him by punishing them, by forcing them to submit. His testing behaviors also had a bullying quality.

The Inner Dimension of Bullying: A Failure in Initiation

Bullying is a result of failing to conquer or master *ourselves*. If our urge to gain victory over ourselves—over our fears and anger—is not channeled appropriately, it manifests in the dark form of aggressively beating down others. The psyche's natural impulse toward maturation gets acted out in a projected, regressed way. The initiation rites of tribal cultures and the challenging activities of youth organizations help facilitate the transition to adulthood with its responsibilities and demands. The young have to *learn* self-conquest and self-mastery for themselves, so the rites or activities have taxing and testing ordeals. Nelson Mandela's circumcision rite at age sixteen was a typical requirement of initiation into adulthood and his tribe. The Native American custom of sending the youth out into the wilderness on a vision quest—prepared to deal with the elements and other dangers if necessary—is comparable. Our culture's loss of initiation rites and of mentoring by elders cannot be ruled out as a significant factor in the growing trend of bullying and other deadly youth violence, including not only shooting sprees but also inner-city gang warfare.

Initiation is such a powerful instinctual, archetypal need that it is no accident that its frustration and absence in *The Lord of the Flies* coincides not only with the collective bullying and killing of Piggy, as this poor scapegoat is called, but also with the descent into depravity of almost all the boys marooned on the island. The title of this classic refers to Beelzebub, who in the Hebrew Bible was a Philistine god and rival to Yahweh and in the New Testament was identified as the devil.

Whether intentionally or not, William Golding alludes to a primitive, dark god complex as the ruling principle that overtakes this wayward band of boys. Their tribal bonding and frenzied activities are attempts to compensate for the absence of adults serving as role models to implement authentic initiation challenges. There are no formal rites of passage, no tests to endure and difficult ordeals to overcome, no secret traditions to be initiated into. As Robert Bly points out, boys cannot be adequately initiated by other boys; only men—knowledgeable elders—can truly guide boys to manhood. Gangs, whether they are of the criminal or inner-city kind, reflect the attempt of mentorless boys to initiate themselves.

It is therefore also no accident that Mafia gangsters, at least in former times if not currently, operated as a secret society of dangerous misfits engaged, with their code of honor, in a kind of tribal bonding and initiation into manhood (albeit a primitive, macho manhood). Bullying and strong-arming are regular features in the Mafia's repertoire of violence and Machiavellian practices. It goes without saying that crime bosses exude a god complex.

In Mario Puzo's book and Francis Ford Coppola's film *The Godfather*—how fitting is this title?—Don Corleone is portrayed as a demigod who rules the criminal underworld. Like Yahweh, he'll make you an offer you can't refuse. He does not seem to fear retribution from a greater god or a law of karma. Seeing himself as an avenger of injustice—this is his Yahwistic claim to redemption that sets his Mafia apart from Russian, Japanese, and other Mafias—he asserts in the film's opening scene that he is not a murderer. To him, the wars between Mafia families are the same as wars between nations: as in the Hebrew Bible, killing in service to a higher principle such as family or self-preservation is not immoral and incurs no bloodguilt.

Later he refuses, at least initially, to get into the narcotics business for a properly Machiavellian reason: it would arouse the hostility of the authorities, who up until that time looked the other way regarding his family's involvement in gambling, a lesser vice. Even Michael Corleone's execution of his own brother in *The Godfather II* is treated as a matter of Machiavellian principle—strictly business and not personal. *The Godfather III* poignantly shows where this principle inevitably leads; at its conclusion, Michael Corleone is a lonely, broken man, not to mention the very thing his father disparaged: a murderer. His self-defeat reminds us of Yahweh's demise in the latter part of the Hebrew Bible.

A Cyclone of Yahwism

Grown-ups who are bullies have never mastered initiation and never became adults in the full, psychological sense. Their consciousness tends to have an unborn quality, and in matters where their character and self-mastery are challenged, they can behave like belligerent adolescents—or, as the case may be, like Yahweh. The rise and fall of Lance Armstrong sadly illustrate this.

There probably would have been no rise had he not cheated by doping; the man whose biological father abandoned him when he was a child would steal initiation into the knighthood of world-class cyclists if he could not genuinely earn it. Unquestionably, a ban on drug use for performance enhancement sets up a Yahwistic dynamic insofar as integrity is regulated by a law. It has been argued that doping, like recreational drug use, should be legalized. If all the athletes admitted to drug use, the public would know about it, and the playing field would be leveled. Some fans might tire of them the way they would with wrestling matches as soon as it becomes apparent that the fight is fixed (though others might not care: it's a theatrical performance, not golf). To raise the bar themselves, athletes might be compelled to advertise their success as drug-free. This might change the rules of the game from inside, voluntarily.

But such was not the given situation, and Armstrong took it upon himself to beat the rules if he couldn't change them. "I certainly was *very* confident that I'd never be caught," he said. Like Yahweh, he believed that laws and rules were just for mortals. (At this point in our discussion, I must admit that I was duped by his athletic abilities and wrote about him accordingly in my book *The Way of the Small*.)

Armstrong's brazenness was also godlike in other forms of risk-taking, as if he were invulnerable, a Superman whom not even kryptonite could harm. He taunted the media—criticizing them for not believing in the miraculous—in his seven Tour de France victories after climbing back from the death sentence of cancer. On *Larry King Live*, he boasted that it would be crazy to dope himself up and risk his life again. In a sworn deposition, as another argument for why he would never do this, he volunteered that he knew that if he were caught cheating, it would jeopardize not only his career but his philanthropic work in cancer research.

It was as if Armstrong were testing fate with his cavalier attitude. Only a man who thinks he is a god would challenge the gods in this way. Commenting on Armstrong's insistence that the doping accusations must be followed up with extraordinary proof, journalist David Walsh said, "Why couldn't it just be 'proof,' that allegations must be followed up by proof? What Lance was saying is that, when you're an icon who sits as high in the firmament as I do, you're going to [need to] have extraordinary proof to bring me down. And it was true. What he was saying was right: different values apply to the gods, and I'm a god."

The most disturbing part of Armstrong's story, however, is not that he doped (apparently, many if not most cyclists in the Tour de France did), nor that he persistently and convincingly lied about it (as they did, too), but that he viciously bullied those who told the truth about it. He wasn't just defensive; he publicly attacked and humiliated them, using the power of his celebrity to make his insults stick and make others look as if *they* were violating *him*. His venom had the vengeful sting of Yahweh. When Betsy Andreu, the wife of Armstrong's former teammate Frankie Andreu, accused Armstrong of doping, he called her a jealous, bitter, vindictive woman. In his interview with Oprah Winfrey, he admitted he was a bully "in the sense that [he] tried to control the narrative" by discrediting friends, peers, and other critics as liars.

Yet even in the interview, he minimized this, as if his behavior's wounding effects upon others were trite. Later explaining such aggression, he said, "I'm a fighter. I grew up as a fighter. . . . I was prepared to say anything." His dedicated service to a war god and in particular to the Yahwistic, Machiavellian ethic that the end justifies the means was absolute. "This is not a story about doping," author Daniel Coyle said. "It's a story about power, and the story became [about] hanging on to that power."

Machiavelli and Yahweh

The aspiration toward redemption is a Yahwistic feature that can be closely connected to bullying. The bully who has a special mission feels justified in steamrolling over others. Of course, his understanding of "redemption" is perversely thwarted and has little to do with traditional, spiritual ideas of redemption. Lance Armstrong was single-minded in his redemptive pursuit to be a world-champion cyclist, and to accomplish this, any warring means he deemed necessary were, in his conscience, permissible. This is how Machiavellian thinking enters the picture: we have a vision of greatness that we are willing to go to war for and which we are committed to win any way we can.

Putting aside for argument's sake the thorny question of Machiavelli's intentions and whether he was an advocate or teacher of evil, as some scholars contend, we will use the term "Machiavellian thinking" or "Machiavellian ethic" in the popular sense to reflect the thinking or ethics of the manipulative, shrewd master of power and statecraft whom Machiavelli describes in his classic, *The Prince*. Neither in this treatise— that incidentally was designed to instruct the newly installed Florentine prince Lorenzo de Medici—nor in his other works did Machiavelli ever quite say, "The end justifies the means." The closest thing he said that resembles this is "For although the act condemn the doer, the end may justify him." Nevertheless, he shows how a cold, utilitarian ethic of gaining and holding on to power makes the world go round—at least, the world as we have known it since ancient times. For his application of this ethic to the rise and fall of various nation-states (he is an astute student of history), he has been hailed as one of the great thinkers of the Renaissance and a founder of modern political science. He is a so-called "realist," explaining the way things work rather than the way they should or could ideally work.

Machiavelli's main premise is straightforward: the prince or political leader builds his princedom or state according to how well he wields an iron hand in forcing others to bend to his will. One might argue that Yahweh was a Machiavellian long before Machiavelli set his pen to paper, and certainly, their methods were similar even if their aims or ends were different. (Yahweh was not interested in the kingdoms or statehood of the Israelites, and although he surely looked after his own needs in the same ways as the prince does, he was also genuinely concerned with what he felt was in their best interest—namely, the Law and their moral righteousness and holiness.) Harold Bloom points out that Machiavelli's prince differs from Yahweh in that the former prefers fear over love as the most reliable way of inducing obedience, while the latter is altogether indifferent to whether he is loved or feared since either results in obedience. In this regard, Yahweh can be even more cold and utilitarian than the prince.

Following are some of Machiavelli's guidelines for a prince who wishes to rule absolutely—guidelines that the Yahwist is intimately familiar with and has no need for Machiavelli to tell him about:

> [When innovators] depend on their own strength and are able to use force, they rarely fail. Thus it comes about that all armed prophets have conquered and unarmed ones failed; for . . . the character of peoples varies, and it is easy to persuade them of a thing, but difficult to keep them in that persuasion. And so it is necessary to order things so that when they no longer believe, they can be made to believe by force. Moses, Cyrus, Theseus, and Romulus would not have been able to keep their constitutions observed for so long had they been disarmed.

Regarding this premise that successful prophets and princes are armed, we shall shortly see that in modern times, a prince is armed not only by weaponry but also by information about his enemy.

> [In] taking a state the conqueror must arrange to commit all his cruelties at once, so as not to have to recur to them every day.

Therein lies a prescription for genocide, among other draconian measures.

[A prince should] have no other aim or thought, nor take up any other thing for his study, but war and its organization and discipline, for that is the only art that is necessary to one who commands. . . .

A man who wishes to make a profession of goodness in everything must necessarily come to grief among so many who are not good. Therefore it is necessary for a prince, who wishes to maintain himself, to learn how not to be good, and to use this knowledge and not use it, according to the necessity of the case.

The latter passage could just as well describe Yahweh's power ethic and how he kept his people under control. Machiavelli believes that a prince should cultivate acts of power rather than wisdom or compassion or any of the other finer, more internal human attributes. "Nothing causes a prince to be so much esteemed," he writes, "as great enterprises and giving proof of prowess." Yahweh's own acts and action orientation display in boldface his desire to gain esteem in this extroverted way. Similarly, what he most valued were his worshippers' external demonstrations of devotion, whether they truly felt it or not. These demonstrations were rewarded, while their absence was punishable by death.

"The Strangest Paradoxical Combination"

Although the Machiavellian ethic is naturally universal, having been practiced for millennia in East and West alike, in the West it is historically and psychologically undergirded by Yahweh's power ethic. In his capacity as the supreme role model, Yahweh made the will to power a customary prerogative. Kings, queens, princes, prime ministers, premiers, and presidents have exercised this prerogative as if God had given it to them, regardless of whether or not they saw themselves as divine monarchs. It is thus also natural that Yahweh's particular power style has leaked into their Machiavellian behaviors.

Insofar as these leaders have unconsciously imitated him, they have been both Machiavellian and Yahwistic. They have not only operated according to Machiavellian methods and a generic god complex—that is, in a way that was harshly competitive, polarizing, and striving toward one-upmanship and dominion over others—but may also have exhibited such specific Yahwistic features as redemption-seeking, bullying, paranoia, and retribution. Four outstanding American examples of this, all of whom were on a mission of one kind or another, include Senator Joseph McCarthy, FBI director J. Edgar Hoover, Richard Nixon, and Donald Trump. Of these, Nixon was the most complex and Shakespearean—a prince who fell at the pinnacle of power and, many have argued, within arm's reach of greatness.

Nixon's political mission was largely to forge a "peace with honor" with North Vietnam (though during the 1968 presidential campaign he dishonorably tried to sink LBJ's foreign policy while furtively advancing his own with the Viet Cong). Emerging later in the course of his presidency, the establishment of diplomatic relations with China became his political mission. However, his personal mission, as a number of his biographers have noted, was to prove himself and to overcome a deep-seated insecurity rooted in his childhood.

"Nixon had a terrible inferiority complex," historian James Shenton writes. "He was a dirt-poor Quaker whose abusive father lost the family ranch and was forced to become a grocer. Some sources suggest that Francis Nixon, the father, beat his boy, Richard. Nixon's mother, Hannah, was a strict Quaker who instilled in her son a strong sense of guilt. Hannah taught her son that if he should face damnation, he, himself, would be the cause of it." How uncanny was her foresight, or was she rather projecting onto him a dissociated, dark part of herself, thereby planting the seeds of self-loathing within him? He additionally suffered the childhood trauma of losing two of his four brothers to tuberculosis.

In Nixon's case we can observe two complexes—a Yahweh complex and an inferiority complex—dovetailing with each other, with the former likely compensating for the latter. Whether from the depressive condition of his childhood or simply as part of the constitution of his

Yahweh complex, or both, he was prone to melancholy his entire life, to a "constant grimness," in the words of columnist George Will. Of his complicated personality, his chief domestic advisor John Ehrlichman said, "Sometime, hopefully, there will be a historian or a committee of historians who will listen to *all* the tapes [he secretly recorded], and go into *all* the archives, and then come out and say, 'Richard Nixon was the strangest collection—the strangest paradoxical combination—of any man I ever heard of,' and they'll be right." Like Yahweh with his antinomy of conflicting impulses, Nixon was torn between his aspiration toward greatness and a vindictiveness unfitting for one with such an aspiration.

The entire Watergate episode can be seen as the by-product of a war-god complex whose spirit was constellated collectively as an intersubjective field (similar to the Beatles), infecting Nixon's aides and radiating out from the White House and beyond matters of foreign policy and the Vietnam War. The Committee for the Re-election of the President, whose acronym was CRP but was nicknamed CREEP by Nixon's opponents, was organized like a military task force. Two of its prominent members, Howard Hunt and James McCord, were involved in the Watergate burglaries (of which there were also two). Both men were former CIA operatives. William Saxbe, Nixon's attorney general, described Ehrlichman and White House chief of staff Bob Haldeman, key players in the cover-up if not the burglaries, as a "couple of Nazis." Their zeal was characteristic of a god on the warpath.

Of course, at the hub of the Watergate scandal was Nixon himself. Well before his reelection campaign, he set the militant, Yahwistic tone of his administration with the aides he chose and the instructions he gave them: "Memo to Haldeman. The more I think of it, setting up a special group for the purpose not of cheering but solely of attacking and defending is of the highest priority." As with McCarthy's witch hunt against communist sympathizers and homosexuals and Hoover's alleged manipulation of those whom he had "dirt" on, the war here was to be conducted on the field of information acquisition rather than a concrete battlefield. No less than McCarthy and Hoover, Nixon was held hostage by a paranoid and persecutory Yahweh complex.

Nixon's paranoid tendencies long preceded Watergate and the famous "Enemies List" he kept during his presidency for the purposes of protection and revenge. In his campaign for a congressional seat, he used anti-communist smear tactics to defeat his opponent, Jerry Voorhis, a hardworking, five-term Democratic congressman. As a congressman, Nixon's influential role in the Alger Hiss espionage case catapulted him to fame (Hoover provided him with FBI reports much like he later did with McCarthy). From the Hiss episode, Nixon drew conspiratorial conclusions about Jews, intellectuals, and the Ivy League. The following is from declassified White House tapes:

> The Jews are born spies. You notice how many of them are? They're just in it up to their necks. . . . [They have] an arrogance that . . . makes a spy. [The Jew] puts himself above the law. I want a look at any sensitive areas around where Jews involved are. See, the Jews are all through the government and we have got to get in those areas. We've got to get a man in charge who is not Jewish to control the Jewish [sic], do you understand? The government is full of Jews. Second, most Jews are disloyal. Generally speaking, you can't trust the bastards. They turn on you. Remember that any intellectual is tempted to put himself above the law.

> The guys from the best families are most likely to develop that arrogance that puts them above the law.

> If they're from any Eastern schools or Berkeley, those are particularly the potential bad ones.

Nixon referred to Daniel Ellsberg, Leslie Gelb, and Morton Halperin as "the three Jews." All of them also intellectuals with Ivy League degrees, they were connected to the Pentagon Papers that were leaked to the press. This was the event that motivated the Watergate break-ins.

And yet, in spite of his prejudices, Nixon appointed Henry Kissinger, a Jew and a former Harvard professor, as his national security advisor and secretary of state. It was to Kissinger that a sobbing Nixon turned on the night before announcing his resignation, asking him to kneel and pray with him. Likewise, Nixon filled his White House with other Jewish appointees. He also valiantly and decisively airlifted massive military supplies to Israel in the Yom Kippur War, prompting Israeli Prime Minister Golda Meir to credit him with saving her nation. He did this knowing full well that he had received only 8 percent of the American Jewish vote. How Yahweh-like was his ambivalence toward Jews.

By the end of his presidency, the entire liberal establishment and its press had been added to Nixon's Enemies List. To Kissinger he said: "Never forget, the establishment is the enemy. The professors are the enemy. The press is the enemy. The press is the enemy. The press is the enemy. Write that on a blackboard one hundred times and never forget it."

Was it an irony or a presentiment that the press—specifically, *The Washington Post*—would bring down his presidency by exposing Watergate? Eventually Nixon's Yahweh complex and conspiracy fears pushed him beyond the limits of the law. Himself conspiring with Haldeman, he said:

> We're up against an enemy, a conspiracy. They're using any means. We are going to use any means. Is that clear? I don't give a shit about the law. I need a son-of-a-bitch who will work his butt off and do it dishonorably.

> I want the Brookings Institute safe cleared out. Get it done. I want it done. I want it implemented on a thievery basis. Goddammit, get in and get those files. Blow the safe and get it.

Clearly, Nixon fell into the grip of the very vices he railed against. Or rather, he railed against the vices he was already gripped by—a common behavior known as projection. After all, whom was he really speaking about when he said that Jews have "very aggressive, abrasive and obnoxious personalities" driven by "an inferiority syndrome they have got to compensate"? Who was the arrogant lawbreaker in the end?

Nixon demonstrated what historian Richard Hofstadter describes as the paranoid style and anti-intellectualism in American public life. The American psyche is prone to periodic outbursts of both. The paranoid style in particular may be observed in the agitation incited by certain media and in such fearmongering as the Obama citizenship conspiracy theories, whose fire Trump also fanned. Those who engage in this kind of agitation and fearmongering assume they have godlike knowledge—their sense of certainty is absolute—and they exhibit the self-righteousness, judgmental harshness, and aggression of the Yahweh complex. In other words, the paranoid style and the Yahweh complex often go together in American politics.

Paranoia is highly contagious, leaping from one person's psyche into another's. Just like McCarthy's Red Scare spread fear across the land, of both communism and his Senate hearings, Watergate injected paranoia into American politics at its highest level, undermining the public's trust in its leadership.

Nixon revealed his Machiavellian cunning in matters large and small, and for better and worse. "Only Nixon could go to China" has become a catchphrase to indicate that only a politician with an unassailable reputation for upholding certain political values could undertake a seemingly contrary action without jeopardizing his support or credibility. He knew that he could open a dialogue with China because his staunchly anti-communist record and strong hand with North Vietnam would counter any skepticism about whether he had gone soft.

By the same token, when Senator Edward Kennedy asked him in 1972 to authorize Secret Service protection for him because of threatening mail, Nixon took advantage of the situation. Stooping to a pettiness hardly fitting for a world leader and reminiscent of Yahweh's pettiness, he ordered Ehrlichman and Haldeman to plant Secret Service bodyguards to spy on the senator even though he wasn't running for office. Note also the similarity to Yahweh's sadistic streak:

That's going to be fun. Cover him around the clock, every place he goes. We might just get lucky and catch this son of a bitch and ruin him for '76.

After the election he doesn't get a . . . thing. If he gets shot, it's too damn bad. Do it under the basis, though, that we pick the Secret Service men.

Pressing for increased wiretaps and an investigation into the tax records of Kennedy and other leading Democrats, Nixon said, "I could only hope that we are, frankly, doing a little persecuting."

What can we conclude about this tormented, paradoxical man who inflicted on America a "long national nightmare," as Gerald Ford called the Watergate episode? Evidently, he compensated for his childhood trauma, feelings of inadequacy, and later political defeats (especially the one by John Kennedy in the 1960 presidential election) by developing a highly inflated Yahweh complex. This complex fueled his aspiration for redemption and greatness—not necessarily a bad thing in itself, as we shall later see, but its paranoia and Machiavellian ethic justified to him his breaking the law. He felt entitled to get ahead at any cost, even if it meant lying, cheating, and hurting others.

Paranoia is the ultimate expression of disempowerment, and disempowerment is the underbelly of the Yahweh complex—its raison d'être. The Yahweh complex is a defense against powerlessness in our personhood. It attempts to compensate for this the way Yahweh compensated for his inner powerlessness by asserting his external power over Job and the Israelites as a whole. This powerlessness was at the root of what Jung described as God's doubt complex.

Figures like Nixon, McCarthy, Hoover, and Trump use Machiavellian methods to gain control over others. Since they do not feel authentically self-empowered and believe they have to use deceitful or illegitimate ways to get power, there is always a lingering feeling deep down that they don't deserve the power they've amassed. Nixon couldn't rest on his laurels as president. Even at the height of power, he believed he had to resort to dirty tricks to keep it. He might not have specifically instructed his staff to break into the Watergate offices, but his deep-rooted mistrust of others and unbelief in himself created a vacuum of confidence that his staff members unconsciously picked up and acted on.

In the school of Yahwistic-Machiavellian psychology, the end may justify the means, but in the school of history, if the means are not worthy of the end, the mission's legacy will be tainted by its darkness. The school lessons are clear, even if the latter one is uncompromising. In the final analysis, Nixon's was a presidency that, in the schema of Yahweh's evolution described earlier, fell into the stage of the mission's failure (the fifth stage, and I'm referring here to his personal mission, not his political ones). However, unlike Yahweh, Nixon never fully recovered from this failure or transcended it, in spite of writing a number of impressive books after his presidency.

Leonard Cohen said something thought-provoking about such a failure: perhaps the *real* mission *was to fail*. Nixon almost said as much between the lines in his farewell speech at the gathering of his family and his White House staff before boarding the helicopter that took him out of history. He said, "Always give your best, never get discouraged, never be petty. Always remember: others may hate you, but those who hate you don't win, unless you hate them, and then you destroy yourself." If Nixon truly learned this from the Watergate affair, then from a psychological and spiritual point of view, his mission was a success.

10

Legalists, Fundamentalists, and Moral Perfectionists

Religion can be the enemy of God. It's often what happens when God, like Elvis, has left the building. A list of instructions where there once was conviction; dogma where once people just did it; a congregation led by a man where once they were led by the Holy Spirit.

—Bono

The Yahweh complex does not appear in a vacuum or even just in response to familial and social influences, as significant as these may be. It also arises from a history that is imprinted deep in its core like the DNA in our cells. As a collective complex in our collective unconscious, the Yahweh complex houses our Abrahamic history not as a memory—since memories cannot be inherited—but as a predisposition or tendency toward certain patterns of behavior. The complex's tendency toward rigidity, intolerance, and extremes parallels the same in Abrahamic history and both originates in and reinforces it.

Among the most typical forms of this, we may observe the legalism, fundamentalism, and moral perfectionism to which the complex is prone. All closely related to each other, they can have a huge impact on individual and social behavior alike. Let us take a look at these powerful "isms," beginning with legalism.

Psychologist Abraham Maslow observed that the original religious or "peak" experience of mystics or prophets tends to become frozen by future generations who make a dogma out of it, legalistically determining what kind of thinking is proper and what kind is not. "Legalistic" here means inclined toward or demanding the strict adherence to laws or rules and professing that these are absolute or divine. The revelation is sooner or later institutionalized by a church.

With Israel's revelation, this did not occur later because the Law that Yahweh gave to Moses was legalistic in and of itself and included instructions for its own institutionalization. Thus, the Israelite exception only proves the rule: the legalism or institutionalization of religions ensures that they will be transmitted socially and from generation to generation. The Israelite tradition was also exceptional in that Yahweh demanded, as a matter of life and death, that the Law be followed meticulously. *Yahwism by nature tends to be legalistic and preoccupied with the "right" way of doing things.* Later, this would contribute not only to the vast body of laws developed by Western society but also to its litigiousness.

Maslow further notes that some religions develop a schism between the mystics and the legalists. He describes the legalists as those inclined to interpret scripture and its symbols and metaphors literally. They also include those who perform rituals in a superstitious, rote fashion and repeat dogma mindlessly, as well as those for whom the church or organization has become more important than the prophet and his original revelations.

"It's wrong to criticize leaders of the Church, even if the criticism is true," said Dallin H. Oaks, a member of the Quorum of the Twelve Apostles, the governing body of the Mormon Church of Jesus Christ of Latter-day Saints. Such collectivistic and conformist thinking smacks of the patriarchal mindset of all Abrahamic traditions: Father knows best, even when he doesn't. Dostoevsky's grand inquisitor in *The Brothers Karamazov* cynically justifies why he and his kind are determined to preserve the authority of the church even at the expense of religious truth (and how contemporarily he addresses those Jehovah Witnesses who ring our doorbells early Sunday morning to announce the Good News):

> So long as man remains free he strives for nothing so incessantly and so painfully as to find someone to worship. But man seeks to worship what is established beyond dispute, so that all men would agree at once to worship it. For these pitiful creatures are concerned not only to find what one or the other can worship; what is essential

is that all may be *together* in it. . . . And men rejoiced that they were again led like sheep, and that the terrible gift [of freedom] that had brought them such suffering, was, at last, lifted from their hearts. Were we right teaching them this [principle of blind faith]? Speak! Did we not love mankind, so meekly acknowledging their feebleness, lovingly lightening their burden, and permitting their weak nature even sin with our sanction?

In other words, in their supposed service to mankind, the institutions of religion transfer the mystique and power of the divine onto themselves, as this is more easily accessible to the masses.

But the mystics to whom Maslow refers stand in sharp contrast to the masses and their religious leaders. It is hard work to wrestle with the mysteries of life and do so without the comfort of simplistic, pat explanations. In advocating that people think for themselves, mysticism poses a threat to institutional religion. "This cleavage between the mystics and the legalists," Maslow adds, "remains at best a kind of mutual tolerance, but it has happened in some churches that the rulers of the organization actually made a heresy out of the mystic experiences and persecuted the mystics themselves."

This was certainly the case with Catholicism, whose Medieval and Spanish Inquisitions investigated and executed thousands suspected of having mystical or divergent interpretations of the Bible. In its belief that it was safeguarding itself, a belief that could only be founded on an underlying fear and insecurity, Catholicism assumed a Yahwistic authority and prosecuted with a Yahwistic vengeance: "Anyone who attempts to construe a personal view of God which conflicts with Church dogma must be burned without pity," declared Pope Innocent III, whose crusade against the Albigensians for their "heretical" views led to the slaughter of some twenty thousand men, women, and children. Of course, as his self-chosen papal name suggests, he thought he was doing a good deed. "All things truly wicked," Ernest Hemingway said, "start from an innocence."

It should thus come as no surprise that Meister Eckhart and St. John of the Cross, two of history's greatest mystics, were targets of the Yahweh complex and religious intolerance of others. Eckhart, a Dominican monk, was tried for heresy by the Franciscans barely a century after the death of their founder, the gentle, nature-loving St. Francis of Assisi.

This is not to portray the Dominicans as the poor victims of the Franciscans, for the Dominicans were also official inquisitors. There was a Yahwistic rivalry between the two orders as they competed for prestige and power in the church. Eckhart was found guilty of heresy but is believed to have died before receiving this verdict. His articulate *Defense* shows the care he took to answer the "bloodhounds for error," as Eckhart scholar Raymond Blakney described the two Franciscans who were turned loose on him. Jungian analyst Bradley TePaske speaks to their persecutory spirit when he says, "However fundamental to Judaism and Christianity, the legalistic rigidity and punitive wrath of the patriarchal order casts an extremely punishing amoral shadow, a cold overplus of Justice." In Eckhart's case, as with many others, there was less an overplus than a clear violation of justice. Were his judges like Dostoevsky's cynical grand inquisitor, intentionally preserving old dogmas so that the comfort of the masses could continue to prevail, or rather like Pope Innocent III, who really believed he was doing a good thing?

In contrast to Eckhart, St. John of the Cross was persecuted by his own order, the Carmelites. Opposed to reforms in religious observance that he and St. Teresa of Avila had instituted in Carmelite monasteries and convents, his superiors imprisoned him in solitary confinement in a small cell. Their grievance was that he wanted to return their order to its more austere, original "Primitive Rule" that had been relaxed by Pope Eugene IV. This involved reintroducing the abstinence from meat and the obligation of silence. Ironically, John was punished for *not* wanting to deviate from established norms. (He and Teresa, however, additionally introduced St. Peter of Alcantara's practice of going discalced or barefoot, which, needless to say, also didn't go over well with their superiors.) The scars from the lashings he received weekly remained on his shoulders for the rest of his life.

He eventually escaped and returned to his former activities, continuing his reformations by virtue of the fact that the church authorities above his immediate superiors had approved them prior to his imprisonment. The saint that he was, he bore no ill will toward his jailers. As his name implies, the church eventually canonized him.

Theological Correctness: The Bane of Religion

The zeal for theological correctness may be found in varying degrees in all three Abrahamic religions, especially in their more legalistic, orthodox forms. With his intense focus on instilling monotheism into his people, Yahweh himself was concerned with theological correctness (even though theology as such did not become a formal discipline until the Talmudic and Early Church Fathers). Theological correctness in Judaism has been connected mostly to the interpretation and application of the Law. In biblical times the spirit and letter of the Law were one and the same. Changing times demanded a rabbinic (i.e., Talmudic) reinterpretation of the Law, adapting it to new circumstances without watering it down.

In Christianity and Islam, theological correctness became a more vexing problem. Because Yahweh's behaviors in the Hebrew Bible were so human and erratic, and his manifest forms so diverse, ranging from pillars of cloud and fire to Ezekiel's extraordinary vision of him on his chariot-throne, Judaism could never have pinned him down to a specific way of being even if it had wanted to. By contrast, Christianity simplified Yahweh by elevating him to the stature of God the Father, a remote, rarefied, and perfect being keeping a low profile behind the scenes—much like in the latter part of the Hebrew Bible—in order to allow his son, Jesus, to take center stage. (Or, at least, this was his disposition until the New Testament's Book of Revelation, in which he again became gripped by apocalyptic fever.)

But at the same time, Christianity complicated matters with such doctrines as the Incarnation and the Trinity, both of which, as Jung has shown, are so sublime in their deeper meanings that one could hardly have expected the masses to truly understand them. As these doctrines raised confusion, theological correctness became a serious concern. For its part, Islamic monotheism has always been simple, straightforward, and ferocious, with little room for theological deviation. When, for example, the Sufi mystic Mansur al-Hallaj declared, "I am the Truth," implying that he had discovered the divine within himself, the authorities tortured and executed him.

In comparison to Christianity and Islam, there has been little or no persecution of mystics in the Jewish and Eastern religions. Jewish mystics—almost all of them rabbis steeped in the Talmudic tradition—did not have to fear the authorities; in their religion, *they* were the authorities. Nevertheless, Jewish authorities did use their power to correct or banish those who veered too far from what they deemed sound theology. A young Baruch Spinoza, excommunicated for his pantheistic views, was one of their better known cases. (His books were also put on the Catholic Church's *Index Librorum Prohibitorum*, or "List of Forbidden Books.")

Eastern religion has always viewed mysticism through a special lens. Much if not most of the East's scriptures openly discuss or point to mystical insight; mysticism is woven into the very fabric of Eastern religion. Theological correctness and consistency are less a concern precisely because mystical insight is by nature fluid, flourishing mostly in the here and now and in the individual's interior experience.

This is not to say that Eastern religion is less concerned with the institutionalization or social and intergenerational transmission of its knowledge. Nor is it to say that there has been no religious persecution in the East. The ninth-century campaign against Buddhists by the Taoist Chinese emperor Wuzong of Tang is a notable example of such persecution, even if ethnic, socioeconomic, and political factors contributed to this too. But still, religious persecution for ideological or mystical reasons never attained quite the same intensity or degree in the East as it did in the West. The attitude toward mysticism has been inherently more friendly.

The Relativity of So-Called Absolute Truth

Legalists naturally harbor the conviction that they are the true believers, that they alone possess the truth. This is the human counterpart to Yahweh's fierce insistence that he alone is the true God, a declamatory status upheld by many if not most Jews, Christians, and Muslims. His scriptural testaments, his word, are considered the legal proof that these religions have been specially selected to receive his grace. This conviction inflates the followers of all three Abrahamic religions and complicates the relationships each religion has to the others. Judaism does not accept the verity of Christian and Islamic revelation. Christianity accepts the verity of Jewish revelation—what came before its own revelation and serves as its foundation—but not that of Islamic revelation. Its historical view of Jews is that they rejected Christ and have consequently sinned, a source of much anti-Semitism.

With some modifications, Islam accepts the verity of both Jewish and Christian revelation but sees itself as the fulfillment of it in much the same way Christianity views its relation to Judaism. However, too much of Islam vehemently rejects the verity of any other tradition outside of its own. The scientific, economic, and intercultural flourishing of the Islamic Golden Age in the Middle Ages is a distant memory. "Would that contemporary Islam could turn to their religious genius of seven centuries ago for enlightenment!" Jungian analyst J. Marvin Spiegelman writes.

As is the case in regard to theological correctness and mysticism, in the East this issue of who owns the truth is treated differently than in the West. Hindus and Buddhists have little difficulty accepting the verity and value of other traditions, seeing others' avatars merely as further incarnations of the Godhead or messengers of the Absolute. (I remember traveling in India and encountering a yogi who wore a necklace with the symbols of every major world religion on it. When I queried him about it, he said with delight, "All are one, and the One is in all.") To the degree that each Abrahamic religion promotes absolute knowledge as its own private property, we see a deficit of symbolic thinking and a blindness to the workings of the religious imagination that participates equally if differently in every religion. On the other hand, such tendencies toward universalistic thinking may not be desirable among the Abrahamic religions, as they blur ideological boundaries and differences that not only should be made clear but that add to the colorful palette of religious expression and diversity. An example of this will be given shortly in the discussion on moral perfectionism.

At the end of the day, the determination of who is the true believer and what is the truth is, of course, in the eye of the beholder, with the more liberal and tolerant beholder accepting other viewpoints more graciously. Even the Vatican has recently taken positive steps in this direction with its ecumenical movement.

Faith, Doubt, and "Ultimate Concern"

When legalists turn their interpretations of scripture into a simplistic formula for how to live and in Yahwistic fashion judgmentally condemn other ways of living as inferior, sinful, or otherwise wrong, they become also fundamentalists. They apotheosize the fundaments of scriptural teaching at the expense of a balanced view that entertains a range of viewpoints and invites inquiry. They try to stuff something very large into a container too small for it. People tend to fall into a fundamentalist way of thinking to ward off the spiritual poverty or not-knowing that the mystics tell us is central to the human encounter with the divine. They need to fill this void with what they believe are clear and incontrovertible truths. They can tolerate neither complexity nor uncertainty. At heart, fundamentalism is the fear of doubt and is doubt itself. Why would one need to be so correct theologically and to convert others if one weren't unconsciously plagued by doubt? Even more than Satan, doubt is the enemy that fundamentalists seek to vanquish.

But doubt is a healthy and even necessary ingredient of faith. Without it, faith loses its character and becomes a fixed certainty rather than an open-ended receptivity to things unseen. We experience doubt because the divine is, indeed, a mystery; it is not self-evident. This is why theologian Paul Tillich saw faith and existential doubt as two poles of a single experience, that of "ultimate concern." Of course, doubt doesn't feel good, and thus often leads to an impatience that forces us to reach for certainty. Beginning with his recognition in Genesis that humankind was not reliable, Yahweh himself suffered great doubt about his creation. When his flood failed to rectify this problem, he established the Mosaic Law as a way to ensure his people's devotion. He wanted to regulate their faith. Such regulation is also at the root of fundamentalism. Learning to tolerate doubt is the antidote to fundamentalism's tyranny over the mind.

It is in order to avoid doubt that certain kinds of Yahwism exist. The Catholic Church covered up sexual abuse by its clergy because it was afraid of sowing seeds of doubt in a religion that is already under attack by modern, secular values. It ideologically attacked its nuns on the grounds that they were feminists so that it could maintain the old order, reformation of which, by giving women a new status in the church, would have raised doubt that the old papal creed against them must have been wrong. And how could divine authority as vested in the pope be wrong?

With its dependency on literalism and theological correctness, fundamentalism tyrannizes its practitioners as well as those whom they coercively attempt to convert. It robs the individual of their capacity to make autonomous decisions and to have an authentic, interactive relationship with the ideas and images in scripture. In the place of imagination, it substitutes dogma. Erich Fromm describes the mechanism that is set in motion as the individual surrenders their God-given gift of freethinking and free will in order to become one of the grand inquisitor's sheep:

> When man has thus projected his own most valuable powers onto God, what of his relationship to his own powers? They have become separated from him and in this process he has become *alienated* from himself. Everything he has is now God's and nothing is left in him. *His only access to himself is through God.* In worshipping God

he tries to get in touch with that part of himself which he has lost through projection. After having given God all he has, he begs God to return to him some of what originally was his own. But having lost his own he is completely at God's mercy. He necessarily feels like a "sinner" since he has deprived himself of everything that is good, and it is only through God's mercy or grace that he can regain that which alone can make him human. And in order to persuade God to give him some of his love, he must prove to him how utterly deprived he is of love; in order to persuade God to guide him by his superior wisdom, he must prove to him how deprived he is of wisdom when he is left to himself. . . . Thus the attempt to obtain forgiveness results in the activation of the very attitude from which his sin stems. He is caught in a painful dilemma. The more he praises God, the emptier he becomes. The emptier he becomes, the more sinful he feels. The more sinful he feels, the more he praises his God—and the less able is he to regain himself.

In this way does fundamentalism lead to a closed system of psychological and spiritual slavery: an erroneous idea of redemption creates the very sin from which one seeks redemption.

Holiness vs. Perfection

Our particular historical ideas of sin and redemption can further contribute to our psychological and spiritual slavery. One such idea is that of moral perfection, the belief in which has had a pernicious effect. Religious tyranny is very much the tyranny of perfectionism, which can include not only theological correctness but also moral puritanism. Often the two go together.

Striving for moral purity becomes a tyranny whenever it subjects human nature—which includes our instinctual, animal nature— to standards that deprive us of our well-being and joy in life. Moral perfectionism violates both the Aristotelian and Confucian golden mean of moderation and balance, not to mention Buddhism's Middle Way between extreme self-denial and self-indulgence. The medieval rabbinic scholar and sage Moses Maimonides was clearly influenced by Aristotle in his thinking about the moral mean. "The virtues," he writes, "are states of the soul and settled dispositions in the mean between two bad states, one of which is excessive, the other deficient."

As Christianity has stressed God's perfection, its model of the imitation of God—or *Imitatio Dei*, as the core aim of religious practice was classically known—is that we too must strive to be perfect. Maimonides, who also viewed God as perfect, got around this by asserting that by following the mean, "there is no possibility of an excess or a deficiency." We will govern ourselves as God governs nature. In any case, the emphasis upon perfection is much less pronounced in Judaism than in Christianity since the Hebrew Bible vividly documents both God's and man's failures. Though Yahweh himself was perfectionistic, insisting that his laws and rules be obeyed to the letter, he did not set puritanical moral standards for his people or expect them to be morally perfect. The laws and rules themselves were not puritanical. "So don't overdo goodness and don't act the wise man to excess," Ecclesiastes tells us, "or you may be dumbfounded. . . . For there is not one good man on earth who does what is best and doesn't err."

David is an archetypal example of a righteous man who was far from perfect. He committed adultery and murder—again, he arranged the death of Uriah the Hittite, an officer in his army, after impregnating Uriah's wife, Bathsheba—but upon his repentance, albeit not without much retribution, Yahweh forgave him. Here righteousness incorporated the attitude we must have toward others when they've harmed us but have made amends: in the words of the Talmud, "So as He is merciful, so should you be merciful." You should be merciful even to *yourself* when *you* have sinned.

Yahweh demanded holiness rather than perfection: "The Lord spoke to Moses, saying: Speak to the whole Israelite community and say unto them: You shall be holy, for I, the Lord your God, am holy." One may wonder, what is the difference here between perfection and holiness? Perfection is an ideal of flawlessness. Holiness as understood in this passage refers to the Holiness Code, a detailed set of prescriptions within the Mosaic Code (specifically, Leviticus 17 to 26). It more or less repeats the Ten Commandments and includes a host of other practical commandments regarding interpersonal ethics, sex, agriculture, and religious rites. It is a guide to righteous living, not an effort to return to the paradisaic condition or to turn humans into angelic beings.

Christianity, however, takes this practical discipline of being holy to another level. Jesus admonishes us: "You, therefore, must be perfect, as your heavenly Father is perfect." What Jesus in fact did was raise Yahweh's moral standards while lowering his legal standards. To illustrate, we may cite Yahweh's two commandments that one should not covet his neighbor's wife and commit adultery. Maimonides interpreted the term "covet" here as desire accompanied by a deed, the adultery being the actual deed. Jesus, on the other hand, went so far as to stipulate that "everyone who looks at a woman lustfully has already committed adultery with her in his heart," the lust alone being the deed. According to this new moral standard, we are probably all adulterers. At the same time, when confronted with a woman who had been caught committing adultery and asked if she should be stoned, Jesus replied, "Let him who is without sin among you be the first to throw a stone at her." This virtually annulled the old legal standard of executing adulterers—a barbarism that the Talmud soon enough also condemned—by making it applicable to one and all and thus to no one person in particular.

Wasn't this Jesus's point on both counts, with both the moral and legal standards of adultery? It is our nature to sin. The doctrine of original sin—a Christian (and especially Pauline) idea, not a Jewish one—purports that the human condition, including our natural appetites and passions, are linked with man's fall from his paradisaic condition. As a consequence of this, we are all, in Augustine's view, born in a state of "total depravity" or corruption. We are driven to sin and without God's grace cannot refrain from it.

This notion tends to breed a contempt not only for humanity but also for the physical world, since when man fell, Paul tells us, all creation became subject to decay, "groaning in travail together until now." It is as if the world were altogether the opposite of God rather than a natural extension of him. This in turn adds fuel to the necessity for Armageddon, for a new world order that will once and for all eradicate sin. The idea of original sin justifies and heightens the apocalyptic fever that Jesus inherited from his father and plainly exhibited when he said, "I have come into this world to judge it" and "I came to cast fire upon the earth."

So, ironically again, Christianity nullified most of the Mosaic laws only to replace them with a more austere standard: moral perfection. This in fact was an *intensification* of Yahwism, leading to a Yahweh complex *plus*. This means that the Yahweh complex can be more moralistic, perfectionistic, and judgmental than Yahweh himself was, as can be observed in the impact that the Christian credo has had upon its practitioners. Martin Luther writes, "Christ becomes more formidable a tyrant and a judge than was Moses. . . . From childhood on, I knew I had to turn pale and be terror-stricken when I heard the name of Christ; for I was taught only to perceive him as a strict and wrathful judge."

The punitive element in the preaching of fire-and-brimstone types, still popular today, aims to invoke the same terror. If Luther's experience is any indication, this terror seems to altogether extinguish one's receptivity to Jesus's highest principles—namely, love and forgiveness. All that remains, then, in addition to one's terror, is the dark, blinding brilliance of the doctrine of original sin. Erik Erikson describes how Luther's preoccupation with his sinfulness surfaced in confession:

> [He] was so meticulous in the attempt to be truthful that he spelled out every intention as well as every deed; he splintered relatively acceptable purities into smaller and smaller impurities; he reported temptations in historical sequence, starting back in childhood; and after having confessed for hours, would ask for special appointments in order to correct previous statements. . . . [At] one time his superior Staupitz mocked him in a letter in which he said that Christ was not interested in such trifles and that Martin had better see to it

that he have some juicy adultery or murder to confess—perhaps
the murder of his parents.

Naturally, the vileness that the doctrine of original sin attaches to
the instinctual side of life has to be overcome by the struggle for moral
perfection. The more sinful we are, the more we must strive to be perfect.
(Indeed, Paul, possessed by the spirits of both Jesus and Yahweh, made a
vocation from this principle.)

The imitation of God had to be austere in order to be effective, giving
rise not only to Christianity's idealization of sexual abstinence but also
to such ascetic practices as mortification of the flesh, or self-flagellation.
Writing about the medieval lay Christian movement of the Brethren of the
Free Spirit, historian Robert Lerner cites the proceedings of a 1315 inquiry
into the practices of the hooded nuns of Schweidnitz: "One woman said
that she beat herself with the hide of a hedgehog and that others did the
same to themselves with barbed chains and knotted thongs. Another who
had been beaten in the house for eleven months, said that she underwent
such brutal exercise that she now was horribly disfigured and could not
recover from her injuries even though she had entered as a beautiful girl."

Such horror that arises from one's own internalized ideology is every bit
a form of religious tyranny as the kind imposed by external social agencies.

Christianity's elevated moral standards and consequent pursuit of
moral perfection are inherent not only in its ascetic extremism but also its
mainstream traditions. Protestantism made no protest against this austere
moral calculus, as both Martin Luther and John Calvin, to mention only
the two leading reformers, were Yahwists in the intensified sense of the
meaning. In his American tale *The Scarlet Letter*, Nathaniel Hawthorne
explores the tragically damaging effects of Puritan legalism and morality.

Protestantism's austerity is less evident today only because the practice
of moral rectitude in all Western religion has been watered down by the
rise of the very same secularism to which the Reformation contributed—
still another historical irony. Yet even in its more secular forms, Protestant
theology is handcuffed to the idea of original sin. Even a Christian

existential thinker like Søren Kierkegaard was tormented by anxiety and guilt over sin. (Kierkegaard's mixture of these with his additional tendency to lose his connection to the earth and to live only in his head prompted Jung to describe his condition as a complicated intellectual neurosis.)

As with their approach to mysticism, the Eastern religions have a different stance toward moral probity, and their mysticism and morality are related. In embracing the world as it is rather than pursuing a heaven after we die, they know that perfection, though sometimes touted, is at best a lofty ideal. "Water which is too pure has no fish," the *Ts'ai Ken T'an* tells us.

11

The Sacrilege of Holy War

Men never do evil so completely and cheerfully as when they
do it from a religious conviction.

—*Blaise Pascal*

The instinctual aggression underlying humanity's long and bloody
history of war is elemental to its nature and, of course, predates
the Bible. However, the Bible put God's stamp on our aggression by
fusing it with his own and placing it under the banner of his will—most
notably, his will for the Israelites to conquer the Promised Land. In a
similar manner, the Yahweh complex adds to our natural aggression a
sense of sanctity and moral rightness, a conviction that we are on a divine
mission and that God and goodness are on our side. Consequently, when
influenced by this complex, we will not hesitate to enforce *its* authority
and agenda, no matter how violent and heinous the actions it inspires.
All is permitted in the name of God and in the spirit of our god complex,
and we are but their instruments.

This principle underlaid the most notorious of holy wars, the Crusades
against the Muslims and other enemies of Roman Catholicism from
the eleventh to the thirteenth centuries. There are various views on the
motivating factors of the Crusades, including one that they were a defensive
war to liberate the Holy Land from Islamic rule, therefore supposedly taking
a stand *against* imperialism. All the same, we see here an early example of the
Yahweh complex in collective action. "*Deus vult!*"—God wills it!—became
the Crusaders' battle cry. "God himself will lead them, for they will be doing
His work," Pope Urban II said in a speech that had the galvanizing effect
of not only a declaration of war but also the rise of a mass movement. The
popular hymn "Onward, Christian Soldiers" erroneously gives to Jesus the

credit that belongs to Yahweh: "Onward, Christian soldiers, marching as to war, / With the cross of Jesus going on before. / Christ, the royal Master, leads against the foe; / Forward into battle see His banners go!" The cross may have been Jesus's, but the militancy was Yahweh's.

Needless to say, the Crusaders failed to permanently gain possession of the Holy Land or to thwart the expansion of Islam—that is, to do God's work as the pope had decreed they would. In the course of the eight main Crusades (there were others until the end of the seventeenth century), three million died by conservative estimates. In the First Crusade alone, six thousand Jews in the Rhineland lost their lives—the Crusades spawned a most superstitious, virulent form of anti-Semitism—and thirty thousand Jews and Muslims were slaughtered in two days when Jerusalem was captured. One witness reported that at Jerusalem's Temple Mount, the third holiest place in the Islamic world, the blood reached the horses' knees. The Fourth Crusade even involved an attack by Western Christians against the Eastern Christian city of Constantinople, so Yahwistically divisive were these so-called holy wars.

Though the Crusades had some positive effects, these were overshadowed by their negative ones. As religion scholar Karen Armstrong writes,

> [They changed Europe's status as] a primitive backwater, isolated from other civilizations and lost in a dark age that had descended on Western Christendom after the collapse of the Roman Empire in the fifth century. By the end of the crusading venture, Europe had not only recovered but also was on a course to overtake its rivals and achieve world hegemony. This recovery was a triumph unparalleled in history, but it was also a triumph that involved great strain and whose unfortunate consequences reverberate even today. . . . Indeed, nearly a millennium after Urban II's rallying cry, some Muslim fundamentalists still call Western imperialism and Western Christianity by the same name: *al-Salibiyyah*—"the Crusade."

The Diverse Ingredients of Holy War

Holy war is a terrible affliction that has assailed all the Abrahamic religions at one time or another and is still rampant. It commonly takes the form of an obsession over who is the elect, the people chosen to truly represent God on earth. Two or more sides mutually insist, "We are the true followers of God and you people aren't." Holy war can express and reinforce a group's conviction that God is on its side in any argument or difference it has with another group, even if that group is within the same religion. This affliction has thus had serious consequences for the relations not only between the Abrahamic religions but also within each religion alone.

Demonstrating the long reach of Yahweh, holy wars tend to be multigenerational, as if they are passed on through the mother's milk—or through the father's wrath, which is just as hard to resist. The rock band Arcade Fire makes a noble attempt to resist it when, in their song "Windowsill," they sing that they no longer want to live in their father's house and fight his holy wars. The force of the obstacle they have to overcome is matched by the intensity of their anguish.

Holy wars usually involve a complex range of factors, from religious to political and socioeconomic. The nonreligious differences between sides are often conflated with the religious ones. While the former can and must be resolved by rational human efforts, the latter are most difficult to move beyond because they are rooted in irrational beliefs that tend to be impervious to change.

History provides a checkered tapestry of how religious and nonreligious factors merge together to create holy wars, or at least wars with religious zeal. Joan of Arc's mission had the purely political aim of freeing France from English domination late in the Hundred Years' War, yet it was inspired by her visions of the archangel Michael, St. Catherine of Alexandria, and St. Margaret of Antioch. In death she became a martyr, and after death, a saint.

A more recent example is the Syrian civil war, which began in the Arab Spring with pro-democracy protests against President Bashar al-Assad.

However, as Assad cracked down on these and violence escalated into an armed rebellion, the war assumed a sectarian character, setting against each other the country's Sunni majority and Alawite minority, which included Assad and his security forces. Most of the two hundred thousand people Assad slaughtered were Sunnis (journalist Joe Klein accurately assessed him as an "Old Testament tyrant"). Because he targeted a distinct religious group, the UN declared his actions a genocide. And what religious features in specific distinguish Alawites from Sunnis, playing into their other differences with a deadly force? Political scientist Primoz Manfreda explains:

> Alawites practice a unique but little known form of Islam that dates back to the ninth and tenth centuries. Its secretive nature is an outcome of centuries of isolation from the mainstream society and periodical persecution by the Sunni majority. Sunnis believe that succession to prophet Mohammad (d. 632) rightly followed through the line of his most able and pious companions. Alawites follow the Shiite interpretation, claiming that succession should have been based on bloodlines. According to Shiite Islam, Mohammed's only true heir, imam, was his son-in-law Ali bin Abu Talib. But Alawites take a step further in the veneration of Imam Ali, allegedly investing him with divine attributes. Other specific elements such as the belief in divine incarnation, permissibility of alcohol, celebration of Christmas and the Zoroastrian new year make Alawite Islam highly suspect in the eyes of many orthodox Sunnis and Shiites.

This belief that only one side can possess the true understanding of who is qualified to represent the Islamic creed feeds into the hatred between Shiites and Sunnis and provides a religious justification for the wars they have waged against each other, including the eight-year Iran–Iraq War, which was the twentieth century's longest conventional war.

In times past—but not too far past, as the Northern Irish conflict proved—Catholics and Protestants also fought each other. If they did not fight primarily for religious reasons, as was indeed the case in Northern

Ireland, then they nevertheless identified themselves along religious lines, each usually seeing their cause as divinely justified. In seventeenth-century Europe, an estimated seven and a half million people died in the Thirty Years' War, which was driven both by political motivations and ardent religious passions.

Oliver Cromwell's conquest of Ireland, also in the seventeenth century, led to the passage of the Penal Laws against Roman Catholics and confiscation of large amounts of their land, and his brutal military measures have been described as genocidal. His Declaration to the Irish Catholic Clergy reveals the holy-war character of his thinking: "You are part of Antichrist, whose Kingdom the Scriptures so expressly speaks should be laid in blood and [soon you must all] have blood to drink; even the dregs of the cup of the fury and wrath of God, which will be poured out unto you." Cromwell Yahwistically justified this as revenge on the Irish for a massacre of English Protestants that had occurred some years earlier. Clearly, he believed that revenge is a dish best served cold.

Contrary to what one might expect, holy wars in Judaism didn't altogether end with the success of Yahweh's campaign to situate the Israelites in the Holy Land or with their hard-won return from exile in Babylonia. Foreign occupation of the Holy Land was continuously a thorn in the side of Jewish pride, and it inspired a fervent desire to regain Jewish sovereignty. The Maccabean Revolt in 166 BCE was seen as a war to gain religious freedom and to end the oppression imposed by the Hellenistic Seleucids. Historian Reuven Firestone writes that "both the Great Revolt of 66 CE [with the mass suicide of Jewish fighters at Masada] and the Bar Kokhba Rebellion of 132 CE—two of the most horrific and catastrophic events that the Jewish people ever experienced—were driven by Jewish holy war ideas."

To these uprisings against Rome we may add the revolt against Heraclius from 613 to 614 CE, in which Jews joined forces with the pre-Islamic Persian Sassanid Empire to liberate Jerusalem from its occupation by the Christian Byzantine Empire. With the Persians' permission, the Jews effectively controlled the city for the next five years. Viewing their repossession of Jerusalem in a messianic light, they made plans to build a Third Temple and establish a new high priesthood. The revolt therefore acquired, in hindsight, the patina of a holy war. A Third Temple never came about as the Byzantines recaptured the city in 629.

The Jewish inclination toward holy war more or less went into hibernation once the Diaspora took hold and rabbinic consciousness redefined the value of what is holy in ways that unmoored the religion from its dependency on the Holy Land. The Jews simply could not go up against the superpowers who successively incorporated Palestine into their empires. The Talmud didn't explicitly redirect the people's preoccupation with the Holy Land. Rather, it shifted their focus on the Temple—which was the center that most saliently gave the Holy Land its significance—to a religious life and practice of the Law that could endure even after the destruction of Jerusalem and the Temple itself. (The rabbinic sage largely responsible for this shift was Yohanan Ben Zakkai.) In no small measure, this assured Jewish survival in the two-thousand-year Diaspora that followed.

Predictably, the Jewish inclination toward holy war resurfaced with the establishment of a Jewish state in 1948. At heart ethnic and political, the Israeli–Palestinian conflict developed the overtone of a religious one for many Jews and Arabs alike. Both sides feel they have a claim to the land, and that claim, too, blends religious and nonreligious factors. The religious ones go back to the inception of Judaism and Islam. Jews and Muslims both believe that they are the preferred descendants of Abraham. How do each explain their belief?

From the Bible we already know of Yahweh's selection of the Israelites as his chosen people. The Bible also tells us that Abraham had two sons— Isaac and Ishmael—from different mothers, and that Isaac's mother, Sarah, coerced Abraham into sending Ishmael and his mother, Hagar— an Egyptian slave who was Sarah's maid—into the wilderness. Yahweh told Abraham to not be distressed about this, for both sons would be the founders of great nations.

Muslims believe that Muhammad and the northern Arabs descended from Ishmael. This links the Jews and Arabs to a common heritage as

Abraham's descendants. An angel later repeated the same prophecy about Ishmael to Hagar at a moment when she too was distressed. However, according to the Bible, he added that Ishmael "shall be a wild ass of a man, his hand against everyone, and everyone's hand against him, setting himself to defy all his brothers."

The fourteenth-century Islamic scholar Ismail ibn Kathir naturally offers a slightly different version of the angel's words: "He would be a wild man. His hand would be over everyone, and the hand of everyone would be against him. His brethren would rule over all the lands." Ibn Kathir sees Islam's rule over the world as a prophecy appropriate for Muhammad's offspring. The Muslims also redress the story of Ishmael by making him, and not Isaac, the son whom Abraham nearly sacrificed, and the one whose descendants God preferred. From this soil sprouts the competing Jewish and Muslim beliefs that each people is entitled to the Holy Land and, in the case of the architects of the Islamic Empire, that they were entitled to all lands.

But again, the tendency toward holy war affects the relations not only between different peoples but also among themselves. Holy war between opposing factions of a society can tear it apart. For instance, Yigdal Amir, who assassinated Israeli prime minister Yitzhak Rabin, was a product of the extreme Orthodox nationalistic culture that he came from. Amir claimed he was acting in accordance with Jewish law, specifically the "pursuer's decree" that obligates any Jew to stop someone who presents a mortal threat to another Jew. He believed Rabin's policies endangered his fellow Jews and that his government had been elected by a religiously illegitimate coalition of Arabs and Jews. The Israeli court disagreed with his interpretation of this law and sentenced him to life imprisonment. Their implicit message was that the Holy Land can no longer be a haven for holy war, for either Arabs or Jews.

One must assume that if one person in Israel (or wherever else Jews live) has the views of Yigdal Amir, there must be others. The same is true about extremists everywhere: they represent a wider mindset and not just their own.

We know that Timothy McVeigh, who bombed the Alfred P. Murrah Federal Building in Oklahoma City, expressed the views of many in the militia movements that intermittently crop up in the United States. Like Amir and Muslim terrorists, McVeigh was on a holy mission and possessed by a Yahweh complex, even if this mission was couched in secular language and ideology. Everything about him was Yahwistic, from his Roman Catholic upbringing to his bitter, coldly judgmental disposition and agnostic disillusionment, the latter a sign of our godless or anarchic times. Up to the last minute before his execution, he remained impenitent, yet he concluded his life on a religious note: he requested a Catholic chaplain and a prequiem—a Mass for those who are about to die—to be conducted by composer David Woodard. Perhaps also a sign of our times, his final meal consisted of two pints of Ben and Jerry's mint chocolate chip ice cream.

The Hungry Force of Jihadism

The same interface of religious and nonreligious factors that characterize most holy wars gives Islamic holy war, or jihad, its exceptionally volatile combustibility. The religious dimension of this is striking. The Arabic term "jihad" literally means "striving" or "struggle." Two kinds were originally distinguished: the "greater jihad," or the struggle Muslims must wage against sin—a spiritual notion; and the "lesser jihad," or the armed struggle against nonbelievers—a more worldly and militant notion. Both were viewed as integral to redeeming and unifying our divided world.

The greater jihad is naturally more difficult, and is "greater" precisely for this reason. It has an enduring meaning that is dependent not on outer factors but rather on inner values. As the Muslim Bollywood actor Shah Rukh Khan aptly put it, "Fighting and conquering negativity in your heart is the real jihad." If jihad were only this kind of struggle, history would have been very different.

Going beyond merely defensive purposes, the lesser jihad was understood as the advancement of Islam's power. Its aim was unmistakable. Historian T. David Curp writes:

In Islam's first centuries, Muslim scholars and jurists formulated their understanding of the religious *and* political division of the world into the Dar al-Islam, or the House of Peace [or House of Islam], and the Dar al-Harb, the House of War [or House of Unbelief]. While truces between Islamic and non-Muslim polities were acceptable, the Koran taught that these were to be limited in duration. Ultimately, no permanent peace between Muslims and nonbelievers was possible until all nonbelievers submitted to Muslim rule, and the Dar al-Islam encompassed the whole world.

This is far more expansive than Yahweh's ambition to conquer the Promised Land, Christianity's Crusades, or Europe's colonizations. None of these aimed, at least expressly, for domination of the entire world. We find here another illustration of the Yahweh complex plus.

Only the New Testament's Apocalypse compares to modern jihadism's otherworldly orientation. For instance, al-Qaeda's final instructions to the nineteen terrorists who undertook the 9/11 attacks reminded them that theirs was "a battle for the sake of God. The enemies are the allies of Satan, the brothers of the Devil. Do not fear them for the believer fears only God. And when the hour approaches, welcome death for the sake of God. With your last breath remember God. Make your final words 'There is no God but God!'"

As religion scholar Reza Aslan explains, "They were engaged in a metaphysical conflict, not between armies or nations but between the angels of light and the demons of darkness. They were fighting a *cosmic war*, not against the American imperium but against the eternal forces of evil." This way of thinking raises jihad to a whole other level. No longer is it an internal war against sin; nor is it merely the external conquest of non-Muslims. It is a stroke of the sword that transcends both and unites them in a single cosmic act.

Moderate Muslims might say this position is extreme even by the standards of the Qur'an, since only Allah has the power to vanquish the demons of darkness. One wonders: as powerful as a war-god complex and the promise of paradise are, is there something in the world we live in driving jihadists to embrace such extremism? Political economist Ömer Taşpinar tells us that religious fanaticism alone does not explain what makes young people join jihadist movements like ISIS. We can't understand their motivations without understanding how four practical, nonreligious factors merge together with the religious ones:

1. Those who are educated and have high ambitions but no real prospects for advancement are the "frustrated achievers" increasingly tempted by radicalism.

2. The interconnected nature of the world, thanks to information technology and globalization, creates an acute awareness about opportunities elsewhere.

3. Geographic proximity to Europe, a sense of historical rivalry, and constant comparisons of achievements contribute to a sense of relative deprivation.

4. In a sense, Islam as a civilization is a frustrated achiever.

In other words, young Muslims both in Europe and in Muslim countries feel disenfranchised and disillusioned by a lack of opportunity, and the constant reminder of "relative deprivation" tips the scale toward jihad. Here we see the blending together of religious and nonreligious factors that is typical of holy wars.

In the case of modern jihad, the nonreligious factors are the concrete, practical underbelly, as it were, of the religious ones. However, from the viewpoint of the Yahweh complex, the religious and nonreligious aspects here are two sides of the same coin. Are not the acts of jihad similar to Yahweh's acts of terror insofar as they betrayed the way he felt in response to his rejection by his people? The terror was in *him*. Jihadists also act out a terror that reflects their feelings about their position in the world, even if they are unconscious of them.

The situations are different, but the emotions are similar. The Muslim experience of deprivation and disillusionment constellates the Yahweh complex *emotionally*, and that's why it's prone to extremism. Its pattern duplicates Yahweh's: deprivation + disillusionment + apocalyptic fever = mass murder. Wasn't Yahweh also a frustrated achiever, beginning as early as Noah's flood? Apocalyptic fever was the apotheosis of his frustration and rage. We can observe the same every time a suicide bomber blows others and themselves up.

Rage, Retribution, and the Quest for Identity

Holy war today is not limited to "big" events in the lives of nations, to declared wars that have a beginning and an end. Nor is it limited to overt acts of terrorism. Social media has turned holy war into a cultural and geopolitical phenomenon as much as a military and localized one. Journalist Bobby Ghosh offers a short "history of rage and retribution" from 1989 to 2012 that cuts across the lines of traditional warfare:

1989 *The Satanic Verses*: Ayatollah Khomeini calls for author Salman Rushdie's death after his novel is deemed blasphemous.

2004 *Submission*: Dutch filmmaker Theo van Gogh is killed in the wake of his film criticizing the treatment of Muslim women.

2005 Guantánamo: Allegations (later retracted) that the Koran was defiled at the detention camp trigger fatal riots in Afghanistan.

2005 Danish cartoons: Images depicting Muhammad in the newspaper *Jullands-Posten* spark violent protests in several countries.

2006 Papal lecture: Pope Benedict XVI's inclusion of a controversial 14th century quote about Islam is condemned by politicians.

2010 "Ground Zero" mosque: A plan for an Islamic center in Manhattan is a rallying point for US politicians during the election season.

2010 Terry Jones: The Florida pastor's announcement of plans to burn the Koran on the 9/11 anniversary incites global protests.

2012 Koran incineration: The accidental burning of Korans at the US Bagram Air Base in Afghanistan spurs violence. President Obama apologizes.

2012 Blasphemy plot: A Muslim cleric in Islamabad is accused of planting evidence to implicate a young Christian girl in burning the Koran.

2012 *Innocence of Muslims*: Clips of an English-language film mocking Muhammad are posted on the Web.

2012 Sheik Khaled Abdallah: The controversial Egyptian TV host reports on *Innocence of Muslims* on his program.

2012 Cairo demonstration: Angry Egyptians scale the wall of the US embassy and remove the flag in protest of *Innocence of Muslims*.

We may, of course, add to this list other incidents that occurred since 2012. Just in 2015 alone there was the attack on *Charlie Hebdo* magazine in Paris (an event that inspired 3.7 million people and forty world leaders to rally in a "unity" march), the wider massacre that killed a hundred and thirty people, also in Paris, and the shooting in San Bernardino, California.

Holy war is a violent quest for identity or defense of identity aimed at alleviating the violence or war inside ourselves when we feel lost or threatened in a strange new world. Salman Rushdie speaks from his own experience as a victim of holy war and of Ayatollah Khomeini's identity politics, or, as the case may be, Khomeini's Yahweh complex:

> People find their selfhood in terms of what they most object to . . . By having an enemy and by launching yourself in fury against that enemy, you seem to have a better feeling of who you are. . . . It becomes a kind of identity politics. People who are looking to find a narrowly defined but passionately, feverishly, even violently held definition of identity, find it very easily by finding a target and attacking that target.

The problem of holy war is that our identity gets mixed up with God's in less than a truly holy or mystical way. The fact that we are the last to see this, or never see it at all, places holy war among the most hypnotic, diabolical manifestations of a god complex. Of course, there is no such thing as a truly holy war. Perhaps there's a holy *response* to a war initiated by an aggressive enemy, as articulated, for instance, by Lincoln and Churchill. But is war *ever* holy, with its effects of destruction and loss of life, and these mostly over causes that essentially have nothing to do with a mature, evolved understanding of God?

The Surreptitious Nature of Modern Holy War

In another way of thinking, all wars are potentially "holy." Clever propaganda can turn any war into a holy one by simply emphasizing and ceaselessly repeating that it serves a religious cause or fateful calling. Wars in any scenario are usually started by leaders who are inflated with a god complex that makes them, and in turn their followers, feel righteous, infallible, and invincible. To leaders and followers alike, war is holy not only because of the principles that they may believe are at stake but also because it fills them with a numinous zeal and spiritual sense of purpose. Both become drunk with the power of war and warmongering.

Such was indeed the case with Hitler, who delivered more than five thousand mesmerizing speeches promising his followers that his new empire, the Third Reich, would reign for a thousand years. He was definitely on a "holy" mission, even if he didn't use that word: "What we must fight for," he writes in his autobiography, "is to safeguard the existence and reproduction of our race and our people, the sustenance of our children and the purity of our blood, the freedom and independence of the Fatherland, so that our people may mature *for the fulfillment of the mission allotted it by the Creator of the universe*" (italics my own). Notice how smoothly and even eloquently Hitler here gets his message across, as if he were not referring to something as gruesome and atrocious as what would later become known as the "final solution," with its death camps and ovens.

As theologian Charles Henkey, among others, has said, the devil does not come to your door looking like classical images of the devil. He is dressed in a fine suit, holds a bouquet of flowers, and greets you with a friendly, inviting smile. (Think of the way Nazi soldiers lured Jews into deportation trains and then gas shower rooms by telling them they were being "resettled" in labor camps and getting showers to rid themselves of lice.) Hitler and Germany's part in the Second World War would eventually entail the deaths of some seventy-five million people, by one estimate. As observable in this and similar instances, "holy war" is just a euphemism for an altered state of consciousness otherwise known as megalomania, the madness of an unrestrained will to power. It is an empty yet deadly pursuit.

Holy war thus operates as a wily, slick, archetypal force—a kind of trickster, if we were to give it a human face. It clouds our perception and judgment, convincing us that it is holy because it feels like a religious experience (at least until we get on the battlefield and discover up close how deadly or maiming it is—or perhaps, *even and especially then*). The zealous, manic intoxication that holy war induces makes it a tricksterish shape-shifter, enabling it to disguise itself as patriotism or loyalty to any charismatic leader or inspiring cause that may capture our attention.

Because it so easily adapts to new and secular causes that arise as quickly as circumstances permit, holy war occurs today in surreptitious forms. Americans in particular tend to engage in them. The motivating factors of their wars were less opaque in earlier times. In its day, many openly spoke of the Civil War as a holy one. One Northern minister declared, "If the crusaders, seized by a common enthusiasm, exclaimed, *It is the will of God! It is the will of God!*—much more may we make this our rallying cry and inscribe it on our banners." Even the First World War, often described as unnecessary and lacking a worthy cause, became an occasion for President Woodrow Wilson to celebrate the mystery of holiness. When he presented the Treaty of Versailles to the US Senate, he concluded his speech with these words:

The stage is set, the destiny disclosed. It has come about by no plan of our conceiving, but by the hand of God who led us into this way. We cannot turn back. We can only go forward, with lifted eyes and freshened spirit, to follow the vision. It was of this that we dreamed at our birth. America shall in truth show the way. The light streams upon the path ahead, and nowhere else.

For a number of reasons, including its inflated religious perspective, the speech was not well received.

In more recent times, holy war has become a trickier phenomenon, seeping into American politics and social life unnoticed while pitting American against American in ways not altogether unlike the Civil War. Holy war now manifests mostly as highly polarized conflicts between conservatives and liberals, even within parties and not just between them. People are not only passionate but also devout in their moral and political positions: the right to bear arms vs. gun control; pro-life vs. pro-choice; scientific thinking vs. anti-scientific thinking—all are quasi-religious moving parts in our "culture wars" (a moniker for America's domestic holy wars). We even have a war on truth, a war between facts and "alternate facts." Trump's "big lie," a.k.a. his false claim of a stolen election, the assault on Capitol Hill, and the way politicians then rallied behind him all demonstrated the intoxication of holy war.

All the above varieties of infighting are draped in the fervor of holy war and are really a single holy war: the war for the soul of America and for whether this soul will reflect the spirit of democracy or that of a Trumpian autocracy (I purposely use religious language here to illustrate my point). Even if most of these conflicts do not actually involve physical violence like the episode on Capitol Hill did, they are tearing apart the delicate fabric of national unity. Each side of any given conflict struggles to vanquish the other—or the other's views and viability—since anything short of that would not be a clear victory.

We Americans believe in our causes with the ferocity and conviction of Yahweh Sabaoth—one of Yahweh's various biblical names, literally meaning the "Lord of Hosts" or the "Lord of Heavenly Armies." Yahweh Sabaoth walks among us every day and works his dark magic just like he did in the Tower of Babel episode, setting us against each other. Who says that the Hebrew Bible or Old Testament is old?

12

The Embers of Western and Islamic Imperialism

Emotional neglect lays the groundwork for the emotional numbing that helps boys feel better about being cut off. Eruptions of rage in boys are most often deemed normal, explained by the age-old justification for adolescent patriarchal misbehavior, "Boys will be boys." Patriarchy both creates the rage in boys and then contains it for later use, making it a resource to exploit later on as boys become men. As a national product, this rage can be garnered to further imperialism, hatred and oppression of women and men globally. This rage is needed if boys are to become men willing to travel around the world to fight wars without ever demanding that other ways of solving conflict can be found.

—*bell hooks*

As ancient as ancient history itself, imperialism is a force independent of Yahwism, but, like aggression in general, it can draw upon Yahwism most conveniently. In the spirit of ancient Israel, European monarchs exercising the divine right of kings were seen as voice pieces for God, implementing his will on earth. Consequently, their empire-building campaigns were also seen as providential. Of course, Chinese and Japanese emperors too were endowed with the divine right to rule, the former blessed by a Mandate of Heaven and the latter honored as descendants of the sun goddess Amaterasu. Wherever divine right existed, imperialism was not far behind.

However, because the Bible, again, sanctified our aggression by fusing it with God's, Western imperialism exhibited a most ferocious religiosity in its sense of entitlement, leading to unimaginable cruelty. Millions were exploited, enslaved, and murdered in the name of God. In New England, for instance, colonists believing that one of their own had been murdered by a Pequot Indian attacked, together with their Indian allies, a Pequot village, burning alive some seven hundred Indians. The Puritan minister and writer Cotton Mather remarked that the colonists thought this "a sweet sacrifice, and—gave the praise thereof to God." Later, the colonists captured most of the remaining Pequots and sold them into slavery in Bermuda.

The film *Even the Rain* unabashedly shows what happened to Indians in Latin America who refused to convert to Christianity: they were also burned to death. The renowned Spanish theologian Juan Ginés de Sepúlveda argued that the Indians of the New World deserved this kind of treatment because their sins and idolatries were offensive to God. There was no limit to the effort to purify their souls. "The Spaniards in Mexico and Peru," Bertrand Russell writes, "used to baptize Indian infants and then immediately dash their brains out: by this means they secured that these infants went to Heaven."

In spite of Pope Paul III's declaration in 1537 that Native Americans were "true men," even Enlightenment thinkers like Voltaire, Montesquieu, and Hume continued to see them—and Africans—as racially inferior. Whether they believed in God or not, such thinkers were still infected with the Yahwistic ideal of who is chosen and pure and who is not. Often this kind of thinking led to a cultural imperialism if not also an economic one and was cloaked in gestures of goodwill, as if the imperial power were doing the "heathens" a favor. President William McKinley, for example, described the Philippine-American War, one of the worst in terms of cruelty and war crimes on the part of the United States, as follows: "There was nothing left for us to do but to take [the Philippines] and to educate the Filipinos, and uplift and civilize and Christianize them, and by God's grace do the very best we could by them, as our fellow men for whom Christ also died." Waving his magic wand, McKinley thought he could turn a most ugly war into a holy and righteous one. He didn't even realize that the Philippines were the only nation in Asia that was predominantly Catholic.

In their Yahwistic passion to establish God's kingdom on earth, missionaries often paved the way for Western imperialism. First they would set up posts in the New World, and then, hearing of their adventures, explorers would follow. The explorers' stories would in turn inspire European governments and industrialists to build colonies and acquire the land's abundant resources. Exactly such was the case with David Livingstone in sub-Saharan Africa; he was both a missionary and an explorer. Sometimes the governments or industrialists encouraged or sponsored the missionaries in the first place as part of a Machiavellian scheme. George Bernard Shaw writes in regard to the Englishman as a prime force of colonization: "When he wants a new market for his adulterated Manchester goods, he sends a missionary to teach the natives the gospel of peace. The natives kill the missionary: he flies to arms in defense of Christianity; fights for it; conquers for it; and takes the market as a reward from heaven."

Such slyness also pervaded the Yahwistic legalism of Western imperialism. In many instances, laws were used to try to fool the colonized into accepting colonization without costly violence. The Laws of the Indies issued by the Spanish Crown for its American and Philippine colonies guaranteed the protection of natives' rights but in Latin America were clearly not carried out. New Zealand's Treaty of Waitangi is generally accepted as the founding document of the nation. Signed in 1840 by the Maori tribal chiefs and the British government, it stated that the Maoris and British settlers would be co-caretakers of the land (in accord with the understanding of almost all indigenous peoples that no one can *own* the land and that it is there for everyone). This at least is what the Maori version of the treaty stated. The English version stated that the British queen held sovereignty over everything—the land, all property, and even the Maoris themselves.

When sly maneuvers no longer worked, the Yahwistic power of the written word and of the law was unfurled shamelessly. President Andrew Jackson's Indian Removal Act of 1830 forcibly did exactly what its name implied it would do, proving that previous US treaties with Native American tribes weren't worth the paper they were written on. Although

Chief Justice John Marshall ruled in *Cherokee Nation v. Georgia* that the Cherokees could not be forced to give up their land, he also declined to deliver a verdict based on the technicality that the Cherokees had filed suit as a "foreign nation" rather than the more accurate designation as a "domestic dependent nation."

Such Yahwistic preoccupation with the letter of the law not only sacrificed its spirit but also signaled how limited were the Indians' chances to keep their land. In the subsequent Supreme Court case of *Worcester v. Georgia*, Marshall again ruled against forced removal. However, Jackson—a militant, imperial Yahwist if ever there was one (it's no accident that Trump chose to hang his portrait in the Oval Office)—and the State of Georgia ran roughshod over his decision and relocated the Cherokees to Oklahoma, with Tennessee, Alabama, and North Carolina soon following suit. Their mass exodus in 1838 has been memorialized as the "Trail of Tears." (The Chocktaw, Seminole, Creek, and Chickasaw nations were also relocated, though earlier.) Because some four thousand of the sixteen thousand Cherokees who made this journey died from exposure, disease, and starvation, it has been described as a genocide. Howard Zinn's masterful classic *A People's History of the United States* and Eduardo Galeano's heart-wrenching *Open Veins of Latin America* are replete with accounts of this kind; they can be read as a history of Yahwism in the New World.

Yahwistic imperialism is no stranger to Russia, too. With its Eastern Orthodoxy and czarist mentality regardless of the regime in control, Russia is a Yahwistic society. The style of its leaders may reflect that of the pre-Christian Slavic war-god Perun, as mentioned earlier, but overlaid on this and affecting the society as a whole is the more widespread autocratic and chauvinistic ethos of Yahweh. Historically and still today, Russians accept and tolerate the Yahwistic assumption that rules are for the people but not for the rulers; like Yahweh, Russian leaders are exempt from having to uphold the law.

Churchill's famous description of Russia as "a riddle wrapped in a mystery inside an enigma" could just as well have been said about Yahweh.

After all, what did Yahweh want? In his complexity, he allowed his people to be enslaved, then led them to freedom and transformed them into a militant nation of conquerors, only to then send them into foreign exile so he could once again save them. More simply, we could say he wanted to be prominent in their lives. And what does Russia want? What did President Vladimir Putin want when, with more than 90 percent of Russians approving, he annexed Crimea in 2014? Journalists Michael Crowley and Simon Shuster tell us:

> [He was determined to] restore Russia's place in the ranks of great powers. . . . Putin has developed a personal ideology, made up of at least one part personal theology and another part manifest destiny. Putin is Russian Orthodox, a deeply conservative faith with an ancient liturgy, ties to saints of the Middle Ages and an allergy to social change. History haunts the Orthodox: the Russian czars saw themselves as protectors of the world's Orthodox people—the 19th century Crimean War was fought largely on those grounds—and Putin is increasingly taking up that cause. During the blustery March [2014] speech to parliament, Putin invoked the legacy of another Vladimir—the 10th century ruler Vladimir the Great, a prince of Kyiv who converted the pagan Slavs to Christianity. "His spiritual feat of adopting Orthodoxy predetermined the overall basis of the culture, civilization and human values that unite the peoples of Russia, Ukraine and Belarus," Putin said. At the end of that speech Putin signed a treaty formalizing the Russian annexation of Crimea, the peninsula where Vladimir the Great was baptized in the year 988.

Putin's ideology could be clearly traced back to the czars, whose mandate to be "protectors of the world's Orthodox people" was ultimately derived from Yahweh's role with the Israelites. Wherever there is a chosen people, there is also a special manifest destiny and calling to prominence. Was it really a surprise that Putin didn't stop with Crimea and in 2022 invaded Ukraine, very likely with the same ideology inflating him (rather than on the grounds of ending a genocide by a Ukrainian Nazi regime, as he falsely claimed)? In his eyes, his Yahwistic mission justified his bullying and brutal attack on his militarily weaker neighbor; he evidently heard and answered the call for a holy war.

What *was* surprising was the evil of his unrestrained, scorched-earth policy and complete disregard for the many lives lost—on *both* sides—so he could get what he wanted. He appeared to be consumed by a ruthless war-god complex that left room in his psyche only for what a number of Western leaders have observed is a cold shell of a human being, if there was any humanity within him to begin with. On the other hand, the long history of tyranny sadly shows that he is all too human.

The Rise and Fall of the Islamic Empire

Nowhere is the belief in being chosen for a special mission of prominence more salient than in the history of Islamic imperialism. The Islamic Empire was not a centralized empire like the Roman or British Empire but consisted of a series of caliphates, regional empires, dynasties, sultanates, and states, some of which existed contemporaneously. This empire spanned from the seventh to the twentieth centuries, peaking around the twelfth and thirteenth centuries and beginning its gradual decline thereafter (though some historians date the beginning of its decline later, depending on the historical markers used). Its rise coincided with Islam's Golden Age, a high achievement in civilization too often forgotten by both Muslims and non-Muslims.

Of this achievement and its breadth of innovation, economists William Cooper and Piyu Yue write:

> For 400 years, from the mid-9th century to the mid-13th century, Islamic culture became unparalleled in its splendor and learning. The accomplishments of Islam's Golden Age are numerous, including unrivaled intellectual activities in all fields: science, technology,

theology, philosophy, and literature—particularly biography, history, and linguistics. The tales of the Arabian Nights ("One Thousand and One Nights") was compiled during this period. The Muslim belief that Arabic, the language of the holy Quran, was the language of Allah himself, led to standardization of the language throughout the Islamic Empire as the language of faith and power. The so-called "Arabic" numerals began to replace the cumbersome Roman numerals, and the concept of zero was introduced for the first time. Muslim scholars also made many other important and original contributions to mathematics, astronomy, medicine, and chemistry (an outgrowth of alchemy) and studied a wide variety of minerals and compounds.

Important advances in agriculture were also made in the Golden Age, including preserved and improved ancient networks of wells, underground canals, and waterwheels. New breeds of livestock were introduced; the spread of cotton and new strains of wheat was hastened; and the art of making paper was borrowed from the Chinese. The Middle East became the center of world trade and Baghdad became a luxurious and commercial world city. Science, technology, medicine, astronomy, and architecture flourished. Literature, history, poetry, and religious studies reached great heights. The achievements of the Islamic Empire in religious mission, military success, and cultural advancement represented one of the greatest civilizations of the time.

Cooper and Yue add that the Golden Age occurred while Europe was still in the Dark Ages and that its advances in science and technology later provided the impetus for the European Renaissance. Thinkers like al-Kindi—"the Philosopher of the Arabs" who wrote with equal facility about philosophy, psychology, astronomy, optics, medicine, chemistry, mathematics, cryptography, music theory, and more—were Renaissance men before there was a Renaissance. And al-Kindi was just one among a host of Muslim polymaths. Medieval Europe even depended on Arabic translations of many otherwise unknown Greek works.

But even at the height of Islam's cultural achievements, its imperial practices were ferocious and savage. By the eighth century, Islamic influence stretched from Portugal and Spain through all of Northern Africa to India and Indonesia. While the Ottoman Empire was considerably tolerant of Christians and Jews, the various conquests of India were among the cruelest manifestations of Yahwism.

"The Mohammedan conquest of India," historian and philosopher Will Durant writes, "is probably the bloodiest story in history. The Islamic historians and scholars have recorded with great glee and pride the slaughters of Hindus, forced conversions, abduction of Hindu women and children to slave markets and the destruction of temples carried out by the warriors of Islam during 800 AD to 1700 AD." These actions weren't explicitly genocidal like the military campaigns of the Israelites, nor could they be justified as defensive like the Crusades that aimed to recapture Jerusalem from the Muslims but wreaked widespread and unnecessary devastation. Nevertheless, they exercised the same sense of entitlement and drive for conquest. They too were viewed as divinely ordained.

Along the eastern and southern edges of the Mediterranean, Christians also suffered from the Islamic Empire's relentless attacks in order to subjugate, pillage, and murder them. As many as a million were enslaved. These attacks made the same lasting impression on Christians that the Crusades did on Muslims. The fourteenth-century Byzantine emperor Manuel II Palaiologos said, "Show me just what Muhammad brought that was new, and there you will find things only evil and inhuman, such as his command to spread by the sword the faith he preached."

When Pope Benedict XVI repeated these words in a speech in the early days of his papacy (an incident briefly mentioned earlier), it sparked a furor, even though it was clear that these were the emperor's words and not his and that they were expressed in context of a larger discussion on faith, reason, and violence. Riots broke out in the Middle East. Muslims protesting in Europe called for the pope's death and waved placards that read, "Islam will conquer Rome" and "Jesus is the slave of Allah." A Catholic priest and nun were murdered. Several churches were set on fire. As clergyman Stephen Andrew Missick said, "Muslims around the world unintentionally confirmed the words of the Byzantine emperor."

Curiously, the Yahwistic theocracy whose export from Arabia gave rise to the Islamic Empire also led to its decline. Historian Bernard Lewis explains that "in the sense of a state ruled by the church or by priests, Islam was not and indeed could not be a theocracy," but it certainly was a theocracy in the sense that, "in the Muslim conception, God is the true sovereign of the community, the ultimate source of authority, the sole source of legislation." However, it wasn't theocracy per se that undermined Islam; after all, theocracy didn't undermine ancient Israel. What undermined it was the theocracy's *thorough insulation* of the tradition, its sealing itself in a kind of time capsule or bubble that could absorb historical change only to a certain point. Lewis identifies the seeds of this condition by comparing the Islamic and Western religions:

> The first and in many ways the most profound difference, from which all others follow, can be seen in the contrasting foundation myths—I use this expression without intending any disrespect—of Islam, Christianity, and Judaism. The children of Israel fled from bondage, and wandered for 40 years in the wilderness before they were permitted to enter the Promised Land. Their leader Moses had only a glimpse, and was not himself permitted to enter. Jesus was humiliated and crucified, and his followers suffered persecution and martyrdom for centuries, before they were finally able to win over the ruler, and to adapt the state, its language, and its institutions to their purpose. Muhammad achieved victory and triumph in his own lifetime. He conquered his promised land, and created his own state, of which he himself was supreme sovereign. As such, he promulgated laws, dispensed justice, levied taxes, raised armies, made war, and made peace. In a word, he ruled, and the story of his decisions and actions as ruler is sanctified in Muslim scripture and amplified in Muslim tradition.

In other words, Islam had a built-in assumption that there needed to be no evolution of the tradition—exposition of the tradition by additional knowledge, yes, but no stretching into the unpredictable challenges of history, particularly those that also challenged the theocratic foundation of Islam. Lewis insinuates that this theocratic foundation guaranteed the "absence of a native secularism in Islam, and the widespread Muslim rejection of an imported secularism inspired by Christian example." By "Christian example," he means Jesus's teaching to "render to Caesar the things that are Caesar's, and to God the things that are God's." Augustine further clarified the differences between the secular "city of man" and the sacred "city of God," showing their common interests and how they can cooperate with each other, mutually promoting peace, social stability, and good behavior.

But Islam had no inherent way to release social development from the ceiling imposed on it by the closed system of its theocracy. Muhammad's success in providing a young Islam with everything he *thought* was needed later became the obstacle to Islam's ability to adapt to new developments. The civilization became inflexible. Nuclear medical scientist Ibrahim Syed specifies how this inflexibility played out:

> Muslim scholars argue that the Qur'an advocates the quest for knowledge of nature by observation, and this inspired the development of scientific method by Muslims. However, in the 12th century when Muslim philosophers began to suggest that truth itself may be revealed by empirical observation as well as from the Qur'an, there was a religious crackdown, the gate of *ijtihad* [independent reasoning] was closed and scientific research largely ceased in the Muslim world. It was eventually pursued in Europe, but not without resistance from religious authorities there. The start of the 13th century saw the beginning of the relative decline of Islamic civilization. This decline was not caused by outside forces. It was not caused by a lack of dedication to Islam. It was caused by Muslim rulers and the *Ulema* [scholars]. It was caused by obscurantism in Islam. This is because rejection of science and scientific method

was rejection of what was to later become the main driving force in industrial wealth and prosperity. Scientific research in the Muslim world declined and the intellectual environment became inhospitable to the open and honest exchange of ideas. . . . There was a feeling in the Muslim world that improvement was unnecessary, except perhaps in the technology of warfare. Gradually all the advancements known to the Muslim world passed to Europe, where the knowledge was eventually utilized to greater effect.

And this, as Lewis would say, is what went wrong with Islam. This problem of resistance to change is still extant in the Muslim world. We see its manifestations in the urge of entire groups to return to or to prolong archaic modes of governance, education, and regulation of public and social life. Such an attitude, historian Arnold Toynbee warns, prevents a civilization from creatively responding to the challenges of history, thus locking it into the certainty of stagnation and decline.

Iran's Apocalyptic Fever and Islam's Wounded Pride

Iran is almost unique among the nations of the world. Aside from Russia with its annexation of Crimea and invasion of Ukraine, it is the only country at the time of this writing that has renewed imperialistic ambitions. It clearly wants to attain hegemony in the Middle East if not the entire world. It is unique even among Islamic nations; the Iranian Revolution marks a departure from Islamic history for a variety of reasons. The departure I'm interested in here is probably the most alarming: the Iranian regime has embraced the traditional idea of the lesser jihad.

It is more than extreme in its aspirations. Apocalyptic fever fires the ideology of both its ayatollahs and nonclerical leaders. They subscribe to Islam's messianic teaching on the end of world, raising the concern that they think they have a righteous role in facilitating it. They see themselves as shepherds of the Apocalypse. This is largely why leaders like Israel's Benjamin Netanyahu fear Iran acquiring nuclear weaponry. If they get it, Netanyahu warns, "all bets are off." (It takes a Yahwist to know a Yahwist, even though Netanyahu's Yahweh complex manifests differently.) He adds that the danger, naturally, is not merely to Israel but also to the United States and the world at large. Iran's resumption of its nuclear program is a frightening prospect given their apocalyptic thinking, and is surely one reason why President Biden placed the renewal of negotiations with Iran among his chief priorities in the first months of his administration.

However, Iran's thinking is only the extreme form of an issue shared by Islam in general—namely, that Islam has not undergone the psychological transformation that the West has via the Reformation, the Renaissance (in particular, its development of humanism), and the Enlightenment (appropriately also called the Age of Reason). It is still contained in a premodern, fundamentalist worldview in which scripture is taken literally as God's word and the notion of looking at it symbolically or mythically is alien. It did not incorporate the separation of church and state, the emergence of democracy, the huge leaps in modern scientific understanding (such as the theories of evolution and the Big Bang), and the spread of cosmopolitanism.

Of course, the more developed Gulf states like Saudi Arabia, Qatar, and the United Arab Emirates, with their futuristic cities and skyscraper skylines, appear to be technologically ultramodern, but have they advanced psychologically in ways as progressive as their technological development? Wahhabism or Salafism, with its puritanical impulse to return to the mindset and practices of the first three generations of Muslims, still plays a significant role in these states. The conflict between Islam and the West reflects not only a "clash of civilizations," as Lewis and others have described this phenomenon, but specifically a clash of *levels* of civilization. "Level" here refers not to cultural refinement or sophistication but to the degree of tolerance for diversity, pluralism, and change. Struggling movements like the Arab Spring showed a hint of promise, but there can be no doubt that other movements like that of ISIS are still medieval in their basic outlook.

But just as much a truth is that we can all be reduced equally to the same primitive level of the war gods who are alive and well within all of us. As Harold Bloom said, our own "war against terror remains a belated repetition of the wars of Yahweh. Our second invasion of Iraq was the unhappiest of replays, even a parody of the Crusades." Do we need the gruesome photographs and videos of torture and prisoner abuse that our soldiers committed at Abu Ghraib to convince us of this? Some polemicists wishing to one-sidedly profile Islam as hatemongering might be prone to cite various passages in the Qur'an that extol jihad. Others might then refute these with contrary passages that inspire brotherly love and nonviolence. However, this attempt to portray Islam as being in one corner or the other is as convincing as would be the many similar passages in the Hebrew Bible and New Testament. All such scriptural passages only show that Judaism, Christianity, and Islam share the same paradoxical God who has two opposite sides.

Yahweh/the Father/Allah is a living contradiction, generating war as a function of what the gods of old did and still do in our psyches. Whether we are speaking of the Germanic Wotan, Slavic Perun, or Abrahamic Yahweh or Allah, the war gods who inspire our murderous rage reside deep in our collective (and in particular, our racial) unconscious. From the seat of our souls, they swallow our identities and impose upon us their will to power. Because our war-god complexes are part of the structure of our psyches, they won't disappear even if imperialism were altogether eradicated by international condemnation and sanctions. "War belongs to our souls as an archetypal truth of the cosmos," Jungian analyst James Hillman writes, "[and it] shall remain until the gods themselves go away."

Nevertheless, as universal as the instinct for war is, the Islamic Yahweh complex—or Allah complex, if you will—exhibits something over and above it. It has a distinct animus that has gathered its steam from the disillusionment that followed the decline of the Islamic Empire. Thomas Singer explains the sense of inferiority, resentment, and envy that are the hallmarks of what he calls the Muslim cultural complex:

In the case of [Muslim extremists], their radical Islamist dream of creating a new "caliphate" can be interpreted as the geographic projection of a wish to restore a wounded, collective Muslim spirit through the creation of an empire that transcends national boundaries. The traumatized collective spirit of the Muslim world has suffered centuries of humiliation at the hands of a rapidly expanding Western civilization that captured the scientific, technological and materialistic initiative that once belonged to the Muslim world.

Of course, this does not justify terrorism or its evil but merely explains the Muslim world's desire to relieve its traumatically wounded spirit and to protect itself from the further trauma it understandably fears from modernization and globalization (or what political theorist Benjamin Barber calls "McWorld"). Terrorism from this point of view is primarily a defense and only secondarily an offense. Needless to say, it fails to truly relieve the pain of the wound and protect against the tide of history. It will take a different kind of effort, a different kind of struggle or jihad—one that is neither militant nor *only* spiritual—to heal the humiliation of the Muslim world and to give it oars to navigate that tide in an authentically self-determined way.

Asked in an interview to name the essential conflict in the Islamic world today, Itamar Rabinovich, a historian and former Israeli ambassador to the US, answered:

> The basic issue goes back to the late eighteenth century when Europe became more powerful than the Muslim powers and Islam was beginning to be defeated by Western military superiority. The question is, do you want to join the West, or do you think you can borrow techniques from the West but not the spirit of the West? So, can they do what the Chinese and Japanese did, which is to say, they acquire from the West what they wanted, keep their own authenticity and be very successful in the world, or stand straddling the line and remain unhappy? This is the basic debate.

The future of peace in the Middle East and between Islam and the West depends on the outcome of this debate within the Muslim world. This outcome, in turn, depends on whether the Muslim world can break out from its arrested position of straddling the line and remaining unhappy—break out the way Yahweh did in his transformation. Yahweh, too, suffered centuries of humiliation, but then recovered from this wound by reconnecting to his wisdom and by moving forward in a new way. Muslims might not recognize this narrative as such in the Qur'an and the life of Allah, but the challenge is identical: the angry, wounded God inside the Muslim soul must be healed.

IV

GOD BLESS YAHWEH

And I will betroth thee unto Me forever; yea, I will betroth thee unto Me in righteousness, and in justice and in lovingkindness, and in compassion. And I will betroth thee to Me in faithfulness; and Thou shalt know the Lord.

—Yahweh, in Hosea 2:21–22

13

The Calling of Winston Churchill

Centuries ago words were written to be a call and a spur to
the faithful servants of Truth and Justice: "Arm yourselves,
and be ye men of valour, and be in readiness for the conflict;
for it is better for us to perish in battle than to look upon the
outrage of our nation and our altar. As the will of God is in
Heaven, even so let it be."

—Winston Churchill

No treatment of the Abrahamic God's impact upon us would be
complete without a balanced view that includes his positive side.
We should not demonize him, since without a dark side, epistemology
tells us, we wouldn't have a contrast by which to appreciate his positive
side. Our perceptions of God would be undifferentiated and monotone.
This might sound overly rational and not especially comforting for those
of us who have suffered greatly, but nevertheless, such polarity seems to be
an underlying and mysterious principle in most, if not all, of the world's
religions.

Among other concerns in this final part of the book, we will look at
how a positive Yahweh complex, if not the living God himself, can be a
source of inspiration in our lives, beginning with Winston Churchill but
certainly not limited to him. Without inspiration from this complex, it is
questionable if Churchill would have been able to stand up to Hitler, as
Lincoln might not have been able to unite the sundered American nation,
as Martin Luther King, Jr., might not have been able to so courageously
spearhead its civil rights movement, and as Mandela might not have been
able to endure twenty-seven years in prison and then lead his nation to
its first democratic election and government. Due to the limited space of

our inquiry, I choose to present the positive Yahweh complex of only two of these political giants.

Churchill's Relationship with Yahweh

The Yahweh complex, like any primitive or dark complex, can be disastrous, but to not have access to it when you really need it can be equally disastrous, and even catastrophic. The reason for this is simply that we need our aggression to protect us when we are faced with a mortal threat. Of course, aggression doesn't need to exist in the form of a complex; animals clearly act aggressively without being in the grip of some complex. Humans, however, are more complicated, and, as indicated earlier, aggression is often psychically merged with some complex that puts a face upon it, so to speak. That face may be human, or it may be the face of a god.

"The Enemy Within," an episode from the original *Star Trek* series, nicely illustrates the importance of aggression. Due to a malfunction in the transporter, Captain Kirk is split into two identical Captain Kirks, except one is uncontrollably aggressive and the other is compassionate but altogether without aggression. The aggressive Kirk needs the compassionate Kirk to be civilized, for without him he wildly roams the ship and in one instance sexually assaults a female crew member. Conversely, the compassionate Kirk needs the aggressive Kirk to help him make tough decisions. Without the ability to be appropriately aggressive, he is weakened to the point of being crippled. In the end, the transporter is repaired, the two Kirks go through it arm in arm, and the original Captain Kirk returns with his dark side reintegrated—this being the moral of the story: we need to healthily integrate within ourselves our dark and bright sides.

"Integration" here does not mean that the dark side is conquered once and for all and is merged into our personality as if it were something like our creative or spiritual side. Rather, it means that we consciously hold it within ourselves as an "inner other," relating to it as the powerful force it is so that we can choose to *use* it if necessary, rather than be used *by* it.

No figure in recent history better exemplifies the distinct vitality and healthy integration of the Yahweh complex than Sir Winston Churchill. Europe and possibly the entire world might today be under the rule of the Third Reich were it not for this great leader's self-acknowledged love of war. He was a natural-born warrior. As a young war correspondent, he saw military action in Cuba, India, the Sudan, and the Second Boer War in South Africa. Held largely responsible for the ill-fated Battle of Gallipoli in World War I (the historical facts show him here in a better light), he resigned as first lord of the admiralty and became a military commander on the Western Front. (This was his failed mission, but unlike Nixon, he was able to overcome it.) All this helped prepare him for his role in World War II. He knew that the only way to fight brute strength was with even greater strength, and as a true warrior, he marshalled his own moral strength to champion his cause.

Churchill's personal development loudly echoed the central theme of Yahweh's development: the young boy Winston was emotionally abandoned. His parents sent him to a boarding school he detested. His pleading letters to them oozed of loneliness, homesickness, and a desire for their love but were rarely answered. He was scorned by an extremely critical, Yahwistic father whom he repeatedly tried to please without success. On one occasion, at age thirteen, he was playing with toy soldiers when his father asked if he'd like to join the army. He said yes, thinking that his father had discerned his qualities of military genius. Later he learned that his father thought he was not intelligent enough to become a lawyer and that the army would be a more suitable choice. In the end, of course, this proved to be a very wise choice given those genius qualities.

Many biographers suspect that Churchill's depression in later life— the "black dog," as he called it—was rooted in this childhood experience. But is it possible that his success was also rooted in it? It is likely that he cultivated his emerging warrior instincts, at least in part, as a way to cope with his rejection and pain, as a way to empower himself. In

Yahweh's instance, his warrior inclinations were developed in order to ensure his chosen people's victory so that they and their progeny would have a homeland, but the underlying factor motivating this may have influenced Churchill too: the drive to win his people's love. Churchill's ambition to save them was probably godlike in more ways than one. In any case, his depression did not seem to be the clinical, biochemically determined kind. Rather, he was overtaken by the spirit of melancholy. He was similar to Yahweh in more ways than one.

Before he became prime minister in 1940, Churchill found himself standing on the sidelines—out of office, advocating unpopular positions, and politically isolated. Some of his Yahwistic judgments were on the wrong side of history. For example, he thought that the Indian independence movement should be crushed and that Gandhi, who was frequently conducting publicized hunger strikes, should be allowed to starve himself to death.

However, his foresight about what was coming in Europe was almost supernatural. He fiercely criticized Chamberlain when the prime minister secured a peace treaty with Hitler; Churchill remained convinced that this would only further embolden Hitler and that Britain needed to prepare for war. Once the war began and Hitler began to bomb civilians in London, Churchill demonstrated Yahwistic resolve—an eye for an eye, a tooth for a tooth—by bombing Berlin. He knew that if this didn't shake Hitler's confidence, it would at least silence those voices in England still advocating appeasement.

In a manner of speaking, we could say that when Churchill committed England to fight Germany till the very end, win or lose, Yahweh went to war against Wotan in a life-or-death struggle to determine which god would prevail. As mentioned in the prologue, Wotan was the Teutonic tribal god whom Jung believed had, in the form of a collective complex, possessed the German people in both world wars. We may here add Jung's description of him as the "god of storm and frenzy, the unleasher of passions and the lust of battle; moreover he is a superlative magician and artist in illusion who is versed in all secrets of an occult nature." Jung could just as easily have been speaking about Hitler. The storm troopers, too, were very much an incarnation of Wotan, who roamed the earth as a restless wanderer, creating strife and unrest everywhere he went. His spirit of conquest and turbulence, Jung hypothesized, eventually seized the entire German nation.

Historians, of course, do not recount this global drama in this language, but there can be no doubt that both Churchill and Hitler saw it in divine or spiritual terms. Churchill often appealed to God's help in his speeches and felt he was personally guided by his hand. He was an impassioned, stalwart believer in what he called "Christian civilization" and "Christian ethics." For him, both of these explicitly included their Jewish foundation and thus had the capacity to elevate the human condition. A philo-Semite, he thought Moses was "one of the greatest of human beings . . . [because he initiated] the most decisive leap forward ever discernable in the human story." Churchill believed, as did the authors of all the Abrahamic scriptures, that God worked through the acts of humans, shaping history through their efforts and accomplishments. As a Christian humanist, he didn't believe in the divinity of Jesus and rarely went to church. Instead, he espoused Jesus's Sermon on the Mount as "the last word in ethics," and consequently held Jesus in as equally a high regard as Moses.

When he met with Roosevelt in 1941 to establish the Atlantic Charter and the two attended a church service for which they were asked to select the hymns, Churchill chose "Onward, Christian Soldiers" (which, as also discussed earlier, was a source of inspiration as Yahwistically militant as any). Later explaining his choice in a radio broadcast, he said:

> We sang "Onward, Christian Soldiers" indeed, and I felt that this was no vain presumption, but that we had the right to feel that we were serving a cause for the sake of which a trumpet has sounded from on high. When I looked upon that densely packed congregation of fighting men of the same language, *of the same faith, of the same fundamental laws, of the same ideals* . . . it swept across

me that here was the only hope, but also the sure hope, of saving
the world from measureless degradation [italics my own].

Clearly, Churchill saw himself and the Allies as serving a purpose that
was ideologically Abrahamic and messianic. In one of his books, he famously
wrote, "I felt as if I were walking with destiny, and that all my past life had
been but a preparation for this hour and for this trial." When he was sixteen
in 1891, a schoolmate recorded his premonitory words: "This country will
be subjected somehow, to a tremendous invasion, by what means I do not
know, but I tell you I shall be in command of the defenses of London, and I
shall save London and England from disaster." He was, as his great-grandson
Jonathan Sandys and journalist Wallace Henley described him in their book
God and Churchill, a "God-haunted man."

But Hitler believed that he too was divinely inspired: "I go the way
that Providence dictates for me with all the assurance of a sleepwalker," he
said in a 1936 speech. It was Providence that he believed had saved him
from the assassination attempt of 1944 and that in general had "willed"
his rise to power and determined his purpose in history as he conceived it.

One might be inclined to say that only one of the two, only Churchill
or Hitler, could have been right about whose side God was on. Yet they
were both right; merely, they were inspired by different gods. Of course,
two sides of a conflict can easily claim that the same god endorses their
cause. In the American Civil War, for example, the North and South both
believed they had God on their side, an irony Lincoln noted in his second
inaugural address. As for Wotan, his defeat by Yahweh in World War II
could naturally have been only temporary, even if on a global scale it was,
we hope, final: Wotanism was to rise again in neo-Nazi movements in
Germany, America, and elsewhere. Gods don't just die; they reincarnate
in our souls whenever our hunger to dominate or rule over others pulls
them in from the collective unconscious.

In the end we must conclude that the Yahweh complex not only is a
culprit of atrocities but also fulfills a historical need. Churchill *needed* his
Yahweh complex, with its drive for war *and* a high civilization, just like

we *needed* Churchill. As the author of Ecclesiastes wrote, "For everything there is a season, and a time for every purpose under heaven." The Yahweh complex is no exception.

14

The Solomonic Wisdom of Abraham Lincoln

But I will ask you—and this shall be my last word—to listen
to a few sentences in which Mr. Lincoln admits us into the
most secret recesses of his soul. It is a meditation written in
September 1862. Perplexed and afflicted beyond the power of
human help, by the disasters of war, the wrangling of parties,
and the inexorable and constraining logic of his own mind,
he shut out the world one day, and tried to put into form
his double sense of responsibility to human duty and Divine
Power; and this was the result. It shows—as has been said in
another place—the awful sincerity of a perfectly honest soul,
trying to bring itself into closer communion with its Maker.

—*John Hay, Lincoln's secretary*

Governance in antebellum America was not for those lacking
imagination, as President James Buchanan demonstrated. Failing
to appreciate the gravity of the question of whether slavery should be
permitted in the territories, he said it was "a matter of but little practical
importance." This shortsightedness was compounded by a stodgy Yahwistic
legalism. "I acknowledge no master but the law," he said. By this he meant
that he deferred to the Supreme Court's *Dred Scott* decision that Congress
did not have the constitutional power to prohibit ownership of slaves
in the territories. It also meant that he believed that states did not have
the legal right to secede but neither could the federal government legally
prevent them from doing so. In effect, Buchanan's hands were tied by his
own beliefs.

It is against the backdrop of Buchanan's rudderless leadership that
Abraham Lincoln's entry onto the stage of national politics must be

viewed. When Lincoln first took over, his pragmatism was his leading edge. He admitted that if he could pursue a course that would save the Union without war, he would do so, even if this meant that slavery would not be abolished. As this became impractical, he developed a course of action that integrated, perhaps not smoothly but nevertheless effectively, his pragmatism with an idealism that many have described as inspired.

His vision for America hinged upon its greatness not only as an industrial or military power but also as a nation of high ethical standards— meaning here, in the famous words of his Gettysburg Address, a nation "conceived in liberty and dedicated to the proposition that all men are created equal." As a moral visionary, he knew that America could be no greater than the individuals who inhabit it. He saw that slavery was a cruel abomination and if continued would seriously undermine the American experiment, or what he called the "last best hope of earth."

Like the Founding Fathers, Lincoln concluded that democratic government cannot embrace all points of view, especially those intolerant to democracy itself. This conviction enabled him to insist that the principles of freedom and equality are nonnegotiable, that they do not depend on the people's choice or their vote but are the precondition of their having the right to choose and vote in the first place. This principled way of thinking gave him the authority to take a stand against the South's excesses and abuse of freedom, even if it required war.

What thus kept the Union together was Lincoln's reliance on a higher law than the literal law of the Constitution, or at least the Supreme Court's interpretation of the Constitution at that time (the *Dred Scott* decision was later superseded by the Fourteenth Amendment to the Constitution, which declared people of African descent as citizens and entitled to equal protection under the law). Furthermore, Lincoln decided that he could, in accord with the war powers of the president, seize slaves as enemy property, knowing full well that the government would not then allow them to be re-enslaved. (He was here influenced by the popular writings of War Department solicitor William Whiting.)

All this points to Lincoln's Solomonic wisdom. Solomon, as we know, is legendary for his wisdom and shrewdness. Confronted with two prostitutes claiming to be the mother of the same baby, he ordered that a sword be brought so that it could be cut in two and that one-half be given to one woman and the other half to the other woman. When one of the women pleaded that he give the other woman the infant, while that woman insisted that it should die so that neither of them had it, Solomon gave it to the first woman, determining that she was its real mother.

Yet the Bible is clear about the source of this wisdom on Solomon's part: "And all Israel heard of the judgment which the king had rendered; and they stood in awe of the king, because they perceived that the wisdom of God was in him, to render justice." With its feminine capacity to relate to others in a way that "gets" who they are in their innermost being, Solomonic wisdom is the wisdom of Yahweh. Solomon was the alleged author of Proverbs, the book in which Yahweh reconnected to his wisdom.

What also distinguishes this kind of wisdom is the knowledge of righteousness and justice and the ability to exercise these in the world. These are the two things Yahweh most required from the Israelites after the avoidance of idolatry. In a way, this wisdom is the knowledge of good and evil that Adam and Eve blundered into before they were prepared to deal with it. Solomon could differentiate the fine-tunings of evil minds like that of the envious woman trying to steal a child, and he could hold the opposites together, using good to combat evil. Edward Edinger comments that this capacity to hold the tension between opposites, a capacity Yahweh also develops in the latter part of the Hebrew Bible, made Lincoln one of history's greatest figures. It also made possible one of the outstanding differences between America and ancient Israel: both nations were founded on spiritual visions, but Lincoln was able to hold his nation together—again, with a feminine capacity to keep things related—whereas Israel splintered in two. Like Solomon, Lincoln saved the baby.

Lincoln's life as a whole is a lesson in holding together opposites. By contrast to Churchill, he was not a highly experienced soldier. Although he had been the captain of an Illinois militia unit in the Black Hawk War, he saw no action (he later said he had "a good many bloody struggles with the mosquitoes"). Yet as president, he became a sophisticated military strategist, and when incompetent generals wouldn't step up to the plate, he did so by firing and replacing them. He also showed good judgment in appointing Ulysses Grant general-in-chief and warding off critics demanding Grant's removal after the Union army, though victorious, suffered more casualties than the Confederates in the Battle of Shiloh. Lincoln said, "I can't spare this man—he fights."

On the other hand, similar to Churchill, he suffered from consuming bouts of melancholy. A characteristic of his Yahweh complex as much as his wisdom was, his melancholy at times "dripped from him," his law partner and biographer William Herndon said. His young son Willie died early in his presidency, and like Coolidge after losing his son, Lincoln fell into a terrible grief. However, unlike Coolidge, he avoided bitterness and maintained a good sense of humor.

The nation's pain became his own as he conducted a war while openly agonizing about its morality and impact. He even called for national days of repentance, which, as historian Garry Wills points out, was extraordinary in view of the fact that this risked demoralizing his side and undermining its will to press on for victory. Yet Lincoln had the gift to inspire while demanding a fierce moral scrutiny that was not without its ambivalence. Although he went to war against the South and disagreed with its position on slavery, he always understood its reasoning. With his policy of malice toward none and charity for all, he compassionately sought to alleviate tensions and lessen differences between the two sides immediately following the war. He encouraged them to forgive each other. Journalist David Von Drehl pulls together the opposites of Lincoln's character:

> Despite interviewing dozens of Lincoln's associates in the months after his death, J. G. Holland, an early biographer, found himself stumped. "There are not two who agree in their estimate of him," he wrote. One would say "he was a very ambitious man"; another would assert "that he was without a particle of ambition." People said that "he was one of the saddest men that ever lived, and that he

was one of the jolliest men that ever lived . . . that he was a man of indomitable will, and that he was a man almost without a will; that he was a tyrant, and that he was the softest-hearted, most brotherly man that ever lived." The real Lincoln, Holland concluded, was the sum of his contradictions.

Lincoln's Solomonic ability to navigate life's dualities is reminiscent of Lao Tzu's teachings about how to live in the Tao—how to manage the eternal dance between the opposites, between yin and yang (or, if you will, their analogs of good and evil, darkness and light, in the Abrahamic traditions). But Lincoln's suffering and virtue were most like Job's. He was a tormented man who in the face of overwhelming obstacles held on to his integrity and convictions. Although he could have succumbed to any of these obstacles, he remained optimistic and resilient.

As author Bruce Feiler has shown, another biblical figure whom Lincoln was akin to was Moses. Both were liberators of slaves. Elizabeth Keckly, Mrs. Lincoln's African American seamstress, called Lincoln "the Moses of my people." He resembled Moses not only in his historical role but in his leadership style as well, a style emanating what sociologist Max Weber described as charismatic authority. Such authority, Weber writes, rests on the "exceptional sanctity, heroism or exemplary character" of the leader and on his followers' belief that he is endowed with supernatural, superhuman, or special powers or qualities of a divine origin. If Lincoln wasn't esteemed in this way before his assassination, he certainly was soon after.

The way Lincoln exercised his power was also in the mold of Moses. Asserting his will for Congress to pass the Thirteenth Amendment to outlaw slavery, he boldly proclaimed, "I am the president of the United States of America, clothed with immense power." He *wore* his Yahweh complex, rather than the other way around. And he wore it the way Moses wore the miracle-inducing rod that God gave him. Moses's power was Yahweh's power channeled through him. There can be little doubt that Lincoln, too, conceived that he was doing God's work on earth, following his will.

Just after the Battle of Antietam, he announced to his cabinet that he had made "a solemn vow before God" that if the Confederates were driven out of Maryland, he would "crown the result by the declaration of freedom to the slaves." His secretary of the Navy described this vow as Lincoln's covenant with God. In addition, both Moses and Lincoln suffered a tragic end, the first seeing the Promised Land only in the distance, and the second barely setting foot on it before being struck down by an assassin. The lives and deaths of both were a paradigmatic prequel to the life and death of Martin Luther King, Jr., a Baptist minister also inspired by a positive Yahweh complex.

As historian Michael Burlingame suggests, Lincoln's paternal image in the eyes of both the people of his time and ours is due to his being identified with the wise-old-man archetype, a universal motif in religion and literature. But he was also a savior figure. Both as "Father Abraham" and savior of the nation, he incarnated the spirit of Yahweh in his protective and redeeming aspects. His was a most powerful and positive Yahweh complex.

However, it is important to remember that having a positive Yahweh complex doesn't mean that you're immune to its dark side. In fact, as Goethe said, "The more the light, the deeper the shadow." Because you are more conscious, you see your darkness more clearly. We must also remember Captain Kirk's discovery, that we need to live with both sides of our condition. A positive Yahweh complex implies that you have its dark side just like others do but have made up your mind to not serve it blindly. If people are about as happy as they make up their minds to be, as Lincoln reportedly said, then they're also as Yahweh-possessed as they make up their minds to be.

Yahwism is not only an unconscious disposition; it can also be a conscious choice, for better or worse. Sometimes we even have to use the positive side of our Yahweh complex—a better angel of our nature, as Lincoln would say—to restrain the lesser and meaner side. Or to take it a step further, we might, if we're conscious and crafty enough, use the dark side to serve the bright one. As onetime governor of New York Mario Cuomo writes, "[Lincoln] could be a devious and supple politician with a Machiavellian cunning. . . . [He] was on occasion a wily and grittily pragmatic politician in the conduct of his presidential duties—even when dealing with constitutional principles. Like FDR he often claimed the end justified the means."

But it was not only FDR whom he was like. In sagaciously employing diabolical means to get good results, he was also, again, like Solomon. After all, the Civil War, one of the first to engage in industrialized warfare, was as diabolical as any, even if it was necessary and just. Lincoln's positive Yahweh complex would never have triumphed had he not so adroitly marshalled the destructive energies of Yahweh, the Lord of War.

15

Bob Dylan's Apocalyptic Sensibility

(A chapter written during the COVID-19 pandemic)

> If we understand the image of the "Apocalypse"—when we see it in its manifestation, both inner and outer—we do not have to be overcome by it or possessed by it. It is awesome, to be sure, but it is humanized by being understood. In my opinion, as our world sinks more and more into possession by this [psychic force], nothing is more important than the existence of a certain number of individuals who understand what is going on.
>
> —*Edward F. Edinger*

Bob Dylan has his finger on the pulse of the biblical God perhaps more than any other figure in popular culture. Rightly or wrongly, he has been hailed as a prophet, decrying the injustices we inflict on each other and goading us to wake up—indeed, in much the same spirit as the biblical prophets did. Even in his younger days, his sober, stoic view of the human condition was informed by the ethos of the Bible.

Like Yahweh himself, he doesn't have a lot of faith in the world, nor is he soft spoken about its evils. His songs can be seen as testaments to Yahweh's suffering heart as he struggled to come to terms with his fallen creation. Dylan's public persona, if not his songs and deeper personality, similarly seems melancholic. No doubt, he has also beheld Yahweh's radiance, and there is much beauty and joy in his lyrics and music, especially in his love songs. Thus did his mentor and friend, the poet Allen Ginsberg, say when asked if Dylan had sold out his fans by adding electric music to his folk repertoire: "Dylan has sold out to God. That

is to say, his command was to spread his beauty as widely as possible."
(Curiously, "*his* beauty" can refer to *either* God *or* Dylan's sense of beauty,
an ambiguity that is thought provoking even if unintended. Truly, where
does talent like Dylan's come from?)

This divine "command" or calling seems to have been incorporated
into Dylan's inner being at a young age, giving him a seriousness of
purpose that made him stand out among rock 'n' roll stars. His solemn
attitude to things divine emanates from his lyrics, as in his simple yet
resonant "Father of Night," a song that he composed at age twenty-nine
and that is supposedly his interpretation of the "Amidah," the central
prayer of Judaism. Bob Johnston said the following about *Highway 61
Revisited*, the album he produced for Dylan when the latter was twenty-
four: "I believe in giving credit where credit's due. I don't think Dylan had
a lot to do with it. I think God, instead of touchin' him on the shoulder,
he kicked him in the ass. Really. And that's where all that came from. He
can't help what he's doin'. I mean, he's got the Holy Spirit about him. You
can look at him and tell that."

As Dylan aged, Yahweh's dark vision of the world increasingly
became his own. Rooted in the view that human nature is profoundly
and permanently flawed (as least in its earthly state), Dylan's apocalyptic
sensibility shows that he has spent time sharpening his pencil under
Yahweh's tutelage. His mood is often ominous, and he warns us of
impending darkness, as in "Not Dark Yet." His eschatology or conception
of "end things" such as death or the end of the world, as in "Death Is
Not the End" or "Things Have Changed," is lifted straight from the New
Testament with its belief that there is an afterlife and that the world will
end violently. The Apocalypse is one of Dylan's most enduring themes,
one to which he returns again and again. As he himself indicates in "Señor
(Tales of Yankee Power)," a song recorded just prior to his Christian
conversion experience, he traveled the road to Armageddon well before
that experience occurred.

Different Shades of the Apocalypse

A few words about the various viewpoints an apocalyptic sensibility can draw upon: The Apocalypse is a complex matter seen discordantly in Judaism and Christianity (Islam more or less subscribes to the Christian view). Its significance in the New Testament is unquestionable; it will be second only to the Incarnation as a rare demonstration of an active God inserting himself into human affairs as he did more regularly in the earlier times of the Hebrew Bible.

Although there appear cloaked references to things specific to that time, such as the Roman Empire, the Apocalypse is for the most part an eschatological concern with the ultimate goal of history: the creation of a "new Jerusalem," a new world order ushered in by Jesus on behalf of his father. The Book of Revelation forecasts a global drama that will unfold over a thousand years and that will involve a fiery war against the devil and his servant, the Antichrist or false messiah. This archetypal struggle between good and evil will be driven forward by a host of characters, including seven angels who will be instructed to "go and pour out on the earth the seven bowls of the wrath of God," each bowl containing a plague.

The Day of Judgment folds into the Apocalypse as its centerpiece. Interestingly, there are two judgment days, or rather, two stages of judgment. Catholic theologians distinguish between the "particular judgment" each of us will undergo as individuals when we die and the "general judgment" or "Last Judgment" we will all witness and participate in together on the occasion of the Second Coming of Christ as forecast in the Book of Revelation. The Apocalypse as understood here is connected with the Second Coming of Jesus.

Contrary to this understanding, Judaism envisions the Apocalypse as the first and only coming of the Messiah (i.e., it is not connected with Jesus, who at best is considered a great rabbi or teacher but not the Messiah). Nor will the Apocalypse necessarily be a destructive, cataclysmic event. Judaism—or at least rabbinic Judaism—sees the end time more benignly. Based on certain passages in the Hebrew Bible, Maimonides pictured it as a nonviolent development leading to world harmony.

Nevertheless, we find in the Hebrew Bible the same theme of judgment that is so prevalent in the New Testament's Apocalypse. The Hebrew Bible tells us: "And many of those who sleep in the dust of the earth shall awake, some to everlasting life, and some to shame and everlasting contempt." (The reason awakening happens on the Day of Judgment at the end time is because the dead were believed to be asleep in a shadowy netherworld known as Sheol, the Israelite equivalent to the Greek idea of Hades. Ideas of the afterlife were, like our ideas of God himself, still evolving.) However, on the whole, this awakening will be most joyful, as in the Christian doctrine of the resurrection of the dead. Yet except for fundamentalists like ultra-Orthodox Jews or the Hasidim, the end of the world is not nearly as central a theme to Judaism as it is to Christianity.

An additional approach to the Apocalypse motif, inclined also toward the individual, treats the end of the world *as we individually know it*—as an inner change that involves a death and rebirth in our lives here and now. This symbolic approach has been employed by writers and artists going back to at least the Renaissance (Boccaccio's *Decameron*, written and set during the Black Death, being but one popular example that is now a classic). The Apocalypse motif in this approach is often used to depict a *personal, inner* death as well as a social or global one, and sometimes there is no reference at all to any social or global event, the inner world of the individual taking precedence. Certainly, such a death can be as hellish as a physical one or anything in the Book of Revelation. A personal apocalypse leads (hopefully) to a psychological and spiritual rebirth—a new understanding of oneself or a renewal in one's life. Writers and artists thus combine apocalyptic material from scripture or the world around them with some Yahwistic experience of upheaval and annihilation in their own souls.

Dylan, though Jewish, leans toward the Christian viewpoint *and* this literary, artistic one, and sometimes he blends the two together. Perhaps his pessimism about humanity and its prospects is influenced, at least in part, by the Christian viewpoint. (In "Not Dark Yet" he confesses that his faith in humankind has disappeared.) Needless to say, the other part would surely be the daily news.

Dylan's Contact with Things Ultimate

Capturing the feverish, apocalyptic mood in both the culture and his personal world, Dylan's two albums in 1965, *Bringing It All Back Home* and *Highway 61 Revisited,* provide good illustrations of apocalyptic imagery in his work. Do they synchronistically and eerily forecast, a year in advance, Dylan's motorcycle accident? (Regardless of how serious it was, and reports about this varied, it echoes Edinger's warning that we must be careful with what we choose to write or talk about, because the unconscious will force us to live it.) But as insinuated in "It's All Over Now, Baby Blue," the last song on the first of these albums, renewal was already implicit: Dylan seems to be saying, "Set out in a new direction, begin your life over"—and he himself did exactly this, as observable with his next few albums.

John Wesley Harding and the later *New Morning,* both rich with apocalyptic allusions (including the latter's title), suggest that Dylan arrived at a relaxed and rejuvenated state similar to Yahweh's just before the Hebrew Bible's climax. He has mellowed and become more grounded and deep, more wise. Edinger informs us that the Apocalypse motif is essentially about the coming or emergence of our higher self. This may mean different things at different times in Abrahamic history and with the differing Abrahamic traditions, but it usually involves a transition to a more evolved level of thinking and awareness. The more we can experience this catharsis consciously within ourselves, the less it will have to be acted out unconsciously through some catastrophe in the world around us. What we don't let in the front door breaks in violently through the back door, and this can be the case with an entire civilization and not only an individual in a motorcycle accident.

One can conceive of Yahweh's different states of mind and heart as parallel if not identical to Dylan's own states. Dylan has become like the god he beholds. Yahweh persistently comes through in his music and lyrics: Dylan can be troubled, grim, even freakish (as in "Ballad of a Thin Man" and "Desolation Row"); melancholically longing for something lost or unknown (as in his cantorial singing in "One More Cup of Coffee"); lonely, fiery, tormented, despaired, and self-divided (all of these palpable in "Where Are You Tonight? (Journey Through Dark Heat)"); stormy (as in "When the Night Comes Falling From the Sky"); disillusioned by the emptiness and bleakness of everything (as in "Tryin' to Get to Heaven" and "Ain't Talkin'"); and last but not least, mellow and wise (as in "Watching the River Flow," "I Shall Be Released," "Trust Yourself," and "Every Grain of Sand"). Dylan himself believes that he has been transfigured in a biblical sense. Transfiguration involves a metamorphosis of one's inner condition that can be likened to Jesus's transformation on Mount Tabor where he was seen radiating bright light and standing beside Moses and the prophet Elijah. Dylan does not allude to witnessing such physical occurrences, but he does emphasize a clear break between his former identity and a new, transpersonal sense of self.

On the other hand, Dylan did have a visceral response to what he described as a visionary experience of Jesus one night in a hotel room. He perceived Jesus's numinous presence and intuitively knew it was him. "I truly had a born-again experience, if you want to call it that," Dylan said. This marked the beginning of his Christian period. His concerts took on an evangelical tone. At one of them he exhorted his audience: "Are you ready for the judgment? Are you ready for the terrible swift sword? Are you ready for Armageddon? Are you ready for the day of the Lord?"

Infused with the wrath of God, his song lyrics have this quality as well (as in "Precious Angel," in which he ponders if his friends can conceive of the darkness that will descend upon them and drive them to beg God in vain to end their lives). Or perhaps such lyrics can be viewed as having the zeal of the Jewish prophetic tradition. But either way, Christian or Jewish, they are strongly apocalyptic. He was singing about his awakening to the living force of the divine—in the personage of Jesus—and, very much in the spirit of the prophets, he was singing about his alarm at our impoverished spiritual condition.

His first of three evangelical albums during this period is *Slow Train Coming*, whose title is an apt metaphor for a coming Apocalypse. Here is an instance in which the Apocalypse theme of the New Testament merged with Dylan's personal, inner apocalypse: the album was recorded on the heels of his divorce, a painful time in his life by all accounts. If the album's content is about Jesus, its tone is distinctly Yahweh's—passionate and full of fire and brimstone in the style of the Jewish prophets. As for the title song, "Slow Train," its punchy mix of gospel and rock with female backup singers and a dynamic horn arrangement, together with its musical phrasing, rhyme, and moral condemnation of social evils, is so perfect and powerful that, as songwriter Alvin Muckley put it, even God got off his throne when he heard it.

Often an apocalyptic sensibility is closely allied with a sensibility about evil. Biblically speaking, the evil in human nature is why an Apocalypse is needed. But this is not only a biblical principle; it is also a psychological one. Our individual souls or psyches are the battlefield of Armageddon upon which we are to confront the evil impulses within each of us (e.g., *schadenfreude* or pleasure in another's suffering, limitless greed, racism and other forms of hatred, envy to the point of spoiling another's happiness or success, etc.).

Dylan is intimate with this principle of combating the evil within ourselves. "Each man struggles within himself," he told an interviewer about his aforementioned song "Where Are You Tonight? (Journey Through Dark Heat)." "That is where the fight is. . . . If you can deal with the enemy within, then no enemy without can stand a chance." In the narrative of the song, he fights with his inner enemy until both of them are exhausted and collapse by the road, much like Jacob wrestling with the angel till dawn. Jung similarly asserts that to realize our fullness or wholeness, we *must* confront our dark side: "The coming of the Antichrist is not just a prophetic prediction—it is an inexorable psychological law." Evil will surface wherever and whenever it can. Dylan's is a positive Yahweh complex precisely because it has empowered him to confront evil in his own soul and in the collective soul of humanity, and he does so in an artistic way that inspires us to do the same.

Finally, it should be acknowledged that almost every major rock musician or band has had at least one apocalyptic number. Of course, the line between an apocalyptic song and one that voices some other kind of darkness is occasionally blurred, but always, the apocalyptic one supports us when we ourselves are in an apocalyptic mood, when we are struggling with something in us or around us that is dying and we are unsure about what, if anything, will follow. Apocalyptic music and lyrics are, perhaps above all else, *emotionally* apocalyptic. They confirm and reinforce one's feeling that their world is ending, whether that feeling is fear, dread, anxiety, hopelessness, sadness, despair, or even resignation. For a partial list of apocalyptic songs in rock 'n' roll, including the abundance of them in Dylan's body of work, see appendix II.

16

How to Live with Our Yahweh Complex

The possession of complexes does not in itself signify neurosis, for complexes are the normal foci of psychic happenings, and the fact that they are painful is no proof of pathological disturbance. Suffering is not an illness; it is the normal counterpole to happiness. A complex becomes pathological only when we think we have not got it.

—C. G. Jung

"*How to Dismantle an Atomic Bomb* is an odd title for an album," Bono said at the 2006 Grammys at which U2 won the Album of the Year Award. "Actually I was talking about my father, Bob," he continued. "He was the atomic bomb in question." Elsewhere Bono described his father as "an unwanted figure of authority—a sergeant major." Even his last words were angry ones. Bono said, "[When he died] his demise set me off on a journey, a rampage, a desperate hunt to find out who I was, and that resulted in a lot of these songs."

Was Bono's desperate journey inward his way of coming to terms with a Yahwistic father and the latter's impact on him? Was creating the album, with its themes of death, love, war, faith, and family, his form of therapy? It is fitting that the album concludes with the bold, uplifting "Yahweh," sung like a prayer to the biblical God's positive side while hinting at his paradoxical nature.

What is noteworthy about Bono's account is that he had to work through the effects of his *father's* Yahweh complex on *him*, Bono. The father's sins were visited upon the son. Not only the complex but its effects are multigenerational. That's why it's morally imperative that we wrestle with this complex: it affects the people we live and work with, the people who depend upon us and whom we love. And of course, it's imperative for our own development. What good would it do if after reading about the Yahweh complex in all the pages of this book, there were no practical ways to deal with it?

This final chapter offers some ways to cope with this insufferable and often diabolical part of ourselves. It is one of two "how to" components of the book, the other being the first chapter. It consists of a series of reflections—not all my own—held loosely together, with each a stepping stone for further exploration.

Psychotherapy

> The hardest thing is facing yourself.
>
> —*John Lennon*

In my daily work as a psychotherapist, it breaks my heart to see the misery that individuals, couples, and families suffer as a result of the toxicity poured into the vessels of their relationships. When the Yahweh complex in particular leaps into the relationships between people who supposedly love each other, their situation can become very tormented and ugly, not to mention complicated. The use of authority or power in the name of love sets up a tyrannical dynamic for those who are at the mercy of the one or ones with the complex. They have to find a way to emotionally survive, and sometimes they cannot. Sometimes they develop a habitual defense that is equally Yahwistic in its anger or aggression, and at other times they react in a passive-aggressive, depressed, or traumatized way. The original wound multiplies as it reduplicates its defensive pathology among family members. Usually by the time such patients come to the therapist's office, their situation has become intolerable, which is actually a good thing as this can be the beginning of change.

As one form of psychotherapy, Jungian analysis helps us to explore the nature of our complexes as they surface in our behaviors, relationships, and dreams. The value of understanding what complex is distinctly at play is that this expands our consciousness and capacity to confront and take a stand against it (not unlike the way Job took a stand against Yahweh). In indigenous cultures like the Native Americans', the shamans often believe that knowing the name of the demon that possesses us and calling it by that name will not make it go away but will give us a certain power to deal with it. Similarly, the understanding that our suffering comes from a complex (which is one way to think about what shamans mean by "demon") is *already a form of disidentification and separation from it.* We begin to see this "inner other"—rather than ourselves or other people—as the source of the problem.

Such objectivity empowers us to face the complex. Then, a further understanding of the *psychology* of this complex, i.e., what makes it tick, helps us to recognize the situations that trigger it. This in turn helps us to develop skills specifically tailored to those situations. We learn to dialogue and wrestle with the complex, which is a huge asset, since we can never altogether get rid of it.

The sad truth about archetypal complexes is that they're like the Eagles' Hotel California: we can check out whenever we want, but we can't leave. They don't go away. They are too deeply ingrained in the structure of the psyche to be eliminated once and for all. We can deny their existence, but that won't free us from their effects. The Yahweh complex in particular is interwoven with our instincts of aggression or what neuroscientists call the "lizard brain" or limbic system of the brain. This renders it into an immensely powerful force. As we have seen, Western and Islamic civilization itself has too often been altogether swallowed by it.

The most we should realistically hope to change is *the way we relate* to our complexes. All that is really needed here in order to lead a fulfilling life is a conscious and self-possessed relationship to our demons, as opposed to being unconsciously possessed by them. If we don't *have* the complex, whichever one it is, it will have *us*.

Central to this process is an analysis of our ego. This complements our objective understanding of the Yahweh complex with a subjective appreciation of how we as individuals fall into its grip. Although the Yahweh complex is archetypal and thus experienced with more or less the same traits by everybody, it is constellated by circumstances unique to each of us. The factors that triggered it for my father, for example, were different than the ones that trigger it for me or that may trigger it for you.

It is probably true that some of us have a greater predisposition toward having certain archetypal complexes than do others, just like some of us have an innate talent for playing a particular musical instrument. Nevertheless, understanding the unique story of our ego development—what in mythology is known as the hero's journey—helps us to accept ourselves and our dark proclivities in a contextual way. We come to appreciate how we became who we are and how we learned to function the way we do. In this, we see how parental, familial, or peer factors pressured and perhaps traumatized us with some experience similar to Yahweh's, thus constellating the Yahweh complex. We will never be fully prepared and able to manage its eruption without understanding our own personal history. Again, it is *not our fault* that we have a miserable Yahweh complex. We are responsible only for how we respond to it; our responsibility is to wholeheartedly apply our response-ability.

Analysis of the ego is also crucial in order for us to assimilate the painful feelings and primitive affects that the Yahweh complex evokes. As we have discussed, the Yahweh complex is connected to a wide range of emotions, anger and rage probably the primary ones. We learn to recognize what the Yahweh complex feels like within ourselves when it goes off (indeed, sometimes like a bomb).

Similar to knowing the name of the complex, knowing the name of what we're feeling can give us some power as we come face-to-face with it. In the moment that the Yahweh complex erupts, we tend to get gripped and swept away by our emotions. Were we able to deal with them more consciously, we might not get so gripped and swept away. By naming them, we become more conscious of them. If, for example, we suddenly feel an urge to hypercriticize our spouse or child or employee, and we can identify and name this urge, it right away gives us a leg up. Confucius called this principle "rectification of names," and although he conceived of it in terms of identifying people's social roles, it can be easily applied to the roles our emotions play. This can give us a choice in how we deal with them.

Anger is most tricky because it is not only an emotion but a raw affect. The angrier we become, the more difficult it is to relate to the other person as a human being. Anger, especially when it becomes rage, obliterates relatedness. It is true that we also connect to others through anger, but the connection has an impersonal quality. Rage in particular is like a hurricane, tornado, or other primal force of nature. It overwhelms us and makes us its instrument. Because of its intensity, anger is experienced more in the body than most other emotions are, though there can be no doubt that emotions like shame or sadness are experienced bodily, too.

Anger tends to come after we feel hurt, even though we may not experience it that way since the reaction time between the hurting and the anger may be very quick. Anger may also come in response to the *fear* of being hurt. This fear, also a raw, primal affect, can fuel a defensive anger. This seems to be true all across the animal kingdom. (I remember once driving on a country road in the woods and encountering a big bear in front of me. I came to a full stop just a few feet away. How angry she became! Her ferocious growl, however, was clearly fear based and intended to scare me off. But being scared herself and without the protection of a metal car, she ran off first.) Using anger to defend against fear explains why Yahweh was so often angry in the Bible's portrait of him; fear of abandonment or abandonment itself seems to have been the driving force behind his wrath. In any case, it's up to us to explore our own emotions regardless of which of them come first.

A final comment here on the nature of anger may be gleaned from Freud's famous observation that depression is anger turned inward. It has also been suggested that anger is depression turned outward. Although neither of these dictums is always true, the latter has special merit for understanding the Yahweh complex. For instance, when the sadness from being wounded in love leads to depression, we may turn to anger, believing it to be a better alternative. Wasn't Yahweh deep down a depressed God, blustering in rage as a way to manage—or rather, avoid—the pain of his woundedness in love? Nothing is more self-defeating than the eruption of the Yahweh complex as a defense against love. Because we have been wounded in love, we no longer wish to be vulnerable. But love cannot take root and grow without vulnerability.

For reasons such as this, Jung writes that "a complex can be really overcome only if it is lived out to the full. In other words, if we are to develop further, we have to draw to us and drink down to the very dregs what, because of our complexes, we have held at a distance." There are no shortcuts here; as the saying goes, a shortcut is the longest distance between two points.

There are defenses more refined than anger that are used to avoid or mask painful feelings from our wounds. Chief among them are hypervigilance; testing, dominating, or punishing the other; regulation of the other through rules (as observable in Yahweh's preoccupation with ritual etiquette and the Mosaic laws); and setting high ideals leading to perfectionism. The Yahwist is a child of such rigors. But as we learn to tolerate our emotions and affects with awareness and sensitivity as opposed to identifying with them and impulsively acting them out, our defenses gradually drop. Such vulnerability is a strength, not a weakness. It requires a strong, flexible ego that can endure the confrontation with the dark side of the psyche, the same dark side as Yahweh's. *One needs a strong ego to withstand the onslaught of the unconscious.* Thus should psychotherapy be concerned as much with the ego as it is with the unconscious (contrary to what some may think).

In a way similar to the analysis of the ego, an awareness of our superego helps us to loosen the tight hold the Yahweh complex can have upon us. If the rage of the complex rises up from the primitive, instinctual, affect-laden part of our psyche, the id, then by contrast the voice of Yahwistic reason descends upon us from the superego, our moral conscience. Like the id, the superego is collective in nature; everybody has one (unless, of course, they're a sociopath), and it tends to operate in a generally standard way with all of us, helping us discern right from wrong. However, the collective nature of the id and superego makes them especially susceptible to the Yahweh complex, a phenomenon rooted in the collective unconscious. A harsh inner voice that habitually evaluates us and our actions indicates a Yahwistic superego. Demanding moral purity or perfection, it passes judgment on us scrupulously and mercilessly. This in turn can foster a rigid moralism on our parts.

However, such a superego also steps beyond moral probity. It strives to micromanage us and exert a critical opinion on matters that have nothing to do with morality. It wants to keep us in line so that we don't commit the sin of proudly overestimating ourselves, and in so doing it compels us to sacrifice what is best about ourselves. "Who do you think you are to believe that you can be an artist?" this inner critic might say to a talented young person anticipating her first art exhibit. This impulse is fear based and defensive, trying to protect us from rejection and failure, the original traumatic events in Yahweh's life.

But the inner critic can also be cruel and sadistic in the scornful way it puts us down. Often its voice may sound like that of our father or mother, but that is only the earthly vehicle it has chosen in the course of our development (indeed, Freud conceived of the superego as an internalized parent). Most likely, that father or mother was also scrutinized by such a voice, which speaks again to the multigenerational aspect of the Yahweh complex: it comes down to us through the history of our families. A masculine voice tends to make us feel guilty for what we *do*, whereas a feminine voice is inclined to shame us for who we *are*, an attack that strikes closer to our core. But there are no hard and fast rules here, other than the ones the Yahwistic superego imposes upon us.

After anger, the inner critic (or its outer version as the critic of others) is the single most common feature of the Yahweh complex, sometimes even trumping anger. It is also the most toxic feature, poisoning our relationship to ourselves and sabotaging us from the inside. Psychoanalyst Ronald Fairbairn calls this feature the internal saboteur (or anti-libidinal ego). Rage that is acted out upon others is often a displaced fury at how this critic makes us feel about ourselves. Jung's method of active imagination is an effective way of dealing with this autonomous part of ourselves: we engage it in an inner dialogue, challenging its authority and taking a stand against its evil. Again, calling the demon by its name will not make it go away, but it will empower us to at least separate ourselves from it.

We should note that our dialogue is to be with the Yahweh-within-us, not an external Yahweh who is the god of the Hebrew Bible and whom many still worship as their deity and redeemer. That can be done but is more along the lines of prayer. Contemplative prayer, too, can be effective in inoculating us against the Yahweh complex's assaults; but for the purposes of our individuation or personal development, we should be careful about blurring psychological and theological lines. Talking with God should not become a reason to take our eyes off the inner dimension of this problem within us.

No psychotherapy can be effective unless what we learn from it becomes a practical part of our everyday existence and not just an epiphany within ourselves. Psychotherapy, a somewhat artificial construct, is a rehearsal for real life. In particular, the interpersonal dimension of the Yahweh complex is so prevalent that to the degree it is left unattended, our inner transformation remains isolated and abstract. Emotional expression in a noncombative, I–Thou way enables us to achieve what Yahweh himself could not until the conclusion of the Hebrew Bible. To be able to say to a person who has wounded us, "I am hurt; this is what I feel" implies a kind of consciousness and integrity that perhaps can be expected only from others who have also pursued inner work, but nevertheless, such vulnerability is always a vital asset if we wish to become complete, dimensional beings rather than merely perfect ones.

Finally, psychotherapy should not lose sight of the fact that the Yahweh complex is a god complex not only in its pursuit of power but also in its spiritual aspiration. As we have seen, in its positive side it inspires us to discover our innate godhood, our potential to transcend ourselves in service to higher ideals. Only in its negative side does it frustrate that aspiration, confusing our godhood with our egohood. For its spiritual impetus alone, it might be a good thing that we can never completely exorcize the Yahweh complex from our inner workings.

The Stuff that Dreams Are Made Of

> The unconscious mind sees correctly even when conscious reason is blind and impotent.
>
> —*C. G. Jung*

Dreams are an age-old and wonderful way to explore the psyche. They can also help us manage the psyche's eruptions, including the eruption of the Yahweh complex. Unquestionably, much rests on our ability to interpret dreams and on our theoretical and practical approach to them, as different schools have different approaches. While it is not an absolute prerequisite to have familiarity with the Yahweh complex in order to interpret either of the two dreams I will present here, some knowledge of it is helpful in appreciating their finer nuances.

The fact that Yahweh, the chief god of Western and Islamic civilization, has some connection to these dreams *in a symbolic or parallel way* furnishes their interpretation with rich historical, religious, and mythological material. Such dreams expressing a *likeness* of Yahweh, if not directly referring to him, are by no means uncommon. They are archetypal dreams rooted in the collective unconscious but dependent on the dreamer's personal associations in order to be understood in the unique context of their everyday life. As an exception, there can occur certain enigmatic and seemingly impenetrable dreams for which we can proffer little or no interpretation, and they need to be held in the silent awe of our not-knowing. The second dream presented here falls into this category.

The first dream was reported to me by a forty-three-year-old male patient who is a successful screenwriter in the entertainment industry in

Hollywood (and naturally, I have his permission to include it here). To preserve his privacy, we will call him David. The only thing we need to know about him at the outset is that his dream occurred at a transitional moment in his life when he was attempting to shift his career from exclusively writing to writing *and directing* his own screenplays. This was a formidable challenge given the nature of the entertainment industry, and he had some anxiety about it. The dream:

> I am in school. [The film director] Peter Jackson is my teacher. I sit at the back of the class with my friend. We are supposed to be writing in our journals/exercise books. My friend is completely messing about, and I am joining in with him, although in truth I am also writing down artistic snippets—bits of poems and musings amongst doodles and nonsense. Peter Jackson catches us, and is very angry. He shouts at me, accusing me of messing around and not doing my writing work properly. I protest that I am doing some worthwhile work, but Peter Jackson won't hear it. I feel intimidated by him but also defiant and confident that my work has merit on its own terms.

Here are David's associations:
- I admire Peter Jackson and his accomplishments. He created the film industry in New Zealand.
- As a child, I loved his horror movies. His early work reminds me of what I'm trying to do now, to direct my own horror screenplay.
- [In the dream] he is not emotionally attuned, not emotionally intelligent. He is very rigid and doesn't listen to others. He is not a good teacher because he gets angry, asserting his authority in a crude way.
- [In the dream] he's like my father.
- [In the dream] he's a model of the single-minded, tyrannical director. He's monomaniacal.

Clearly, Peter Jackson, whom David didn't know personally, is presented in the dream as a Yahwistic figure. He is a creator but emotionally primitive, rigid, and wrathful. He's a monomaniacal authoritarian. In fact, he is cast in the role of Yahweh; in his emotional style and intimidating effect on the dreamer, he *is* Yahweh. Unlike David, his personality emanates the Yahweh complex. Film director Francis Ford Coppola described the director's job anyways as the last refuge that allows someone to be like God, creating something from nothing and being in charge of everything. Except David's inner Peter Jackson does this in a brittle, controlling, hostile way, much like Yahweh.

Also, we should not underestimate the importance of David's association of *this* Peter Jackson with his own father, a figure who was often critical of him. David and I had previously spoken much about his relationship with his father, so this was part of the mix here as well. The dream was an expression of both his Yahweh complex and his father complex.

Why did David have this dream? What might he have learned from it? The dream announces its pedagogical purpose by establishing its setting as a school. This could be seen as somewhat regressive; what's a forty-three-year-old man doing back in school? But if it is regressive, it would be what psychoanalyst Ernst Kris calls a regression in the service of the ego. Jung also argues that such regression is a "genuine attempt to get at something necessary." It has a positive purpose.

David's dream represents the school that teaches the wisdom of the unconscious. It pits him against the inner tyrannical director who criticizes and tries to undermine him. Again, the inner critic or Fairbairn's "internal saboteur" is at work. But David's dream tells him that he has the wherewithal, the inner resources, to stand up to it. His character has the mettle to endure his anxiety and his own attacks against himself, not to mention the external attacks that he may encounter in his industry as he transforms himself into a director. The dream comes to help him recognize his self-worth and to boost his self-confidence. He can and must withstand the aggression of his Yahweh complex.

The second dream to be discussed is President Barack Obama's, occurring before he went to law school and during his first trip to Kenya to connect with his family and roots. The dream offers some interesting parallels that *resemble* Yahweh's features and function *as if* they constitute a positive Yahweh complex with a strong sense of purpose. The dream took place in 1988 when Obama was twenty-seven years old. It's recorded in his memoir, *Dreams from My Father: A Story of Race and Inheritance*. He had it while he was riding on a train, lulled to sleep by its "trembling rhythm."

> I finally fell asleep, and dreamed I was walking along a village road. Children, dressed only in strings of beads, played in front of the round huts, and several old men waved to me as I passed. But as I went farther along, I began to notice that people were looking behind me fearfully, rushing into their huts as I passed. I heard the growl of a leopard and started to run into the forest, tripping over roots and stumps and vines, until at last I couldn't run any longer and fell to my knees in the middle of a bright clearing. Panting for breath, I turned around to see the day turned night, and a giant figure looming as large as the trees, wearing only a loincloth and a ghostly mask. The lifeless eyes bore into me, and I heard a thunderous voice saying only that it was time, and my entire body began to shake violently with the sound, as if I were breaking apart.

Obama provides no personal associations to the dream. Evidently, he himself recognized its transcendent quality and decided to honor the dream in silence, leaving its mystery up to his readers to contemplate. For our purposes, a few words (including some mythological amplification) are in order. Like any dream that has highly symbolic imagery, as this one does, there may be multiple interpretations that vary from each other. In the end, only the dreamer can attest to whether an interpretation feels right. What I will offer here are only a few possibilities, but regardless of right or wrong, they illustrate how imaginative and unpredictable the unconscious mind can be, and yet how we can rely upon it for solid help or advice when the ego is most in need of it.

To begin, in light of who Obama eventually became, we can intuit from the dream the fateful calling that, so to speak, chased him down. Perhaps the unconscious knew something that his conscious mind had no way of knowing. "It is time," the giant stalker says to him in a thundering voice. Time for what? To enroll in Harvard Law School and become the first Black president of the prestigious *Harvard Law Review*? To become a community organizer in Chicago and a constitutional law professor at the University of Chicago? To become a US senator and president—the first African American president and leader of the free world? Was this a precognitive dream, a forecast of what was in store for him?

As mentioned in the chapter on Freud, both Freud and Jung developed an interest in parapsychological phenomena. Jung in particular concluded that the unconscious has the ability to defy the law of cause and effect so that a future event can be announced or hinted at before it happens.

Who was this giant, and what did he share in common with the biblical Yahweh? Plenty. Here is the Hebrew Bible's description of an encounter between Yahweh and Moses:

> Moses said, "Show me your glory, I beg you." And he [Yahweh] said, "I will let all my splendor pass in front of you, and I will pronounce before you the name Yahweh. I have compassion on whom I will, and I show pity to whom I please. You cannot see my face," he said, "for man cannot see me and live." And Yahweh said, "Here is a place beside me. You must stand on the rock, and when my glory passes by, I will put you in a cleft of the rock and shield you with my hand while I pass by. Then I will take my hand away and you shall see the back of me; but my face is not to be seen.

What this passage doesn't say but is implied is that Yahweh is *big*. This is not the only place in Jewish religious literature that this is indicated. The *Shiur Komah*, a text written probably in the second century CE, describes God's shape as distinctly human but gigantic. Obama's dream and Moses's encounter are obviously different experiences, but the *size* of the two supernatural beings and the *huge importance* that their revelations or disclosures had for the two men are similar. In both instances, the supernatural beings displayed a deadly serious sense of purpose.

We have an idea of who Yahweh is, but do we have any idea of who Obama's stalker is? It might be helpful if we knew what kind of mask he was wearing, since we know that African cultures can have masks for almost every single important function and transition in life, ranging from ensuring a good harvest to ceremonies for marriage or death. Less commonly known is the traditionally African belief that by donning a certain kind of mask, one takes on the spirit or identity of whom the mask was originally intended for. A war mask, for example, would be suitable for a warrior going to war. However, the only hints we have about this giant stalker are Obama's comments that the mask was "ghostly" and the eyes that bore into him "lifeless." Actually, these are the elements in the dream that, after the announcement that "it is time," most intrigue me. It is as if this mask and these eyes belonged to another world, possibly the afterlife or some other eternal condition.

But what made the mask ghostly and the eyes lifeless in the first place? Was it war? Was Obama's stalker a tribal war god, like Yahweh— maybe even Yahweh himself, in an African persona? After all, Kenya's population is 85 percent Christian, and Obama himself is Christian; that is to say, there's no insurmountable conflict between the Abrahamic God and African traditions, as Bantu Christianity has demonstrated (this is the Christianity that many slaves brought with them on the ships that took them from their homes to America). If the stalker was a warrior or war god or Yahweh himself, maybe he came because the young, fatherless Obama needed to adopt a more warrior-like attitude toward the adventure of whom he was to become. The thunderous voice and serious words of the stalker seem to have had an authoritative but not unkind fatherly quality. Perhaps this dream belongs with what Obama had in mind when he titled his book *Dreams from My Father*, except the "father" here would not have been his personal father but rather an archetypal Father.

Another compelling parallel between the two supernatural beings is the concealment of their faces. Putting aside here the above cultural factors for wearing a mask, was the stalker also protecting Obama from the frightful sight of his face? If he was an incarnation of Yahweh, there would have been good reason for this. As we were told above, no man could see his face and live.

Yet another similarity is that both supernatural beings appear to be more or less naked (the King James Version of the Bible goes so far as saying that Yahweh's "back *parts*" were exposed, implying also his buttocks). Then, in both the dream and the Hebrew Bible, there are references to the leopard, a dangerous predator. ("A leopard lies in wait by their towns," the prophet Jeremiah says in his warning to sinners.) The leopard and other wildcats often appear in dreams as well as folklore. In some cultures, including African ones, they are shamanic or totem animals—"spirit animals"—with magical powers. This may be its role in Obama's dream if we view its appearance as an announcement that the stalker is coming.

And what about the villagers who were terrified of the stalker? They seemed to know beforehand who was coming, and they fled for their lives, for the safety indoors. This could have been a scene right out of the Hebrew Bible. Often when Yahweh appeared, people died. In Dylan's "Highway 61 Revisited," Abraham is warned that if he does not sacrifice his son, he should run the next time God shows up. Again, "The fear of the Lord is the beginning of wisdom."

More important than all the unanswerable questions above is that both the stalker and Yahweh are larger than life yet profoundly concerned with life. Both are invested in the doings of mortals and want to have a role in these doings, and both are willing to expose themselves—to be "naked"—so that they may be better known. These parallel experiences of Obama and Moses are remarkable considering that they are separated by more than three millennia. Much has socially and otherwise changed, yet the religious character of human nature has endured in its most basic forms. The stuff that dreams are made of comes from the same place as the stuff of our religions, myths, folklore, and fairy tales. To these we could today add movies, which the Swedish filmmaker Ingmar Bergman said is the medium most suited for illustrating dreams because it is so visual and yet, like dreams, unimpeded by the laws of physics.

All told, with the dreams of both David and Obama, we can observe how the psyche operates. Life presented them with a problem or challenge, and this triggered a response from the psyche in the image of a film director with a Yahweh complex (in David's case) or of a giant with Yahweh-like features (in Obama's case). True to Yahweh's nature, this response was both negative and positive, both dark and bright, both menacing and helpful. There is reason to fear *and* embrace Yahweh. Again, in his own words: "I form the light, and create darkness: I make peace, and create evil: I the Lord do all these things." Our dreams can help us to navigate these opposites. Therein lies their wisdom and power.

RAIN

> The only trustworthy thing in the universe is really a conscious individual human being. We are all relatively untrustworthy because we have an unconscious. . . . How Yahweh energy is going to manifest itself, whether it manifests creatively or destructively, depends very largely on the nature and degree of consciousness of the ego through which it expresses itself.
>
> —*Edward F. Edinger*

Another approach I have found helpful for working with our Yahweh complex is Buddhist teacher Michele McDonald's technique of RAIN, as it elegantly organizes the same inner work undertaken in psychotherapy but in a simple, straightforward, Buddhist way. This can have the effect of calming and neutralizing the Yahweh complex at least temporarily, and if practiced regularly, then regularly. The notion that an Eastern religion could contribute to our struggle with a Western and Islamic god complex is, I suppose, an irony. However, there's a reason why an Eastern method of enlightenment would soothe a tempest like Yahweh: it fosters not only a detached, objective watchfulness (what is today widely celebrated as mindfulness) but also compassion, not only for others but for ourselves, and even for the tormented Yahweh-within-us. After all, it was in order to teach us how to manage turbulent states of mind that the Buddha developed his own psychological observations and methods.

McDonald's wonderfully simple method to manage our problems and conflicts integrates the core principles of Buddhism. It encourages us to cultivate a practice that captures the four main ingredients of what she describes as the "nourishing art of mindful inquiry." RAIN is her acronym for this art; I will slightly modify it here for our purposes:

- *R* means we *Recognize* when we are about to act (or have acted) upon some unproductive emotion, desire, or attitude.

- *A* means we *Accept* this about ourselves by acknowledging and owning it as ours.

- *I* means we *Investigate* or take *Interest* in its dynamics—how we get caught up in it, how it affects us, and how it creates unnecessary suffering for ourselves or others.

- *N* means we then *Non-identify* or *Not identify* with this emotion, desire, or attitude and actively give up our attachment to it.

We see here a method that addresses the very same factors that psychotherapy does. The first step implies that we recognize the Yahweh complex as an autonomous inner force, whether we call it by that name or some other. A cognitive behavioral therapist, for example, might call it an anger management problem. What is important here is that it is identified. A rose is a rose by any other name, to paraphrase Shakespeare. The second step, also very important, is to recognize the feelings and affects that the Yahweh complex brings up in us. It demands us to turn inward instead of acting out. Finally, we should aim to recognize the situations that trigger the complex. We watch out for them so that we can gain a measure of predictability and preparedness.

Acceptance is a more difficult step, as it requires the humility and repeated effort to own this condition, to admit that, yes, we do have it, and it doesn't make us look good. As Shakespeare, again, said, here through the personage of Prospero, "This thing of darkness I acknowledge mine." We must accept the propensity of the complex to dominate us and to warp our perception.

The first step of any twelve-step program is for one to admit that they cannot control their addiction or compulsion. Jung, who influenced Bill Wilson, one of the founders of the twelve-step model, saw acceptance as a central principle in our personal development: "We cannot change anything until we accept it. Condemnation does not liberate, it oppresses." Buddhist teacher and psychologist Tara Brach echoes Jung on this principle: "Radical Acceptance is the willingness to experience ourselves and our life as it is. A moment of Radical Acceptance is a moment of genuine freedom." Indeed, recognizing and accepting that the Yahweh complex is deeply and inextricably ingrained in our psyches has a certain liberating implication: we don't need to get rid of the complex or to perfectly master it; we just need to change our unconscious relationship to it into a conscious one. Healing here isn't about curing but about managing the complex and learning to live with it.

Investigation would explore the particular ways the Yahweh complex manifests individually with each of us. To better understand its collective, archetypal nature, one can read the Hebrew Bible. The Yahweh-in-us is a mirror image of the Abrahamic God. I won't say more about this here since this book is entirely an investigation of this complex.

To non- or not-identify with the complex, we must wrestle with the contrary tendency to allow ourselves to get swallowed by it, the way Jonah was swallowed by the whale (stubborn Jonah was a Yahwist even more than Yahweh was). When we identify with the complex, we share its convictions. This is akin to falling asleep or falling into the unconscious: we don't recognize that the Yahweh-in-us has taken over. "Be careful in your choice of hypnotists," psychologist Sidney Jourard warns us. The struggle to stay awake or alert to the complex's effects makes this the most difficult of the four steps in the RAIN exercise. It is itself an exercise in meditation and mindfulness, required to take place not only on a meditation cushion but also in our daily activities in the everyday world.

The method of RAIN shares certain features with the alchemical procedure of *solutio*, which was mentioned in the chapter on the Beatles: based on water imagery, both dissolve the Yahweh complex's grip on us. RAIN is diametrically opposite in nature to the complex itself. Yahweh's four greatest flaws were that he could not recognize, accept, investigate, and non-identify with his emotional needs and the fiery rage ignited by the frustration of them. By going to the heart of our suffering as he did with his, we heal it.

If we are afflicted with the Yahweh complex and in a situation that can at any moment get out of hand, scrolling through the four steps of RAIN can be a kind of mantra to quickly recenter and ground us. True to the spirit of Buddhism, this method helps us to tame our minds and open our hearts.

"The Rainmaker"

> The sage manages affairs without action.
>
> —*Lao Tzu*

The following is a true story told to Carl Jung by a friend, sinologist Richard Wilhelm. It highlights the Taoist principle of *wu-wei*, or nonaction. As a means to shape events harmoniously, this principle is vital for understanding how the Tao works and plays. It is not a passive form of nonaction but a conscientious—though effortless—channeling of the Tao or, as it were, the Unconscious as understood by Zen Buddhists.

The story:

There was a great drought where Wilhelm lived in China. For months there had not been a drop of rain, and the situation became catastrophic. The Catholics made processions, the Protestants made prayers, and the

Chinese burned joss sticks and shot off guns to frighten away the demons of the drought, but with no result.

Finally the Chinese said, "We will fetch the rainmaker." And from another province, a dried-up old man appeared. The only thing he asked for was a quiet little house somewhere, and there he locked himself in for three days.

On the fourth day, clouds gathered, and there was a great snowstorm at the time of the year when no snow was expected, an unusual amount, and the town was so full of rumors about the wonderful rainmaker that Wilhelm went to ask the man how he did it.

In true European fashion he said, "They call you the rainmaker. Will you tell me how you made the snow?"

And the little Chinaman said, "I did not make the snow. I am not responsible."

"But what have you done these three days?"

"Oh, I can explain that. I come from another country where things are in order. Here they are out of order. They are not as they should be by the ordinance of heaven. Therefore, the whole country is not in Tao, and I am also not in the natural order of things because I am in a disordered country. So I had to wait three days until I was back in Tao, and then naturally the rain came."

Nonviolent Communication

> Any judgment of another person diminishes the likelihood
> of our needs being met. . . . The more people hear blame and
> judgment, the more defensive and aggressive they become.
>
> —*Marshall B. Rosenberg*

Psychologist Marshall Rosenberg developed a simple technique to work with deeply entrenched patterns of behavior. It's an exercise that revolves around our communication style. At first it may seem artificial and formulaic, but it becomes more natural with practice and is a tool that can be easily adapted to one's own personal style. I have used it in my work with many couples, and it works. It slows down their communication process and grounds it in a dialogue based on empathy and compassion. The exercise quickly takes us right out of our complex, whichever one it may be, and breaks its spell over us.

Any two people can practice it together, taking turns in their roles as speaker and listener. The listener responds to the speaker by stating what she or he has heard them say, and the exercise does not continue until the speaker verifies that the listener had heard them accurately. I have here simplified Rosenberg's presentation of this model, which, again, I use with couples in my work or, when the occasion arises, by myself with another. The more complete version of it can be found in Rosenberg's book *Nonviolent Communication: A Language of Life*. This is how it goes:

EXPRESSING CLEARLY
1. *"When I see/hear . . ."*
2. *"I feel . . ."*
3. *". . . because I need/value . . ."*
4. *"Would you be willing to . . . ?"* (specific action)

RECEIVING EMPATHICALLY
1. *"When you see/hear . . ."*
2. *"You feel . . ."*
3. *". . . because you need/value . . ."*
4. *"Would you like . . . ?"* (specific action)

The dialogue proceeds from observations to feelings to needs and finally to a request. Note how the expression is made with "I" statements instead of blaming or accusatory "you" statements that tend to make the listener defensive.

When Others Afflict Us with Their Yahweh Complex

> Knowing your darkness is the best method for dealing with the darkness of other people.
>
> —*C. G. Jung*

Three ways to quickly recognize another's Yahweh complex in the moment:

1. Their angry reaction is disproportionately greater than what the situation calls for; it is larger than life and acts as a godlike force that inflates them.
2. Their communication style is strikingly impersonal—either overheated or ice cold, either attacking or not, but regardless of which, it's impersonal. There is no consideration for the other's feelings. The complex turns the other into an object or target and the individual afflicted by it into its instrument.
3. The complex exhibits a fierce will to power. It demands things to be ideal and exactly the way it wants to them to be.

You can't expect someone in the grip of a complex to talk sensibly or rationally; they're too agitated and emotionally charged. The best we can do is to agree with them to temporarily take a break and reconvene later when they, and possibly we too, are in a calmer, more receptive state, and *then* have a discussion. Again, collective complexes are highly contagious, so we should not assume that we are immune from catching their condition.

How to Tell How Much Someone Is Gripped by the Yahweh Complex

> An inflated consciousness is always egocentric and conscious of nothing but its own existence. It is incapable of learning from the past, incapable of understanding contemporary events, and incapable of drawing right conclusions about the future. It is hypnotized by itself and therefore cannot be argued with. It inevitably dooms itself to calamities that must strike it dead.
>
> —*C. G. Jung*

Three factors indicate the severity of one's identification with the Yahweh complex:

1. The person with a high degree of identification probably has a childhood history of abandonment, neglect, or other trauma that precipitated the Yahweh complex's emergence from the collective unconscious.

2. The greater the person's wound, the greater their need for an arsenal of power and defenses. With its armor of self-protection, a war-god complex rigidly compensates for deep-seated terror around vulnerability and dependency needs. They unconsciously act out their terror while anger at their predicament, taken out on others, is raised to the zone of rage.

3. A person severely afflicted, either generally speaking or in a particular episode, is strikingly unconscious of how engulfed they are in a psychological complex and how inappropriately and unattractively they are behaving. The Yahweh complex imbues them with a sense of entitlement that colors their perceptions and feelings and seduces them into believing they're absolutely right, even when they obviously aren't.

Confronting Evil

> The life and strength of our authority springs from moral
> and not physical forces.
>
> —*Winston Churchill*

If some confrontation or involvement with a person possessed by the Yahweh complex turns dark or even evil ("evil" here defined as it is in the prologue), here are some things to consider. We must not become overidentified with our fight or position against the evil action or behavior; otherwise, we become inflated. This is from Richard Wilhelm's commentary on the ancient Chinese *I Ching* or *Book of Changes*:

> In a resolute struggle of the good against evil, there are, however, definite rules that must not be disregarded, if it is to succeed. First, resolution must be based on a union of strength and friendliness. Second, a compromise with evil is not possible; evil must under all circumstances be openly discredited. Nor must our own passions and shortcomings be glossed over. Third, the struggle must not be carried on directly by force. If evil is branded, it thinks of weapons, and if we do it the favor of fighting against it blow for blow, we lose in the end because thus we ourselves get entangled in hatred and passion. Therefore it is important to begin at home, to be on guard in our own persons against the faults we have branded. In this way, finding no opponent, the sharp edges of the weapons of evil become dulled. For the same reasons, we should not combat our own faults directly. As long as we wrestle with them, they continue victorious. Finally, the best way to fight evil is to make energetic progress in the good.

We must have sympathy for the Yahweh part of ourselves, not hatred or contempt, which only further agitate it. If we hate our shadow or hold it in contempt, we won't be able to transform our relationship with it. Wilhelm further comments, "Hatred is a form of subjective involvement by which we are bound to the hated object."

Darkness and evil arise when we have not fully digested the parts of us that are cruel, whether to others or ourselves or both.

Listen to U2's "Sleep Like a Baby Tonight." Listen to its lyrics. They're about the boys who throughout history were sexually abused by Catholic priests—a long episode that reflects one of the worst cover-ups in history. It is essentially a cover-up of the evil combination of Yahwistic power and sexual depravity, the cover-up itself a moral crime in addition to the sexual one. But this problem was not limited to Catholic priests. We know that the predatory behaviors of a large number of scoutmasters in the Boy Scouts of America were just as egregious. Implicitly, that too, like all other sexual abuse of children by trusted authority figures, is what the song is about.

If he heard it, I imagine God again got off his throne, as he might have when he heard Dylan's "Slow Train." Both are songs about evil that occurs on a grand scale yet goes unnoticed even though it takes place right under our noses. "Hell is empty," Shakespeare famously said. "All the devils are here."

This is, again, from Wilhelm's commentary on the *I Ching*:

> When misfortune has spent itself, better times return. The seed of the good remains, and it is just when the fruit falls to the ground that good sprouts anew from its seed. . . . A law of nature is at work here. Evil is not destructive to the good alone but inevitably destroys itself as well. For evil, which lives solely by negation, cannot continue to exist on its own strength alone.

On *Learning* How to Live with
Our Yahweh Complex

Integration of the unconscious invariably has a healing effect.

—*C. G. Jung*

To integrate the Yahweh complex means to contain and tolerate the affects and urges it spawns while consciously suffering them. Again, we don't integrate it as if it were something like our creative side; we work with it as an inner other. This is an acquired, learned skill and not innate. And like anything that must be learned, there is a learning curve. Anticipating this allows us to be patient—not only with it but with ourselves. After all, a ferocious complex that began its march through history three thousand years ago will not be easily tamed.

There is a learning theory that can help inspire us to develop the required patience and to gauge our progress. It posits four stages of learning in order to become competent at any task:

1. One is unconsciously incompetent.
2. One becomes consciously incompetent.
3. With effort, one then becomes consciously competent.
4. Finally, with mastery, one becomes unconsciously competent.

May we eventually learn to tame the Yahweh complex with unconscious competence.

EPILOGUE

Globalization and the Yahweh Complex

> When faced with a totally new situation, we tend always to
> attach ourselves to the objects, to the flavor of the most recent
> past. We look at the present through a rear-view mirror. We
> march backwards into the future.
>
> —*Marshall McLuhan and Quentin Fiore*

If Yahweh were to conquer the world again, what might this look like?
I say "conquer the world *again*" because in biblical times and from
ancient Israel's perspective, he already became the ruler of the world.
Today he would, of course, come back in a different form—namely,
through our Yahweh complex. If enough of us have this complex, he may
rule the world again. If we have it in a positive way, that may not be such
a bad thing. Imagine a world run according to the ethical principles of
Churchill, Lincoln, King, and Mandela. But if we have it in a dark way,
unconsciously and destructively acting it out, then his conquest could
be maniacal, and the world could become gripped by apocalyptic fever.
It cannot be stressed too much that, given our capacity today to truly
destroy ourselves and the world, this has different implications than at
any previous time in history.

Many today feel that the world is already in a maniacal, apocalyptic
condition, or at least in the early throes of it. Certainly, it is ripe for
the eruption of collective complexes—complexes that originate in the
collective unconscious, in the history of a culture or civilization. The
Yahweh complex is just such a complex. With its roots in the Abrahamic
religious imagination, its collective nature consists of not only its broad
sweep, affecting Jews, Christians, and Muslims alike, but also the
characteristics of the god upon whom it is modeled.

Yahweh himself was very much a collective-oriented god, concerned more with national peoplehood than with the individual's salvation, more with a Law for the many than with what goes on in a person's soul (unlike Krishna in his tutelage of Arjuna, for example). His personality was driven by primitive, collective drives, making him like a Leviathan or a hurricane or some other blind, overwhelming force of nature. The Yahweh complex likewise stirs up and exploits our most collective features: our base emotions, our power drive, our competitiveness, our amoral instincts, our prejudices, and our tendencies toward conflict. What is an apocalypse? An apocalypse is what would happen if our darker impulses were to get out of hand and be unleashed in the world without limitation and regard for human life or the life of the world itself.

In this way, the Yahweh complex is unfortunately too well matched with our current global situation: its collective mindset folds in too easily with the same in the world today. Global commerce, modern geopolitics, and technological innovations like the internet may have turned the world into a "global village," but there can be no doubt that the communication theorist Marshall McLuhan—who coined this term in 1962—would have been of two minds about its current state. He would have praised the increasing interconnectedness of humanity, but he would have been dismayed by the decay of genuine dialogue, critical self-reflection, and cultural literacy. The more collective and conformist we become in our thinking, the less we think for ourselves. The less we think for ourselves, the more diminished we become in our spiritual development and capacity to change. Mass media, mass movements, mass-mindedness, and mass man seem to all go together. Thus is ours a perfect social environment for collective complexes to be triggered and stimulated.

My own fear is that we are galloping at breakneck speed toward some collective trauma that could end civilization as we know it. This could be the result of an ecological crisis, or the collapse of our global financial system, or a pandemic like COVID-19 wiping out large segments of the world's population, or nuclear or biochemical weapons falling into the hands of terrorists, the latter not only in the usual way we think of them:

although the military doctrine of mutual assured destruction (MAD) inhibited nuclear war among the superpowers throughout the Cold War, it has now been made obsolete by Putin, a thug who has threatened to use nuclear weapons against Ukraine. To this terrorist threat we can add backward, rogue regimes like North Korea and fundamentalist ideologues like Iran's rulers. Can we truly trust the monitoring and policing of these states in view of recent intelligence and military failures?

In any case, only our inflation makes us believe that we are immune to disasters even more deadly and earth scorching than Yahweh's wars and apocalyptic acts. Can we take a history lesson from ancient Israel and avoid our own downfall and exile?

Our survival depends on our ability to recognize, accept, investigate, and non-identify with the god complex that leads us to believe that we can do whatever we please. If we do not seize control of this complex, it will seize control of us—that is, if it hasn't already. We need to take responsibility for ourselves as individuals and as nations. We need true leadership, like that of Churchill, Lincoln, King, and Mandela; but if we don't demand and support it, it will not happen.

There is nothing new in what I am saying here. People have been yearning for this kind of leadership since the 1960s, since McLuhan's day when the trend toward globalization and the world's need for a viable global vision became clearer (think of President Kennedy's 1961 inaugural address in which he boldly advocated for the world to come together in a "grand and global alliance," in a "struggle against the common enemies of man: tyranny, poverty, disease, and war itself").

Anybody with the will to power and the means to enforce it can globalize the world under a single, new order, as globalization is not new either. The Roman and British Empires introduced earlier forms of it. But not anyone can create a globalized world that is voluntarily collaborative and harmonious; the Romans and British surely didn't. It is not easy to create a global village in which wisdom and compassion predominate rather than cut-throat competition and every kind of warfare. Such an endeavor—our *only* alternative on a planet projected to have a human population of 9.7 billion by 2050—requires not just our prayers but also our awakening and our hard work at implementing practical changes.

The Yahweh complex can be a curse or a boon, depending on how we approach it. Let us approach it the way Yahweh approached his predicament when he changed his attitude and consequently his fate. In becoming a moral problem to himself, he transformed from a war god into a more complete, conscientious, humane being. We too can choose between our self-defeat and victory. In the end, the only victory that truly counts, as the sages of old tell us, is the one over ourselves. Only in self-mastery will we find the inner power to get out of our own way and to bring forth what is genuinely godly in our nature—our altruistic values, our ethical principles, our compassion, our appreciation of beauty. If we could place these front and center, we might create a globalized world different from the ones that have passed, a world we would want our children and future generations to inherit.

The Abrahamic dream of a "city on a hill" that is the "light of the world" is not a utopian fantasy but the visionary ideal of a society that is also more complete, conscientious, and humane. Whether we like it or not, and whether we are ready for it or not, God's retreat from history has left it up to us to make this dream or ideal come true. His emancipation from the world has freed us—and forced us—to step into his place as its custodian.

Will we continue to do this in an inflated and destructive way, possessed by a dark god complex, or will we do it in an authentic, spiritual way, in service to our godly qualities? That is the question we must answer at the dawn of this new era of globalization; the sanity and survival of our world depend on it.

APPENDIX I

A List of the Main Features of the Yahweh Complex

We are still as much possessed today by autonomous psychic contents as if they were Olympians. Today they are called phobias, obsessions, and so forth; in a word, neurotic symptoms. The gods have become diseases.

—*C. G. Jung*

Again, few people with a Yahweh complex exhibit all or even most of the following features. Usually, a cluster of them are ample indication that it is at work in their psyches and their environment.

- Anger or rage
- Inflation and arrogance
- The power drive (often leading to megalomania)
- Combativeness
- Vengefulness
- Brutality
- Judgmental criticalness (mostly of others—yet, not uncommonly, just as severely of oneself)
- Perfectionism
- Bitterness
- Disillusionment and melancholy (leading to a pessimistic, gloomy worldview and a bitter, saturnine disposition)
- Splitting (between good and bad and projecting the negative side onto others)
- Fundamentalist thinking and apocalyptic fever
- Omnipotence and omniscience (also leading to megalomania)
- Acts like a know-it-all

- A history of trauma
- Wounded pride
- An intense desire to be admired and praised (usually compensating an underlying insecurity)
- Lack of compassion (empathic failure)
- Sternness and a legalistic, unforgiving attitude (as in Yahweh's demand for strict adherence to the Law)
- Lawlessness (one believes they are above the law and acts accordingly)
- A preoccupation with morality *or* an altogether indifferent amorality
- Narcissistic entitlement (like Yahweh, one even feels entitled to be rageful and vengeful, as if this were a natural right)
- Territoriality and imperial ambitions
- An enemy-oriented heroism (a notion of heroism and greatness that needs an enemy in order to define itself)
- Precalculated, Machiavellian manipulation of others
- A patriarchal attitude and misogyny
- Hierarchal authoritarianism
- Bullying (verbal abuse, browbeating, or, as in Yahweh's case, intimidation through the threat of punishment)
- Pettiness
- A tendency toward paranoia
- Cognitive distortions (e.g., irrational thinking; black-and-white thinking; filtering out the positive; catastrophizing; emotional reasoning; "should" and "must" statements)
- Maniacal glee (like the kind Yahweh indulged in when meting out or threatening to mete out his punishments)

APPENDIX II

A Partial List of Apocalyptic Songs in Rock 'n' Roll

Let the end of the world be inside you, then you don't need
to fear the end of the world out there.

—*Eckhart Tolle*

Why do rock 'n' roll artists have such a strong attraction to the
Apocalypse motif compared to most other artists? We can
conjecture that the music makes the dark subject matter palatable and
emotionally moving in the same ways as do Mozart and Verdi's requiems
with their powerful treatments of the "Dies Irae" or "Day of Wrath"
sequence. The Apocalypse is a religious drama like no other. Only the
"end of the world" can be an appropriate simile for such events of the day
as climate change with its increasing hurricanes, melting ice caps, and
massive, fierce fires.

There is really nothing new about this in the world of rock 'n' roll.
Watch Mother Nature flee in the 1970s, Neil Young complains in "After
the Gold Rush," a song he wrote at the very beginning of that decade. Or
look at the album cover of Supertramp's *Crisis? What Crisis?*, produced a
few years later ("A picture is worth a thousand words," as the adage goes).
Like the Apocalypse, ecological dangers sound the call for moral reflection
and renewal. I think that deep down, this calling is what compels rock 'n'
roll artists to write and sing about the Apocalypse. As an archetypal motif,
it comes up from the deep wellspring of the collective unconscious and
inspires the artist to be a faithful witness to what is going on both globally
and in their own immediate surroundings. It is firstly, then, a metaphor
for the troubled and dangerous condition of the world.

Secondly, as a subjective, inner experience (as we discussed in the
chapter on Bob Dylan), the Apocalypse symbolically marks the end of the

213

artist's world *as they have known it,* paving the way for a psychological and spiritual rebirth. Thus is the Apocalypse motif a metaphor also for what they are personally going through, for what is going on within them, emotionally or otherwise. At least, this is what I hear. If you find yourself in doubt as to why I have chosen certain selections to be part of this collection, please google their lyrics and read them, perhaps while listening to the songs (all of the songs are on YouTube). Then my choice may become clearer. With their lyrics as well as their music, these songs can be painfully intimate and personally disclosing in ways other art forms usually are not.

Of course, inclusion in the list provided here is not to insinuate that apocalyptic songs possess some greater value than rock 'n' roll's other songs. Simply, it shows the differing degrees to which rock 'n' roll artists are creatively driven by the Yahweh complex and its related end-of-the-world, death-and-rebirth, Apocalypse motif.

The list is alphabetically ordered according to the artist's last name or the name of their bands if this is how they are predominantly known. If more than one of the artist or band's albums are cited, they are listed in chronological order. As a partial list, not all of any given musician's apocalyptic songs may be cited, just as there are apocalyptic songs by other musicians who are not cited at all. The selection below consists of songs that in some measure are well known and liked. I include one song from each of the blues, gospel, and rap genres since these are closely related to rock 'n' roll in the overall history of popular music.

The albums that are apocalyptic either entirely or almost entirely are labeled as concept albums, and therefore every song on them is listed. This includes the occasional love song—or apocalyptic song blended with lyrics about failed love—that ties *Thanatos* (the death urge) to its opposite, *Eros* (the life or love urge). This balances the albums and prevents them from altogether sinking into a morass of deadening darkness—or not, as the case may be and may *necessarily* be. Deadening darkness is what the Apocalypse is about; we may need it in order for us to come through to the other side. Note how even the song and album titles often have an apocalyptic ring.

- AC/DC: "Hells Bells" (*Back in Black*, 1980. The song's narrative is told from the viewpoint of Satan. The album was recorded shortly after the death of Bon Scott, the band's lead singer.)
- Ryan Adams: "Political Scientist," "Afraid Not Scared," "This House Is Not for Sale," "Anybody Wanna Take Me Home," "Love Is Hell," "Wonderwall," "The Shadowlands," "World War 24," "Avalanche," "My Blue Manhattan," "Please Do Not Let Me Go," "City Rain, City Streets," "I See Monsters," "English Girls Approximately," "Thank You Louise," and "Hotel Chelsea Nights" (*Love Is Hell*, 2004, a concept album whether consciously designed as such or not. Reflecting on it, Adams reportedly said, "Those songs are me going out of my head. I made this totally bombed-out record about killing yourself."); "Doomsday" (*Prisoner*, 2017)
- Adele: "Skyfall" (*Skyfall: Original Motion Picture Soundtrack*, 2012. This song, co-written with Paul Epworth, is in the James Bond film with the same title.)
- Arcade Fire: "Wake Up" (*Funeral*, 2004); "Black Mirror," "Keep the Car Running," "Neon Bible," "Intervention," "Black Wave/ Bad Vibrations," "Ocean of Noise," "The Well and the Lighthouse," "(Antichrist Television Blues)," "Windowsill," "No Cars Go," and "My Body Is a Cage" (*Neon Bible*, 2007, a concept album); "Reflektive Age," "Reflektor" (featuring David Bowie), "We Exist," "Flashbulb Eyes," "Here Comes the Night Time," "Normal Person," "You Already Know," "Joan of Arc," "Here Comes the Night Time II," "Awful Sound (Oh Eurydice)," "It's Never Over (Hey Orpheus)," "Porno," "Afterlife," and "Supersymmetry" (*Reflektor*, 2013, a concept and double album); "Age of Anxiety I," "Age of Anxiety II (Rabbit Hole)" (includes "Prelude"), "End of the Empire I–IV (I. Last Dance, II. Last Round, III. Leave the Light On, IV. Sagittarius A)," "The Lightning

I, II," "Unconditional I (Lookout Kid)," "Unconditional II (Race and Religion)" (the latter features Peter Gabriel), and "We" (*We*, 2022, a concept album)

- Audioslave: "Like a Stone" (*Audioslave*, 2002. Chris Cornell, the band's songwriter and lead singer, said that this song is about finding God and "concentrating on the afterlife you would hope for," meaning that "your heaven is what you make it"; it is shaped according to the eye of the beholder. Struggling with depression and addiction much of his adult life, Cornell committed suicide in 2017.)

- The Beatles: "Help!" (*Help!*, 1965); "A Day in the Life" (*Sgt. Pepper's Lonely Hearts Club Band*, 1967); "Yer Blues," "Helter Skelter" (*White Album*, 1968. Charles Manson famously interpreted "Helter Skelter" as an apocalyptic song. McCartney stated that it is about the rise and fall of the Roman Empire— specifically, "the fall, the demise, the going down."); "Let It Be," "The Long and Winding Road" (*Let It Be*, 1970)

- Black Sabbath: "Black Sabbath," "The Wizard," "Wicked World" (*Black Sabbath*, 1970. "Wicked World" is a CD bonus track); "War Pigs" (*Paranoid*, 1970)

- David Bowie: "Five Years," "Rock 'n' Roll Suicide" (*The Rise and Fall of Ziggy Stardust and the Spiders from Mars*, 1972); "The Next Day," "Dirty Boys," "The Stars (Are Out Tonight)," "Love Is Lost," "Where Are We Now?," "Valentine's Day," "If You Can See Me," "I'd Rather Be High," "Boss of Me," "Dancing Out in Space," "How Does the Grass Grow?," "(You Will) Set the World on Fire," "You Feel So Lonely You Could Die," and "Heat" (*The Next Day*, 2013, a concept album); "Blackstar," "'Tis a Pity She Was a Whore," "Lazarus," "Sue (Or in a Season of Crime)," "Girl Loves Me," "Dollar Days," and "I Can't Give Everything Away" (*Blackstar*, 2016, a concept album released on Bowie's sixty-ninth birthday, two days before he died. He knew he had liver cancer and secretly planned the album to be his swan song. It has been speculated that it reflects his psychological process of preparing to die.)

- Jackson Browne: "Late for the Sky," "Fountain of Sorrow," "Farther On," "The Late Show," "The Road and the Sky," "For a Dancer," "Walking Slow," and "Before the Deluge" (*Late for the Sky*, 1974, a concept album described in *Rolling Stone* as an "exploration of romantic possibility in the shadow of apocalypse"); "The Barricades of Heaven," "Information Wars," "Alive in the World," "It Is One" (*Looking East*, 1996)

- Johnny Cash: "The Man Comes Around" (*American IV: The Man Comes Around*, 2002. See also the listings below of Nine Inch Nails and U2.)

- Nick Cave and the Bad Seeds: "(I'll Love You) Till the End of the World" (*Until the End of the World: Music from the Motion Picture Soundtrack*, 1991. The song is on the soundtrack of Wim Wenders's film with the same title.)

- Chicago: "Prologue, August 29, 1968," "Someday (August 29, 1968)" (*Chicago Transit Authority*, 1969. Although these comprise a two-part piece primarily about the riot that erupted at the 1968 National Democratic Convention when police forcefully attempted to stop a peaceful protest against the Vietnam War, their lyrics also clearly refer to an ultimate Apocalypse.)

- The Clash: "London Calling," "Four Horsemen" (*London Calling*, 1979); "Armagideon Time" (*Black Market Clash*, 1980)

- Leonard Cohen: "The Future," "Waiting for the Miracle," "Closing Time," "Anthem," "Democracy" (*The Future*, 1992); "You Want It Darker" (*You Want It Darker*, 2016)

- Creedence Clearwater Revival: "Bad Moon Rising" (*Green River*, 1969)

- Crosby, Stills & Nash: "Wooden Ships" (*Crosby, Stills & Nash*, 1969)

- Sheryl Crow: "Redemption Day" (*Sheryl Crow*, 1996); "Crash and Burn" (*The Globe Sessions*, 1998)
- The Dave Mathews Band: "Rhyme & Reason" (*Under the Table and Dreaming*, 1994)
- Def Leopard: "When the Walls Came Tumbling Down" (*On Through the Night*, 1980)
- The Doors: "The End" (*The Doors*, 1967. This song is also on the soundtrack of Francis Ford Coppola's film *Apocalypse Now*.)
- Bob Dylan: "Masters of War," "A Hard Rain's A-Gonna Fall," "Talkin' World War III Blues" (*The Freewheelin' Bob Dylan*, 1963); "The Times They Are A-Changin'," "With God on Our Side," "Only a Pawn in Their Game," "When the Ship Comes In" (*The Times They Are A-Changin'*, 1964); "Chimes of Freedom," "My Back Pages" (*Another Side of Bob Dylan*, 1964); "Gates of Eden," "It's Alright, Ma (I'm Only Bleeding)," "It's All Over Now, Baby Blue" (*Bringing It All Back Home*, 1965); "Ballad of a Thin Man," "Highway 61 Revisited," "Desolation Row" (*Highway 61 Revisited*, 1965); "This Wheel's on Fire" (co-written with Rick Danko of the Band) (*The Basement Tapes*, recorded between 1967 and 1975, released as an album in 1975); "All Along the Watchtower," "I Dreamed I Saw St. Augustine," "Drifter's Escape," "The Wicked Messenger" (*John Wesley Harding*, 1967); "If Not For You," "Day of the Locusts," "Time Passes Slowly," "Went to See the Gypsy," "Winterlude," "If Dogs Run Free," "New Morning," "Sign on the Window," "One More Weekend," "The Man in Me," "Three Angels," and "Father of Night" (*New Morning*, 1970, a concept album whether consciously designed as such or not. As its title suggests, it represents a post-apocalyptic period of self-renewal); "I Shall Be Released" (*Bob Dylan's Greatest Hits*, Vol. II, 1971); "Knockin' on Heaven's Door" (*Pat Garrett & Billy the Kid*, 1973); "Going, Going, Gone"

(*Planet Waves*, 1974); "Idiot Wind" (*Blood on the Tracks*, 1975); "Changing of the Guards," "Señor (Tales of Yankee Power)," "Where Are You Tonight? (Journey Through Dark Heat)" (*Street Legal*, 1978); "Gotta Serve Somebody," "Precious Angel," "I Believe in You," "Slow Train," "Gonna Change My Way of Thinking," "Do Right to Me Baby (Do Unto Others)," "When You Gonna Wake Up," "Man Gave Names to All the Animals," and "When He Returns" (*Slow Train Coming*, 1979, a concept album and Dylan's first and most Christian one); "The Groom's Still Waiting at the Altar," "Dead Man, Dead Man," "Trouble" (*Shot of Love*, 1981); "Jokerman," "License to Kill," "Union Sundown," "I and I," "Man of Peace" (*Infidels*, 1983); "When the Night Comes Falling From the Sky," "Dark Eyes" (*Empire Burlesque*, 1985); "Caribbean Wind" (*Biograph*, 1985); "Death Is Not the End" (*Down in the Groove*, 1988); "Political World," "Ring Them Bells," "Disease of Conceit" (*Oh Mercy*, 1989); "Unbelievable," "TV Talkin' Song," "2 X 2," "God Knows," "Cat's in the Well" (*Under the Red Sky*, 1990); "World Gone Wrong" (*World Gone Wrong*, 1993); "Not Dark Yet" (*Time Out of Mind*, 1997); "Things Have Changed" (*The Essential Bob Dylan*, 2000); "Ain't Talkin' " (*Modern Times*, 2006); "I Feel a Change Comin' On" (*Together Through Life*, 2009); "Pay in Blood," "Early Roman Kings," "Tempest" (an ode to the sinking of the *Titanic* with direct reference to the Book of Revelation and the motif of divine judgment) (*Tempest*, 2012); "Black Rider," "Crossing the Rubicon," "Murder Most Foul" (an ode to the assassination of John Kennedy with direct reference to the Antichrist) (*Rough and Rowdy Ways*, 2020)

- The Eagles: "Hotel California," "New Kid in Town," "Life in the Fast Lane," "Wasted Time," "Wasted Time (Reprise)," "Victim of Love," "Pretty Maids All in a Row," "Try and Love

Again," and "The Last Resort" (*Hotel California*, 1976, a concept album that may be considered apocalyptic in view of its strong theme of America's loss of innocence and its excess and decadence. As Don Henley explained, given that the band was named after America's national bird, they felt obliged to make a "bicentennial statement using California as a microcosm of the whole United States, or the whole world, if you will, and to try to wake people up and say, 'We've been okay so far, for 200 years, but we're gonna have to change if we're gonna continue to be around.'")

- Eminem: "Lose Yourself" (*8 Mile: Music from and Inspired by the Motion Picture*, 2002. This song is also on *Curtain Call: The Hits*, 2005. It is about Eminem's seizing the opportunity of rebirth after deathlike years of inner-city life, including a suicide attempt in 1997. He appeals to us to seize our own moment.)

- Florence + the Machine: "Dog Days Are Over," "Blinding" (*Lungs*, 2009); "Seven Devils" (*Ceremonials*, 2011); "Choreomania," "Cassandra," "Heaven Is Here," "Daffodil," "My Love" (*Dance Fever*, 2022)

- Peter Gabriel: "Here Comes the Flood" (*Peter Gabriel*, 1977); "Red Rain" (*So*, 1986); "My Body Is a Cage" (a cover of Arcade Fire's song) (*Scratch My Back*, 2010)

- Marvin Gaye: "What's Going On," "What's Happening Brother," "Flyin' High (In the Friendly Sky)," "Save the Children," "God Is Love," "Mercy Mercy Me (The Ecology)," "Right On," "Wholy Holy," "Inner City Blues (Make Me Wanna Holler)," "God Is Love" (a different version than the one above), and "Sad Tomorrows" (*What's Going On*, 1971, a concept album well ahead of its time with its promotion of ecological awareness. The last two songs are CD bonus tracks); "In Our Lifetime" (*In Our Lifetime?*, 1981)

- Genesis: "Supper's Ready" (*Foxtrot*, 1972)
- Eliza Gilkyson: "Slouching Towards Bethlehem" (this is not a cover of Joni Mitchell's song with the same title) (*Roses at the End of Time*, 2011)
- Tony Gilkyson: "Death in Arkansas" (This song by the guitarist of the bands Lone Justice and X was released as a solo performance on YouTube in 2010 and covered by Eliza Gilkyson, his sister, on her *Roses at the End of Time*.)
- Guns N' Roses: "Welcome to the Jungle," "Paradise City," "Sweet Child o' Mine" (*Appetite for Destruction*, 1987)
- The Jimi Hendrix Experience: "Up From the Skies" (*Axis: Bold as Love*, 1967); "Burning of the Midnight Lamp," "1983 . . . (A Merman I Should Turn to Be)," "House Burning Down," "All Along the Watchtower" (a cover of Bob Dylan's song) (*Electric Ladyland*, 1968)
- Don Henley (from his solo career after the Eagles): "The End of the Innocence," "Little Tin God," "If Dirt Were Dollars" (*The End of the Innocence*, 1989)
- Imagine Dragons: "Radioactive" (*Night Visions*, 2012)
- Jethro Tull: "Locomotive Breath" (*Aqualung*, 1971, an album largely about the decadence of religion, though Ian Anderson, the band's songwriter and lead singer, maintains that it is not a concept album); "Black Sunday," "And Further On" (*A*, 1980); "Beastie" (*Broadsword and the Beast*, 1982)
- Billy Joel: "We Didn't Start the Fire," "Storm Front," "Leningrad" (*Storm Front*, 1989)
- Elton John: "Sixty Years On," "Border Song," "The King Must Die" (*Elton John*, 1970. All tracks on the album were co-written with lyricist Bernie Taupin. Some have suggested that "Border Song" is anti-Semitic because of its complaint to Moses about the latter's people. Taupin claims it's about his alienation due to urban life and is not connected to his

Jewish roots. Eric Clapton, Aretha Franklin, Willie Nelson, and others have recorded covers of the song.)

- King Crimson: "21st Century Schizoid Man (including "Mirrors")," "I Talk to the Wind," "Epitaph (including "March for No Reason" and "Tomorrow and Tomorrow")," "Moonchild (including "The Dream and the Illusion")," and "The Court of the Crimson King (including the "Return of the Fire Witch" and "Dance of the Puppets")" (*In the Court of the Crimson King*, 1969, a concept album in the form of a dreamlike narrative)
- Led Zeppelin: "When the Levee Breaks" (*Led Zeppelin IV*, 1971. This is a reworked country blues song inspired by the Great Mississippi Flood of 1927, written and first recorded by Memphis Minnie and Kansas Joe McCoy in 1929.)
- John Lennon: "Well Well Well" (*John Lennon/Plastic Ono Band*, 1970. Lennon's screaming in the song, which emits a cathartic, inner death-and-rebirth quality, has been attributed to his treatment of primal therapy—then in vogue—with psychologist Arthur Janov; see listing for Tears for Fears below.)
- Gordon Lightfoot: "Black Day in July" (*Did She Mention My Name?*, 1968. This is a song about the Detroit race riots that began on July 23, 1967. Although Lightfoot is mostly a folk artist, this number has a folk-rock sound.)
- Bob Marley and the Wailers: "Midnight Ravers" (*Catch a Fire*, 1973); "So Much Trouble in the World" (*Survival*, 1979); "Redemption Song" (*Uprising*, 1980. This is Marley's last recorded song before he died of cancer at age 36.)
- John Mayer: "Waiting on the World to Change" (*Continuum*, 2006)
- Barry McGuire: "Eve of Destruction" (*Eve of Destruction*, 1965)
- Sarah McLachlan: "Witness," "Angels" (*Surfacing*, 1997)
- Don McLean: "American Pie" (*American Pie*, 1971. McLean has described this as a morality song about the end of

the American dream in the 1950s and '60s.); "Chain Lightning" (This is not a cover of Bruce Springsteen's song with the same title.) (*Chain Lightning*, 1978)

- Meat Loaf: "Bat Out of Hell," "Heaven Can Wait" (*Bat Out of Hell*, 1977. All tracks on the album were co-written with Jim Steinman.)
- Midnight Oil: "Beds Are Burning" (*Diesel and Dust*, 1987)
- Joni Mitchell: "Shadows and Light," "God Must Be a Boogie Man" (*Shadows and Light*, 1980); "Passion Play (When All the Slaves Are Free)," "Slouching Towards Bethlehem" (The latter is based on W. B. Yeats's poem "The Second Coming.") (*Night Ride Home*, 1991)
- The Monkees: "Goin' Down" (Originally released as the B-side to the "Daydream Believer" single, 1967. Written by Micky Dolenz, Davy Jones, Peter Tork, Michael Nesmith, and Diana Hildebrand. Video performance available at https://www.youtube.com/watch?v=xnzrGr78Mws. Also available on CD, *The Monkees: Greatest Hits*, recorded 1966–1987, released on the Rhino label in 1995. The song was used in the soundtrack for an episode of the AMC series *Breaking Bad*.)
- Van Morrison: "Rough God Goes Riding" (*The Healing Game*, 1997)
- Nine Inch Nails: "Hurt" (*The Downward Spiral*, 1994. Johnny Cash's cover of this song on his album *American IV: The Man Comes Around* prompted Trent Reznor, who wrote the song, to graciously say, "[It] isn't mine anymore."); "The Day the World Went Away" (*The Fragile*, 1999)
- Nirvana: "Smells Like Teen Spirit," "In Bloom," "Come as You Are," "Breed," "Lithium," "Polly," "Territorial Pissings," "Drain You," "Lounge Act," "Stay Away," "On a Plain," "Something in the Way," and "Endless, Nameless" (the latter hidden on later CD pressings) (*Nevermind*, 1999, a concept album whether consciously designed as such or not)

- Phish: "Friends," "Breath and Burning," "Home," "Blaze On," "Tide Turns," "Things People Do," "Waking Up Dead," "Running Out of Time," "No Men in No Man's Land," "Miss You," "I Always Wanted It This Way," "More," and "Petrichor" (*Big Boat*, 2016, a concept album whose title refers to Noah's ark)

- Pink Floyd: "Speak to Me," "Breathe (In the Air)," "On the Run," "Time," "The Great Gig in the Sky," "Money," "Us and Them," "Any Colour You Like," "Brain Damage," and "Eclipse" (*The Dark Side of the Moon*, 1973, a concept album); "In the Flesh?," "The Thin Ice," "Another Brick in the Wall, Part 1," "The Happiest Days of Our Lives," "Another Brick in the Wall, Part 2," "Mother," "Goodbye Blue Sky," "Empty Spaces," "Young Lust," "One of My Turns," "Don't Leave Me Now," "Another Brick in the Wall, Part 3," "Goodbye Cruel World," "Hey You," "Is There Anybody Out There?," "Nobody Home," "Vera," "Bring the Boys Back Home," "Comfortably Numb," "The Show Must Go On," "In the Flesh," "Run Like Hell," "Waiting for the Worms," "Stop," "The Trial," and "Outside the Wall" (*The Wall*, 1979, a concept and double album billed as a rock opera about a traumatized, depressed rock star whose social isolation leads to the creation of a metaphorical wall. The album is based on the experiences of band members Roger Waters and Syd Barrett.)

- The Police: "Bring on the Night" (*Reggatta de Blanc*, 1979); "When the World Is Running Down, You Make the Best of What's Still Around" (*Zenyatta Mondatta*, 1980); "Spirits in the Material World," "Every Little Thing She Does Is Magic," "Invisible Sun," "Hungry for You (J'aurai Toujours Faim de Toi)," "Demolition Man," "Too Much Information," "Rehumanize Yourself," "One World (Not Three)," "Omegaman," "Secret Journey," and "Darkness" (*Ghost in the Machine,* 1981, a concept album based on Arthur Koestler's book with the same title)

- Elvis Presley: "How Great Thou Art" (*How Great Thou Art,* 1967. This song, a gospel rendition of the hymn by Carl Boberg, is essentially about the glory of the Second Coming of Christ and hence is apocalyptic. Presley received fourteen Grammy nominations and three awards for his gospel recordings.)
- Prince: "1999" (*1999,* 1982)
- Radiohead: "Lucky" (*OK Computer,* 1997)
- REM: "It's the End of the World as We Know It (And I Feel Fine)" (*Document,* 1987)
- The Rolling Stones: "Paint It Black" (*Aftermath,* 1966); "Sympathy for the Devil" (*Beggars Banquet,* 1968); "Gimme Shelter" (*Let It Bleed,* 1969); "Might as Well Get Juiced" (*Bridges to Babylon,* 1997); "Back of My Hand" (distinctly a blues song), "Laugh, I Nearly Died," "Sweet Neo Con," "Driving Too Fast" (*A Bigger Bang,* 2005); "Living in a Ghost Town" (This 2019 single is about the COVID-19 pandemic and was recorded during it.)
- Simon and Garfunkel: "The Sound of Silence" (*Wednesday Morning, 3 A.M.,* 1964); "Silent Night/7 O'Clock News" (*Parsley, Sage, Rosemary and Thyme,* 1966); "Bridge Over Troubled Water" (*Bridge Over Troubled Water,* 1974)
- The Smashing Pumpkins: "Doomsday Clock" (*Zeitgeist,* 2007)
- Patti Smith: "Amerigo," "April Fool," "Fuji-san," "This Is the Girl," "Banga," "Maria," "Mosaic," "Tarkovsky (The Second Stop Is Jupiter)," "Nine," "Seneca," "Constantine's Dream," and "After the Gold Rush" (a cover of Neil Young's song) (*Banga,* 2012, a concept album described by Smith as "a reflection of our complex world—a world that is rife with chaos and beauty")
- Bruce Springsteen: "Badlands," "Adam Raised a Cain," "Something in the Night," "Candy's Room," "Racing in the Street," "The

Promised Land," "Factory," "Streets of Fire," "Prove It All Night," and "Darkness on the Edge of Town" (*Darkness on the Edge of Town*, 1978, a concept album); "Murder Incorporated" (recorded in 1982, released in 1995 on *Greatest Hits*); "Nebraska," "Atlantic City," "Mansion on the Hill," "Johnny 99," "Highway Patrolman," "State Trooper," "Used Cars," "Open All Night," "My Father's House," and "Reason to Believe" (*Nebraska*, 1982, a concept album); "Land of Hope and Dreams" (*Live in New York City*, 2001, with the E Street Band. Studio version on *Wrecking Ball*, 2012. Springsteen described this song as a hymn and as one of his best.); "Lonesome Day," "Into the Fire," "Waitin' on a Sunny Day," "Nothing Man," "Countin' on a Miracle," "Empty Sky," "Worlds Apart," "Let's Be Friends (Skin to Skin)," "Further On (Up the Road)," "The Fuse," "Mary's Place," "You're Missing," "The Rising" (Springsteen described this song as a prayer), "Paradise," and "My City of Ruins" (*The Rising*, 2002, with the E Street Band, a concept album in commemoration of 9/11); "Devils & Dust," "All the Way Home," "Reno," "Long Time Comin'," "Black Cowboys," "Maria's Bed," "Silver Palomino," "Jesus Was an Only Son" (told from the perspective of Mary as a distressed mother losing her son), "Leah," "The Hitter," "All I'm Thinking About," "Matamoros Banks" (*Devils & Dust*, 2005, probably a concept album about the Iraq War); "We Are Alive" (*Wrecking Ball*, 2012)

- Steely Dan: "King of the World" (*Countdown to Ecstasy*, 1973)
- Sting (from his solo career after the Police): "Love Is the Seventh Wave," "Russians," "Children's Crusade," "We Work the Black Seam" (*The Dream of the Blue Turtles*, 1985); "Jeremiah Blues (Part I)," "The Wild Wild Sea" (*The Soul Cages*, 1991)
- Supertramp: "Easy Does It," "Sister Moonshine," "Ain't Nobody but Me," "A Soapbox Opera," "Another Man's Woman," "Lady,"

"Poor Boy," "Just a Normal Day," "The Meaning," and
"Two of Us" (*Crisis? What Crisis?*, a concept album, 1975);
"Fool's Overture" (*Even in the Quietest Moments . . .*, 1977)

- Talking Heads: "(Nothing but) Flowers" (*Naked*, 1988)
- Tears For Fears: "The Hurting," "Mad World," "Pale Shelter," "Ideas
  as Opiates," "Memories Fade," "Suffer the Children,"
  "Watch Me Bleed," "Change," "The Prisoner," and "Start
  of the Breakdown" (*The Hurting*, 1983, a concept album
  about child abuse, trauma, and depression); "Shout," "The
  Working Hour," "Everybody Wants to Rule the World,"
  "Mothers Talk," "I Believe," "Broken," "Head Over Heels/
  Broken (Live)," and "Listen" (*Songs from the Big Chair*,
  1985, a concept album whose title refers to the chair of
  the psychotherapist in much the same fashion that the
  band's name refers to psychologist Arthur Janov's method
  of "primal scream" that aimed to replace the fears caused
  by trauma with the tears of emotional release, a form of
  therapy that John Lennon underwent with Janov himself);
  "Woman in Chains" (featuring Oleta Adams), "Badman's
  Song," "Sowing the Seeds of Love," "Advice for the Young
  at Heart," "Standing on the Corner of the Third World,"
  "Swords and Knives," "Year of the Knife," and "Famous
  Last Words" (*The Seeds of Love*, 1989, a concept album
  that, coming on the heels of the previous two, speaks to
  the process of the darkness of trauma changing into the
  light of healing and love)
- Ten Years After: "I'd Love to Change the World," "Let the Sky Fall"
  (*A Space in Time*, 1971)
- U2: "Where the Streets Have No Name," "I Still Haven't Found What
  I'm Looking For," "With or Without You," "Bullet the Blue
  Sky," "Running to Stand Still," "Red Hill Mining Town,"
  "In God's Country," "Trip Through Your Wires," "One Tree
  Hill," "Exit," and "Mothers of the Disappeared" (*The Joshua*

Tree, 1987, a concept album about America, including such themes as the search for meaning, one's relationship to oneself, the epidemic of drug addiction, the children who disappeared during Latin American dictatorships that were condoned or supported by America, and the future of the American vision); "Helter Skelter" (a cover of the Beatles' song), "All Along the Watchtower" (a cover of Bob Dylan's song), "When Love Comes to Town" (featuring B. B. King), "Love Rescue Me" (lyrics co-written with Bob Dylan), "God Part II" (it is inferred that Part I is John Lennon's "God" on his first solo album, *John Lennon/Plastic Ono Band*, 1970) (*Rattle and Hum*, 1988); "Until the End of the World" (*Achtung Baby*, 1991. This song is also on the soundtrack of Wim Wenders's film with the same title, and is different than Nick Cave's song with a similar title on the same soundtrack.); "The Wanderer" (featuring Johnny Cash) (*Zooropa*, 1993); "Vertigo," "Miracle Drug," "Sometimes You Can't Make It on Your Own," "Love and Peace or Else," "City of Blinding Lights," "All Because of You," "A Man and a Woman," "Crumbs from Your Table," "One Step Closer," "Original of the Species" (also influenced by John Lennon), and "Yahweh" (*How to Dismantle an Atomic Bomb*, 1988, a concept album)

- Tom Waits: "Earth Died Screaming" (*Bone Machine*, 1992); "How's It Gonna End" (co-written with Kathleen Brennan, Waits's wife) (*Real Gone*, 2004)
- The Wallflowers: "One Headlight," "6th Avenue Heartache" (*Bringing Down the Horse*, 1996); "Letters from the Wasteland," "I've Been Delivered," "Up From Under" (*Breach*, 2000); "Everybody Out of the Water," "Three Ways," "Too Late to Quit" (*Red Letter Days*, 2002); "The Passenger," "God Says Nothing Back" (*Rebel, Sweetheart*, 2005) (Jakob Dylan, the band's songwriter and lead singer, is Bob Dylan's son.)

- The Who: "Overture," "It's a Boy," "1921," "Amazing Journey," "Sparks," "Eyesight to the Blind (The Hawker)," "Christmas," "Cousin Kevin," "The Acid Queen," "Underture," "Do You Think It's Alright?," "Fiddle About," "Pinball Wizard," "There's a Doctor," "Go to the Mirror!," "Tommy, Can You Hear Me?," "Smash the Mirror," "Sensation," "Miracle Cure," "Sally Simpson," "I'm Free," "Welcome," "Tommy's Holiday Camp," and "We're Not Gonna Take It" (*Tommy*, 1969, a concept and double album billed as a rock opera about a traumatized boy); "Behind Blue Eyes" (*Who's Next*, 1971)

- Amy Winehouse: "Rehab," "You Know I'm No Good," "Me and Mr Jones," "Just Friends," "Back to Black," "Love Is a Losing Game," "Tears Dry on Their Own," "Wake Up Alone," "Some Unholy War," and "He Can Only Hold Her" (*Back to Black*, 2006, a concept album insofar as it is autobiographical)

- Neil Young: "After the Goldrush," "Don't Let It Bring You Down" (*After the Goldrush*, 1970); "See the Sky About to Rain," "Revolution Blues" (written from the viewpoint of Charles Manson, whom Young personally knew), "On the Beach" (*On the Beach*, 1974); "Rockin' in the Free World" (*Freedom*, 1989); "Falling from Above," "Double," "Devil's Sidewalk," "Leave the Driving," "Carmichael," "Bandit," "Grandpa's Interview," "Bringin' Down Dinner," "Sun Green," and "Be the Rain" (*Greendale*, 2003, a concept album and rock opera)

AUTHOR'S NOTE

In a certain way, this book is a natural sequel to an earlier one, *The Divine Mind: Exploring the Psychological History of God's Inner Journey.* That book tells the story of what happened to the biblical God. This book tells the story of what happened to us *because* of what happened to the biblical God. By "us" I mean all of us who live in a culture that has been historically shaped by Judaism, Christianity, or Islam. Regardless of whether or not we believe in God, or in this particular God, this historical factor has both profoundly and subtly influenced who we are.

It is not necessary for you to have read the earlier book in order to appreciate this one. Should you be interested, it could just as easily be read after, especially in view of its discussion of the mature, mystical God that the primitive, biblical one evolved into. Either way, his story offers much insight into who we, too, can evolve into, since his journey is a metaphor for our own. Though this book may be considered the sequel, that one explores the ultimate, mystical antidote to our god complex. This antidote is our own innate and inner godhood, also known as our higher self—the part of us that is the most authentic and the least inflated, and to which we all have access if we are open to it.

ACKNOWLEDGMENTS

Edward Edinger once wisely said, "Be careful what you write because you'll have to live it." Writing a book about a tormented god and his ghostly apparitions in history and culture had its own torments and haunting effects. A number of people compensated for these simply by enriching my research and writing process, and I want to thank them. Some of their contributions never made it into the final product for editorial reasons, but the contributors nevertheless deserve to be thanked.

John Köehler is everything one could hope for in a publisher. With an innovative approach that is very proactive in engaging the author in all aspects of production, he runs a dynamic operation. I'm honored that he accepted my book for inclusion in the Köehler collection.

The Köehler team is remarkable. Joe Coccaro, executive editor, smoothly ushered in and guided the publishing process. Hannah Woodlan was a most skillful editor with a fine eye for subtle details while not losing sight of the big picture. Lauren Sheldon, a gifted graphic designer, created a book cover that is, as John put it so well, "supernatural."

Kimberley Cameron of Kimberley Cameron & Associates was not only a sharp and shrewd agent but also a creative partner with an uncanny sense of what would work well in the book and what would not. Known as the "Queen of Titles," she came up with the book's subtitle. She is also one of the most kind and patient people I've ever met.

Deborah Natoli, a thoughtful and generous friend, was especially helpful in the final phase of birthing the book. Stacy Kauffman of Annie Jennings PR was a tireless advocate not only for this book but also previous ones.

Randall Mishoe kindly made available to me his insightful and fascinating diploma thesis, "The Yahweh Complex: A Case Study in Protestant Fundamentalism." Undertaken in 2003 at the C. G. Jung Institute

– Boston (now known as the C. G. Jung Institute of New England), it is the first extensive clinical treatment of the Yahweh complex and an important contribution to the fields of psychology and religion.

My loving brother, George Gellert, brought to my attention Calvin Coolidge's depression. My dear cousin Agi Orsi and close friend Jerry Barclay never failed to ask how the book was going.

Wendy Goldman Rohm was very generous in sharing material from her own research on Bill Gates. The late Gilda Frantz introduced me to Will Roscoe's work on Native Americans and their sexual attitudes, so contrary to those of our patriarchal traditions. I am grateful to Andrew Abrams for introducing me to the notion of a lonely god. Conversations with Matilde Marcolli led to my discovery of an Allen Ginsberg anecdote that I intended for the chapter on living with the Yahweh complex.

Paul Falzone brought the film *Malice* to my attention. Vanessa Glasberg encouraged me to read Eliot Rodger's manifesto on the internet. Márton Csókás reminded me of Shakespeare's presentation of Lady Macbeth and kindly made available material on the Italian and French Mafias. Samoan Barish made me aware of the letters and turbulent relationship between Freud and Sándor Ferenczi. She also introduced me to Barbara Grizzuti Harrison's *An Accidental Autobiography*. Chris Miller turned me on to Eminem.

Jeremy Poole, official national tourist guide of South Africa and tour guide with Smartours, gave me an appreciation of Nelson Mandela that burned in my heart. Norman Weinstein, my good friend since childhood, is responsible for making the arrangements for both of us for that memorable trip to Africa.

And last but certainly not least, I remain forever indebted to Jack Miles for his Pulitzer Prize–winning book, *God: A Biography*. Together with Jung's *Answer to Job*, it dramatically changed my thinking on the Abrahamic God and his profound transformation in the Hebrew Bible.

Notes

Excerpts from the Hebrew Bible are taken from *Tanakh, The Holy Scriptures: The New JPS Translation According to the Traditional Hebrew Text* (Jewish Publication Society, Philadelphia, 1985), hereafter cited as NJPS. (*Tanakh* is an acronym of the first Hebrew letter of each of the Hebrew Bible's three subdivisions: Torah ["Teaching," or the Five Books of Moses], Nevi'im ["Prophets"], and Kethuvim ["Writings"]—hence, *TaNaKh*.) Excerpts are also taken from the Holy Bible, King James Version, hereafter cited as KJV; the Holy Bible, Revised Standard Version, hereafter cited as RSV; *The Jerusalem Bible*, Reader's Edition (Doubleday, Garden City, NY, 1966), hereafter cited as JB; and *The New Oxford Annotated Bible with the Apocrypha*, Revised Standard Version (Oxford University Press, New York, 1977), hereafter cited as NOAB. No translation is cited when any translation suffices for the purpose intended.

All referenced websites were accessed from 2016 to 2023.

Epigraphs

"When there is a light in the darkness": C. G. Jung, Mysterium Coniunctionis: An Inquiry into the Separation and Synthesis of Psychic Opposites in Alchemy (1955–56), Vol. 14 of The Collected Works of C. G. Jung, trans. by R. F. C. Hull, Princeton University Press, Bollingen Series XX, Princeton, NJ, 1970, par. 345. The actual quote of John 1:5 in KJV is "And the light shineth in darkness; and darkness comprehended it not."

"The degree of character flexibility": Wilhelm Reich, *Character Analysis,* 3rd edition, trans. Vincent R. Carfagno, ed. Mary Higgins and Chester M. Raphael, Farrar, Straus and Giroux, New York, 1945, 1972, p. 156.

"The god that you most revere": Patricia Berry, "A Hole in the Heart: Why We Fail at Love," Public Programs, C. G. Jung Institute of Los Angeles, October 22, 2010.

Prologue: The God of Our Fathers

"God is no saint": Jack Miles, *God: A Biography,* Vintage Books/Random House, New York, 1996, pp. 6–7.

"How bold one gets": Sigmund Freud, letter to his fiancée, Martha Bernays, June 27, 1882, in *Letters of Sigmund Freud 1873–1939,* ed. Ernst L. Freud, trans. Tania Stern and James Stern, Hogarth Press, London, 1961.

"His sneezings flash lightning": Job 41:10–7, NJPS.

"I know it when I see it": Potter Stewart, in the US Supreme Court case, *Jacobellis v. Ohio,* 378 US 184, 1964. See https://en.wikipedia.org/wiki/I_know_it_when_I_see_it.

"was certainly a volcano-god": Sigmund Freud, *Moses and Monotheism,* Vintage Books/Random House, 1939, p. 39. Freud is here drawing upon the work of historian Eduard Meyer, *Die Israeliten und ihre Nachbarstämme* (1906).

He is known as Yahweh (or Jehovah): However, the medieval word "Jehovah" does not accurately represent any form of God's name as it was ever used in Hebrew. See NOAB, p. xiv.

As journalist Lance Morrow writes: Lance Morrow, *Evil: An Investigation*, Basic Books/Perseus Books, New York, 2003, p. 28.

"The fear of the Lord is the beginning of wisdom": Ps. 111:10, KJV. Also repeated in Prov. 9:10 and elsewhere.

"The Lord is a man of war": Exod. 15:3, KJV and RSV.

"not a theological god at all": Northrop Frye, endorsement on the back cover of *The Book of J*, trans. David Rosen, interpreted by Harold Bloom, Grove Weidenfeld, New York, 1990.

The Wotan complex that took hold of Nazi Germany: See C. G. Jung, "Wotan" (1936), in *Civilization in Transition*, Vol. 10 of The Collected Works of C. G. Jung, trans. R. F. C. Hull, Princeton University Press, Bollingen Series XX, Princeton, NJ, 1978. See also Michael Gellert, "The Eruption of the Shadow in Nazi Germany," Psychological Perspectives, 1998, 37, Issue 1, pp. 72–89. Also available at http://www.michaelgellert.com/pdfs/eruption-of-shadow-in-nazi-germany.pdf.

we can think of archetypes as instincts of the psyche: See C. G. Jung, *Psychological Types,* Vol. 6 of The Collected Works of C. G. Jung, trans. R. F. C. Hull and H. G. Baynes, Princeton University Press, Bollingen Series XX, Princeton, NJ, 1971, par. 624; C. G. Jung, "Instinct and the Unconscious" (1948), in The Structure and Dynamics of the Psyche, Vol. 8 of The Collected Works of C. G. Jung, trans. R. F. C. Hull, Princeton University Press, Bollingen Series XX, Princeton, NJ, 1978, pars. 270, 277.

"Jack Miles . . . notes his unique history of isolation": Miles, *op. cit.*, p. 231.

Other scholars add that he was lonely: Rabbi Pinchas Peli's idea that God created the universe and man because he was lonely is known from lectures he gave in Israel. Psychologist Marie-Louise von Franz discusses the loneliness of different gods in her volume *Creation Myths* (New York: Spring Publications, 1972), pp. 117–18. Independently of this, I am grateful to Andrew Abrams for first introducing me to this notion. However, this idea is by no means new nor distinctly Jewish. The Celtic gods created man because they too were lonely. The Hindu *Rig Veda* informs us of the origin of the cosmos in the divine's desire for kinship: "Thereafter rose Desire in the beginning, Desire, the primal seed and germ of Spirit. Sages who searched with their heart's thought discovered the existent's kinship in the non-existent." ("The Creation Hymn," *Rig Veda* 10, 129:4, trans. Ralph T. H. Griffith, 1896, http://www.sacred-texts.com/hin/fend/rv10129.htm.) God's loneliness was a theme in soulful Negro spirituals and early African American poetry. The following is from James Weldon Johnson's poem "The Creation": "And God stepped out on space, / And He looked around and said, / *I'm lonely – / I'll make me a world.*" Yet after making it, he was still lonely. And so, "With His head in His hands, / God thought and thought, / Till he thought, *I'll make me a man!*" (*The Book of American Negro Poetry,* ed. James Weldon Johnson, Harcourt, Brace and Co., New York, 1922)

"I the Lord thy God am a jealous God": Exod. 20:5, KJV.

Yahweh's orchestration of the Babylonian captivity of some ten thousand citizens: the number ten thousand taken from "The Jewish Temples: The Babylonian Exile," Jewish Virtual Library, https://www.jewishvirtuallibrary.org/the-babylonian-exile.

Miles shows how this victorious climax contrasts with the conclusion of the Old Testament: Miles, *op. cit.*, pp. 18, 16, 411–12. Miles explains how the Hebrew Bible (sometimes also referred to as the Jewish Bible) and the Christian revision of it, known as the Old Testament, are two different versions of the same scripture, giving, for all intents and purposes, alternate histories of what happened to both the Israelites and their God. Not only does the arc of their story vary according to which narrative you read, but also the meaning of events in the larger scheme of things varies. Both the Hebrew Bible and the Old Testament consist of three parts, but arranged differently. Thus:

The Hebrew Bible:	*The Old Testament:*
I. The Five Books of Moses	I. The Five Books of Moses
II. The Prophets	II. The Writings
III. The Writings	III. The Prophets

Both agree on the foundation of the Bible—on the Five Books of Moses—but the Old Testament reverses the order of the last two categories. Why? We can only speculate, but the demands of history give us some hints. Miles suggests that the main thrust behind the Christian editor's rearrangement was presumably his wish to better announce the New Testament by concluding the Old Testament with the prophets. This would more tangibly connect them to the Christian belief that the life of Christ fulfills their prophecies. The Old Testament editor was as conscientious about linking the Hebrew and Christian scriptures to each other as were the New Testament authors. See also Michael Gellert, "God in the Hebrew Bible vs. the Old Testament," Appendix I in *The Divine Mind: Exploring the Psychological History of God's Inner Journey*, Prometheus Books, Amherst, New York, 2018, pp. 211–14.

The Bible portrays him strolling there: Gen. 3:8, NJPS.

Or so the Talmud states: Rabbi Simeon ben Yohai, Jerusalem Talmud, Taanit 1:1. Also qtd. in Jacob Neusner, *The Talmud: What It Is and What It Says*, Rowman & Littlefield, Lanham, MD, 2006, p. 15. The exact quotation is "To every place to which the Israelites went into exile, the presence of God went with them into exile."

When Adam and Eve fell, they took God down with them: This is not a novel idea. The Kabbalistic *Zohar*, or *Book of Splendor*, raises the question of who threw whom out of the garden of Eden and radically concludes that it was man who threw God out. See the *Zohar*, Be-Reshit 1:53b, Pritzker Edition, 11 vols., trans. Daniel C. Matt, Stanford University Press, Stanford, CA, 2004, Vol. 1: pp. 297–98. The specific passage is "Rabbi El'azar said, 'We do not know who divorced whom: if the blessed Holy One divorced Adam, or not. But the word is transposed: *He drove out Et*—precisely! Who drove out *Et*? *Adam*. *Adam* actually drove out *Et*!'" In the *Zohar*, *Et* is a name for the *Shekhinah*, a concept that, like Chochmah, whom we shall shortly discuss, represents the feminine side of God.

His "stiff-necked" people (as he now calls them): Deut. 9:13, NJPS.

"Lo, I am bringing against you": Jer. 5:15, 17, NJPS.

"Assuredly, parents shall eat their children": Ezek. 5:10, 12–13, NJPS.

"A sword, a sword is sharpened": Ezek. 21:9–10, 15, RSV.

"The hand of the Lord lay heavy": 1 Sam. 5:6, 5:9, NJPS.

"I was brokenhearted": Ezek. 6: 9, NJPS.

Compels him to reflect on his dark side: See C. G. Jung, *Answer to Job* (1952), in *Psychology and Religion: West and East*, Vol. 11 of *The Collected Works of C. G. Jung*, trans. R. F. C. Hull, Princeton University Press, Bollingen Series XX, Princeton, NJ, 1973. Also available as a separate volume published by Princeton University Press, Bollingen Paperback Editions, Princeton, NJ, 1973.

"if Job gains knowledge of God": Jung, *Answer to Job*, par. 617.

"Whoever knows God": *ibid.*

"The encounter with the creature": *ibid*; par. 686.

"I form the light, and create darkness": Isa. 45:7, KJV.

As Jung explains, an antinomy: Jung, *Answer to Job*, par. 567.

As biblical scholar Richard Elliott Friedman points out: *The Disappearance of God: A Divine Mystery*, Little, Brown, Boston, 1995, Chapter 5, "The Struggle with God," section entitled "Merciful and Gracious God," pp. 106–8. This book was also published as *The Hidden Face of God*, HarperCollins, New York, 1996. The phrase Friedman quotes is from Exod. 34:6–7, translation his own except for the word "forgiving," which is used in most translations and for which he substituted "bearing." (I prefer "forgiving" because "to bear" means to tolerate and carry, while "to forgive" goes a step further by mercifully releasing the other from the burden of their transgression.) Friedman cites the following locations at which God's description of himself is reiterated in one form or another: Num. 14:18–19; Jon. 4:2; Joel 2:13; Ps. 86:15, 103:8, 145:8; 2 Chron. 30:9; Neh. 9:17, 9:31; and Mic. 7:18.

Friedman further reminds us that the text is replete: God blessed Sarah: Gen. 11:30, 17:16, 21:2; he consoled Hagar: Gen. 21:17–18; he spared Sodom: Gen. 18:16–33; he spared Isaac and blessed Abraham: Gen. 22:1–18; he blessed Jacob: Gen. 27–50 (the visionary foresight is in Gen. 49); he protected Joseph: Gen. 39–50; he emancipated his enslaved people: Exod. 1–40; he forgave David: 2 Sam. 11–12 (the episode of David murdering his general is described here, and the retribution, forecast in 2 Sam. 12:11–12, continues through the following chapters until 2 Sam. 19); and he oversaw the end of the Babylonian exile: Ezra 1–10 and Neh. 1–13.

"And God saw all that He had made": Gen. 1:31, NJPS.

It helped introduce the idea of progress: See Thomas Cahill's treatment of this in *The Gifts of the Jews: How a Tribe of Desert Nomads Changed the Way Everyone Thinks and Feels*, Nan A. Talese/Doubleday, New York, 1998. See also Mircea Eliade, *The Myth of Eternal Return or, Cosmos and History*, trans. Willard R. Trask, Princeton University Press, Bollingen Series XLVI, Princeton, NJ, 1971.

It helped create a blueprint for democracy: See Max I. Dimont, *Jews, God and History,* Signet, New York, 1962, pp. 47–48. Along the same lines, Harvard president Samuel Langdon wrote in 1775, "The Jewish government was a perfect republic" (qtd. in Bruce Feiler, *America's Prophet: Moses and the American Story*, William Morrow/HarperCollins, New York, 2009, p. 60).

Part I: Yahweh in Our Souls

"An archetypal force has no true care": James Hillman, "Puer Wounds and Ulysses' Scar," in *Puer Papers*, ed. James Hillman, Spring Publications, Dallas, Texas, 1987, p. 112.

Chapter 1: How to Recognize the Yahweh Complex

"Don't live in the past, my brother says": Barbara Grizzuti Harrison, *An Accidental Autobiography*, Houghton Mifflin, Boston, 1997, p. 76.

"Now I know what a ghost is": Salman Rushdie, *The Satanic Verses,* Viking Press, New York, 1985, p. 540.

"The gods have become diseases": C. G. Jung, "Commentary on 'The Secret of the Golden Flower' " (1957), *Alchemical Studies,* Vol. 13 of *The Collected Works of C. G. Jung*, trans. R. F. C. Hull, Princeton University Press, Bollingen Series XX, Princeton, NJ, 1970, par. 54.

"circles of thoughts and interests of strong affective value": Sigmund Freud, "Preliminary Hypotheses and Technique of Interpretation," Sixth Lecture, *A General Introduction to Psycho-Analysis,* (1915–17), in *The Major Works of Sigmund Freud,* Vol. 54 in *Great Books of the Western World, Encyclopaedia Britannica*, trans. Joan Riviere, editor in chief Mortimer J. Adler, Chicago, 1994, p. 488.

"A collective problem": C. G. Jung, *Memories, Dreams, Reflections,* Vintage Books/Random House, New York, 1965, pp. 233–34. Erik Erikson also remarks upon the complex range of factors influencing individual problems: "Any historical and personological item is always determined by many more forces and trends working with and upon each other than a sparing explanation can cover. Often a certain extravagance in searching for all possible relevances is the only way to get an inkling of the laws which determine the mutual influence upon each other of some factors, and the mutual exclusion of others" (Erik H. Erikson, *Young Man Luther: A Study in Psychoanalysis and History* [1958], W. W. Norton, New York, 1962, p. 51).

At worst, this can lead to the kind of mass movement that Jung described as a "psychic epidemic": Jung writes: "Indeed, it is becoming ever more obvious that it is not famine, not earthquakes, not microbes, not cancer but man himself who is man's greatest danger to man, for the simple reason that there is no adequate protection against psychic epidemics, which are infinitely more devastating than the worst of natural catastrophes. The supreme danger which threatens individuals as well as whole nations is a *psychic danger*. Reason has proved itself completely powerless, precisely because its arguments have an effect only on the conscious mind and not on the unconscious. The greatest danger of all comes from the masses, in whom the effects of the unconscious pile up cumulatively and the reasonableness of the conscious mind is stifled. Every mass organization is a latent danger just as much as a heap of dynamite is. It lets loose effects which no man wants and no man can stop" (C. G. Jung, *The Symbolic Life: Miscellaneous Writings,* Vol. 18 of *The Collected Works of C. G. Jung, op. cit.,* par. 1358). On psychic epidemics as developments of a "sort of collective possession" (i.e., a collective complex or archetype), see "The Undiscovered Self (1958)," *Civilization in Transition,* Vol. 10 of *The Collected Works of C. G. Jung,* trans. R. F. C. Hull, Princeton University Press, Bollingen Series XX, Princeton, NJ, 1978, par. 490.

He observed a classical example of this in the case of Nazism: see C. G. Jung, *The Archetypes and the Collective Unconscious,* Vol. 9, Part I of *The Collected Works of C. G. Jung,* trans. R. F. C. Hull, Princeton University Press, Bollingen Series XX, Princeton, NJ, 1977, par. 227; "After the Catastrophe (1946)," *Civilization in Transition,* par. 432; and "Epilogue to 'Essays on Contemporary Events' (1946)," *ibid.,* par. 471. See also my article, "The Eruption of the Shadow in Nazi Germany," in *Psychological Perspectives,* Vol. 37, Issue 1, Los Angeles, 1998, pp. 72–89.

He explains that the German people developed an inferiority complex: C. G. Jung, "Diagnosing the Dictators" (1938), originally published in *Cosmopolitan,* now available in *C. G. Jung Speaking: Interviews and Encounters,* eds. William McGuire and R. F. C. Hull, Princeton University Press, Bollingen Series XX, Princeton, NJ, 1993, p. 122.

The god complex was first identified by psychoanalyst Ernest Jones in 1913: All material on his crucial contribution is based on Ernest Jones, "The God Complex: The Belief that One Is God, and the Resulting Character Traits," Chapter 5 in *Essays in Applied Psycho-Analysis,* International Psycho-Analytical Press/International Psycho-Analytical Library, No. 5, London, 1923, pp. 204–26. This chapter was originally published in the *Internationale Zeitschrift für Psychoanalyse,* 1913. Also available at https://archive.org/stream/essaysinappliedp032427mbp/essaysinappliedp032427mbp_djvu.txt.

By 1934, Jung was, along with Jungian analysts Erich Neumann and James Kirsch: See Erich Neumann, in *Analytical Psychology in Exile: The Correspondence of C. G. Jung and Erich Neumann,* ed. Martin Liebscher, trans. Heather McCartney, Princeton University Press, Philemon Series, Princeton, New Jersey, 2015, pp. 21, 49.

As Jung later does: See C. G. Jung, letter to Robert C. Smith, June 29, 1960, *C. G. Jung Letters,* eds. Gerhard Adler and Aniela Jaffé, trans. R. F. C. Hull, Vol. 2, 1951–1961, Princeton University Press, Bollingen Series XCV, Princeton, NJ, 1975, pp. 570–73. Jung here states that the god complex "is an emotionally 'toned' complex like the father- or mother-complex or Oedipus complex. . . . 'God' within the frame of psychology is an *autonomous complex, a dynamic image.*" Also available in Edward F. Edinger, *The New God-Image: A Study of Jung's Key Letters Concerning the Evolution of the Western God-Image*, Chiron Publications, Wilmette, Illinois, 1996, pp. 138–40. I am grateful to Randall Mishoe, whose work is cited below, for directing me to this passage.

"We can identify a state of inflation": Edward F. Edinger, *Ego and Archetype: Individuation and the Religious Function of the Psyche*, Penguin Books, Baltimore, 1974, p. 14. First published by G. P. Putnam's Sons, New York, for the C. G. Jung Foundation for Analytical Psychology, New York, 1972. Edinger's quotation "'Vengeance is mine,' saith the Lord" is based on Deut. 32:35, Rom. 12:19, and Heb. 10:30, RSV.

Yahweh introduced the notion of progress into a Near Eastern world: See Thomas Cahill, *The Gift of the Jews: How a Desert Tribe of Nomads Changed the Way Everyone Thinks and Feels*, Nan A. Talese/Anchor Books, New York, 1998.

"The question is, 'Do I have a 'God Complex?'": *Malice*, dir. Harold Becker, Columbia Pictures, 1993. Available at http://www.huffingtonpost.com/2013/10/01/alec-baldwin-i-am-god-malice_n_4019992.html. Italics added according to film version.

"Stop! Now this one upsets me": *Whiplash*, dir. Damien Chazelle, Sony Pictures Classics, 2014. Available at http://www.sonyclassics.com/awards-information/whiplash_screenplay.pdf. The script used here is based on the screenplay and not the actual film, which has different names for some of the characters.

The Israelite whose execution Yahweh ordered: Num. 15:32–36.

The fifty thousand Israelites he slaughtered: 1 Sam. 6:19.

"Yahweh the Law-giver who is also judge and persecutor": J. Randall Mishoe, "The Yahweh Complex: A Case Study in Protestant Fundamentalism," an unpublished diploma thesis written for the C. G. Jung Institute–Boston, 2003, pp. 38, 56, 106. I am very grateful to Dr. Mishoe for his kindness in sharing his excellent thesis with me.

as did Jung: Jung wrote that Yahweh's "thunderings at Job so completely miss the point that one cannot help but see how much he is occupied with himself" (C. G. Jung, *Answer to Job* [1952], in *Psychology and Religion: West and East*, Vol. 11 of *The Collected Works of C. G. Jung*, trans. R. F. C. Hull, Princeton University Press, Bollingen Series XX, Princeton, NJ, 1973, par. 587).

Yahweh suffered from a narcissistic personality disorder: Mishoe, pp. 47–50. For other forms of grandiosity, apart from perfectionism, Mishoe cites, on p. 48, Nancy McWilliams, *Psychoanalytic Diagnosis: Understanding Personality Structure in the Clinical Process*, Guilford Press, New York, 1994, p. 177. These forms include self-righteousness, pride, contempt, defensive self-sufficiency, vanity, and superiority, all of which Yahweh also demonstrates.

"splitting of instinct and spirit": *ibid.*, p. 5.

"The complex may shatter one's life": *ibid.*, p.105.

"conflict of being torn": *ibid.*, p. 108.

Jungian analyst Manisha Roy illustrates: Manisha Roy, "When a Religious Archetype Becomes a Cultural Complex: Puritanism in America," *The Cultural Complex: Contemporary Jungian Perspectives on Psyche and Society*, eds. Thomas Singer and Samuel L. Kimbles, Brunner-Routledge/Taylor & Francis Group, Hove, United Kingdom and New York, 2004, p. 72. See also my review of this excellent anthology in *Psychological Perspectives,* Vol. 48, Issue 2, 2005, pp. 321–25.

He admitted as much in Isaiah: Isa. 45:7, KJV.

"If He cannot trust His own servants": Job 4:18–20, NJPS.

Perun was . . . a brutal, detached, temperamental god whose attributes can be observed in the Russian leadership style: see Stanislav V. Shekshnia, Sheila M. Puffer, and Daniel J. McCarthy, "Cultural Myths and Leadership in Russia," Faculty & Research Working Paper, INSEAD, Fontainebleau, France, 2007, p. 4. Available at http://www.insead.edu/facultyresearch/research/doc.cfm?did=2717. Perun's citadel was on top of the World Tree, which in Slavic and other mythology connected the world with the underworld below and the heavens above.

Cognitive distortions, according to cognitive behavioral therapist David Burns: David D. Burns, *The Feeling Good Handbook: Using the New Mood Therapy in Everyday Life,* William Morrow, New York, 1989.

The Hebrew Bible is very much the story of God's childhood and adolescence: In *God: A Biography* (Vintage Books/Random House, New York, 1996), Jack Miles presents a different chronology of Yahweh's development, seeing his retreat from history in the Writings—the third and final part of the Hebrew Bible—as his old age. This is probably because he treats each of the scriptures of Judaism, Christianity, and Islam as a self-contained, complete document in its own right. He thus approaches the Hebrew Bible as a complete arc of God's development, whereas I approach his life span as spreading across the entire history and canvas of the Abrahamic religious imagination. In my view, the Abrahamic God reaches mature adulthood not in the Writings but in the medieval mysticism of all three Abrahamic traditions—namely, the Kabbalah, Christian mysticism, and Sufism. The fact that his temperament in the Writings resembles old age is because the adolescent moratorium also tends to be saturnine and withdrawn. See Michael Gellert, *The Divine Mind: Exploring the Psychological History of God's Inner Journey,* Prometheus Books, Amherst, New York, 2018.

What Erik Erikson calls the adolescent moratorium: Erik H. Erikson, *Childhood and Society,* W. W. Norton, New York, 1963, pp. 262–63; *Young Man Luther: A Study in Psychoanalysis and History* (1958), W. W. Norton, New York, 1962, pp. 43, 99–104.

Literary critic Harold Bloom's incisive *Jesus and Yahweh,* for instance, notes the following traits: Harold Bloom, *Jesus and Yahweh: The Names Divine,* Riverhead, New York, 2005, pp. 99, 106, 110, 111, 117, 121, 132, 133, 137, 138, 148, 149, 154, 159, 169, 172, 175, 176–77, 213–14.

"really busted up": Michael Richards, *Late Show with David Letterman,* November 20, 2006. Available at https://www.youtube.com/watch?v=EC26RI-Ria8.

"I'm not a racist. That's what's so insane about this": *ibid.*

"get to the force field of this hostility": *ibid.*

In an interview, Smith's mother said: Carolyn Smith, interview with Sherry Williams and 6ABC Digital Staff, "Will Smith's Mother Speaks About Oscar's Confrontation: 'First Time I've Ever Seen Him Go Off,'" "6ABC Action News," ABC, March 29, 2022.

Punish them by sending epidemics, droughts, or poisonous serpents: On epidemics, see Num. 14:37 and 2 Sam. 24:15; on droughts, see Jer. 14:1–16 and Hag.1:1–11; and on poisonous serpents, see Num. 21:6.

Drowning the Egyptian army in the Sea of Reeds: Exod. 14:5–31.

Stopping the sun's movement across the sky: Josh. 10:12–14.

The actual commandment is: This commandment is repeated twice in the Hebrew Bible, at Exod. 20:7 and Deut. 5:11. This translation is from the KJV.

"We are still as much possessed by autonomous psychic contents": C. G. Jung, "Commentary on 'The Secret of the Golden Flower,'" *op. cit.*, par. 54.

His father, Hutton Gibson, was a known Holocaust denier and conspiracy theorist: See https://en.wikipedia.org/wiki/Hutton_Gibson.

He believed she would go to hell: Jeannette Walls with Ashley Pearson, "Mel Gibson Says His Wife Could Be Going to Hell," *Today*, MSN, NBC News, available at http://www.today.com/id/4224452/ns/today-entertainment/t/mel-gibson-says-his-wife-could-be-going-hell/#.VjcTE50C0U.

what has been described as an egocentric individualism: See C. S. Wyatt, "Søren Kierkegaard: The Original Leap of Faith," *The Existential Primer*, 2020, section on "Uncertainty" at http://www.tameri.com/csw/exist/kierkegaard.shtml.

"completely lacks any philosophy of life": Søren Kierkegaard, *From the Papers of One Still Living (fen endnu Levendes Papirer)*, Copenhagen, September 7, 1838. See "First Period: Works of Youth (1834–42), From the Papers of One Still Living," *D. Anthony Storm's Commentary on Kierkegaard* at http://sorenkierkegaard.org/from-papers-one-still-living.html.

"Bitterness is like cancer": widely attributed to Maya Angelou.

Bitterness is what we are left with: This is a core principle of alchemy. See C. G. Jung, *Mysterium Coniunctionis: An Inquiry into the Separation and Synthesis of Psychic Opposites in Alchemy* (1955–56), Vol. 14 of *The Collected Works of C. G. Jung*, trans. by R. F. C. Hull, Princeton University Press, Bollingen Series XX, Princeton, NJ, 1970, par. 330.

According to Nixon aide Egil "Bud" Krogh": qtd. in Peter Carlson, "When Elvis Met Nixon," *Smithsonian Magazine*, December 2010. Available at https://www.smithsonianmag.com/history/when-elvis-met-nixon-69892425/.

Nixon complied and there were a number of occasions: See "Whatever Happened to Elvis Presley's Federal Badge?," History Stack Exchange. Available at https://history.stackexchange.com/questions/47557/whatever-happened-to-elvis-presleys-federal-badge.

"Come, you spirits": William Shakespeare, *Macbeth*, Act I, Scene 5.

She has a delightful persona but underneath: See Christopher Byron, *Martha Inc.: The Incredible Story of Martha Stewart Living Omnimedia*, John Wiley and Sons, New York, 2002.

He fell into a deep depression: See "President Coolidge's Burden," Jack Beatty, *The Atlantic Monthly*, December 2003. Also available at https://www.theatlantic.com/magazine/archive/2003/12/president-coolidges-burden/303175/.

"I do not know why such a price": qtd. in Michael Platt, "The Life of Calvin Coolidge," in *Modern Age* 36, No. 4, Summer 1994. Available at: https://www.gw.edu/_elements/userfiles/file/Platt%20-%20Coolidge%20Modern%20Age.pdf.

Robert Gilbert quotes an associate of Coolidge's: Robert E. Gilbert, *The Tormented President: Calvin Coolidge, Death, and Clinical Depression*, ABC–CLIO/Praeger Publishers, Westport, CT, and London, 2003. Also available in Jack Beatty's article, *op. cit.*

"A living God afflicts our reason like a sickness": C. G. Jung, *The Red Book: Liber Novus*, ed. Sonu Shamdasani, Philemon Series, W. W. Norton & Co., New York, London, 2009, p. 338.

"I am the chosen one": qtd. by Chris Cillizza, "Yes, Donald Trump Really Believes He Is the 'Chosen One,'" CNN, August 24, 2019.

"I'd like to remind everyone": Donald Trump, Twitter, July 11, 2019 (account suspended).

Lance Dodes and a host of other mental health professionals: Lance Dodes, "To the Editors of the *New York Times*," 2017. Available at http://www.drlancedodes.com/new-york-times-letter/.

Dodes later added that in Trump's mind: interview with Lawrence O'Donnell, "The Last Word With Lawrence O'Donnell," MSNBC, January 8, 2020.

As journalist Mehdi Hasan commented: Mehdi Hasan, *The Mehdi Hasan Show*, MSNBC, February 28, 2021.

The biblical episode of the golden calf: See Exod. 32.

"Trump felt compelled to go to war with the world": Tony Schwartz, "I Wrote 'The Art of the Deal' with Trump. His Self-sabotage Is Rooted in His Past," *Washington Post*, May 16, 2017. Available at https://www.washingtonpost.com/posteverything/wp/2017/05/16/i-wrote-the-art-of-the-deal-with-trump-his-self-sabotage-is-rooted-in-his-past/?utm_term=.6eb62f2384c3.

"You have to dominate": Donald Trump, qtd. in "READ: President Trump's Call with US Governors Over Protests," CNN, June 1, 2020. Available at https://www.cnn.com/2020/06/01/politics/wh-governors-call-protests/index.html.

"nobody does petty like the former president": Tim Miller, on "The 11th Hour, MSNBC, February 14, 2022. Miller was the Communications Director for the 2016 US presidential campaign of Jeb Bush, and is an outspoken Republican critic of Trump.

"will be met with fire, fury, and frankly power": Jacob Pramuk, "Trump warns North Korea threats 'will be met with fire and fury,'" CNBC, August 8, 2017. Available at https://www.cnbc.com/2017/08/08/trump-warns-north-korea-threats-will-be-met-with-fire-and-fury.html.

"The failure of prophecy": Jack Miles, *God: A Biography*, Vintage Books/Random House, New York, 1996, p. 230. See also pp. 192–94, 185.

As Jungian analyst Adolf Guggenbühl-Craig argues: See "Deserts of the Soul—Lacunae and Heredity," Chapter 7 in The Emptied Soul: On the Nature of the Psychopath, Spring Publications, Woodstock, CT, 1980, 1999.

Here is how the Czech president Václav Havel understood this principle: qtd. in Lance Morrow, *Evil: An Investigation*, Basic Books/Perseus Books, New York, 2003, p. 194.

Bob Woodward surmised that Trump was not fit to be a president: See *Rage*, Simon & Schuster, New York, 2020.

Psychoanalyst Erich Fromm, who coined the term "malignant narcissism": Erich Fromm, *The Heart of Man: Its Genius for Good and Evil*, American Mental Health Foundation, New York, 2010.

What Fromm, among others, would underscore as his authoritarian personality or character: See Erich Fromm, *Escape from Freedom*, Farrar & Rinehart, New York, 1941 (published as *The Fear of Freedom* in United Kingdom in 1942). Others include Wilhelm Reich, *The Mass Psychology of Fascism*, Farrar, Straus and Giroux, New York, 1946, 1970, and Theodor W. Adorno, Else Frenkel-Brunswik, Daniel Levinson, and R. Nevitt Sanford in their volume, *The Authoritarian Personality*, Harper & Brothers, New York, 1950.

"In 2016, after winning his party's presidential nomination": William Saletan, "The Slow-Motion Humiliation of an Empty Demagogue: The President's Sadism Ends His Own Agony," slate.com, November 6, 2020. Available at https://slate.com/news-and-politics/2020/11/trump-election-results-humiliation.html.

"The president had appeared to White House aides": qtd. by Lawrence O'Donnell, "The Last Word With Lawrence O'Donnell," MSNBC, January 7, 2020.

What psychoanalyst Melanie Klein calls a paranoid-schizoid position: See Melanie Klein, "Notes on Some Schizoid Mechanisms (1946)," in *Envy and Gratitude and Other Works, 1946-1963*,

Free Press/Simon & Schuster, New York, 1975, pp. 1–24. See also Noelle McAfee, "Trump and the Paranoid-Schizoid Politics of Ideality," available at https://www.academia.edu/32991721/Trump_and_the_Paranoid-Schizoid_Politics_of_Ideality, and Chet Mirman, "Border Security and the Self," *Other/Wise* (an online journal of the International Forum for Psychoanalytic Education), September 18, 2020, available at https://ifpe.wordpress.com/2020/09/18/border-security-and-the-self/.

Both of Martin Luther's parents had a Yahweh complex: See Erik H. Erikson's excellent *Young Man Luther, op. cit.*, pp. 57–58, 66–67, 71–74. Erikson in turn cites the chief biographers of Luther.

"I am like ripe shit": Martin Luther, qtd. in Erik H. Erikson, *Young Man Luther, op. cit.*, p. 206. Erikson cites Luther's *Tischreden*, Weimarer Ausgaben, V, No. 5537, and writes that Luther's sons recorded this event.

"At the close of the Middle Ages": Johan Huizinga, *The Waning of the Middle Ages*, Doubleday, New York, 1956, p. 150; also qtd. in Erik H. Erikson, *Young Man Luther*, p. 74. I have capitalized the *I* in "In."

what Jungian analysts Joseph Henderson, Samuel Kimbles, and Thomas Singer call a "cultural complex": See Thomas Singer with Catherine Kaplinsky, "Cultural Complexes in Analysis," *Jungian Psychoanalysis: Working in the Spirit of C. G. Jung*, ed. Murray Stein, "The Cultural Complex," Open Court, Chicago, pp. 22–37, 2010. Also available under the title "The Cultural Complex" at https://aras.org/sites/default/files/docs/00042SingerKaplinsky.pdf. Henderson first coined the term in an unpublished letter to Jung in 1947.

"he's so distant": Joni Mitchell, qtd. in *Memories of Leonard*, available at http://www.memoriesofleonard.com/joni-mitchell/, a noncommercial fan-based website.

"I've taken a lot of Prozac, Paxil": This comment was included in Cohen's later concerts. See Leonard Cohen, *Live in London*, Sony Music Entertainment, Columbia Records, New York, 2009. The concluding sentence about studying the philosophies of religions and cheerfulness is based on a quote Cohen elsewhere attributed to the poet-playwright Ben Jonson. The quote, however, belongs to Oliver Edwards, who made the remark to Samuel Johnson; see E. V. Lucas, "A Philosopher That Failed," in *A Little of Everything*, 1912, available at *Internet Archive*, https://archive.org/stream/littleofeverythi034960mbp/littleofeverythi034960mbp_djvu.txt.

his cryptic description of himself as the little Jew who authored the Bible: Leonard Cohen, "The Future," title song on the album, *The Future*, Leonard Cohen Stranger Music (BMI), Sony Music Entertainment, Columbia Records, New York, 1992.

"Forgiveness is the only way to reverse": widely attributed to Hannah Arendt. More explicitly, she writes: "Without being forgiven, released from the consequences of what we have done, our capacity to act would, as it were, be confined to one single deed from which we could never recover; we would remain the victims of its consequences forever, not unlike the sorcerer's apprentice who lacked the magical formula to break the spell" (*The Human Condition*, Anchor Books, Doubleday, Garden City, New York, 1958, 1959, p. 213).

as studies in gendercide show: For example, in 1990 Nobel Prize-winning economist Amartya Sen calculated that over one hundred million females were missing in the world, with at least another two million added each year (Amartya Sen, "More than 100 Million Women Are Missing," *The New York Review of Books*, December 20, 1990).

"Be fruitful and multiply": Gen. 1:28, RSV.

"The past is never dead": William Faulkner, *Requiem for a Nun*, Act I, Scene III.

Chapter 2: Master of the Universe: The Young Bill Gates

"Bill Gates is an American success story": Don Hewitt, producer of *60 Minutes,* CBS; personal communication between Hewitt and Wendy Goldman Rohm, author of *The Microsoft File: The Secret Case Against Bill Gates,* Crown Business, New York, 1998, who in turn personally communicated this to me in 2011.

As author Wendy Goldman Rohm explains: Wendy Goldman Rohm, *The Microsoft File: The Secret Case Against Bill Gates, ibid.*

he called this a "natural monopoly": *ibid.,* p. 9.

It is no accident that Thomas Hobbes called his classic treatise: Thomas Hobbes, *Leviathan, or, Matter, Form, and Power of a Commonwealth Ecclesiastical and Civil,* Vol. 21 in *Great Books of the Western World, Encyclopaedia Britannica,* ed. Nelle Fuller, editor in chief Robert McHenry, Chicago, 1994.

The judge presiding over the legal case: The judge was Thomas Penfield Jackson; cited in Paul Therrott, "Judge Jackson Exits Microsoft Discrimination Case," www.windowsitpro.com, March 14, 2001.

Needless to say, Gates was himself bullied as a child: Mark Leibovich, "Alter Egos," *Washington Post,* December 31, 2000, https://www.washingtonpost.com/archive/politics/2000/12/31/alter-egos/91b267b0-858c-4d4e-a4bd-48f22e015f70/.

"that's the stupidest thing I ever heard": qtd. in Walter Isaacson, "The Gates Operating System," *Time,* January 13, 1997, https://web.archive.org/web/20000619090559/http:/www.time.com/time/gates/gates5.html.

Microsoft co-founder Paul Allen portrays Gates in his memoir: Paul Allen, *Idea Man: A Memoir by the Cofounder of Microsoft,* Portfolio/Penguin, New York, 2011.

Allen said in a *60 Minutes* interview: "The Co-founder," produced by Shachar Bar-On, *60 Minutes,* CBS, August 7, 2011. Videotapes of staff meetings are included here.

Musk, for instance, has been accused of whitewashing: See "Elon Musk's Crash Course," a *New York Times* Presents/Fx documentary, dir. Emma Schwartz, Hulu, 2022.

contributing $1.75 billion to fight it: Mark Suzman, "Why We're Giving $250 Million More to Fight COVID-19," Bill & Melinda Gates Foundation, gatesfoundation.org or https://www.gatesfoundation.org/ideas/articles/coronavirus-funding-additional-250-million-suzman, December 9, 2020.

included a substantial sum that went to Gavi: Bill Alpert, "Gates Pledges $1.6 Billion for Vaccines. What That Means for Covid-19 and Other Diseases," *Barron's,* June 4, 2020. Available at https://www.barrons.com/articles/gates-foundation-vaccines--covid-19-children-developing-countries-51591284623.

his own investments of $2 billion: cited in Lisa Stiffler, "Bill Gates on Climate, Tech, and the Future of the Planet," *GeekWire,* available at https://www.geekwire.com/2021/heres-bill-gates-not-help-fight-climate-change/.

Chapter 3: Eliot Spitzer's Fall

"It is impossible to calculate the moral mischief": Thomas Paine, *Age of Reason,* Part First, Section 1, 1794.

arguably, its Benjamin Disraeli or Léon Blum: I say "arguably" because Disraeli's father, after a falling-out at the synagogue he attended, had all his children baptized as Christians in order to improve their chances of social and professional advancement. In fact, Disraeli was a practicing Anglican.

During his tenure, he also arrested and prosecuted sixteen people: On Spitzer's prosecution of a prostitution ring as attorney general, see Scott Horton, "The Spitzer Sex Sting: A Few More Questions," *Harper's Magazine*, www.harpers.org, March 10, 2008.

"We were having an amiable chat": Jack Welch, qtd. in Geoff Colvin, "Spitzer's Bully Pulpit: The Fallen Governor's Schoolyard Behavior Caught Up with Him," *CNNMoney*, http://money.cnn. com/2008/03/14/news/newsmakers/colvin_spitzer.fortune/index.htm, March 17, 2008.

In an op-ed piece in *The Wall Street Journal* in 2005: *ibid.*

As governor, Spitzer boasted to a state legislator: *ibid.*

As Spitzer acknowledged in the documentary film, *Client 9*: *Client 9: The Rise and Fall of Eliot Spitzer,* dir. Alex Gibney, Magnolia Pictures, 2010.

"when an inner situation is not made conscious": C. G. Jung, "Christ, A Symbol of the Self," in *Aion: Researches into the Phenomenology of the Self* (1950), Vol. 9, Part II of *The Collected Works of C. G. Jung,* trans. R. F. C. Hull, Princeton University Press, Bollingen Series XX, Princeton, NJ, 1968, par. 126.

"Five years later": Eliot Spitzer, in "Briefing," *Time,* July 22, 2013, p. 11.

"Shouldn't the job of comptroller go to someone": Stephen Colbert, *The Colbert Report,* Comedy Central, July 19, 2013. Available at http://thecolbertreport.cc.com/videos/dpebt7/political-sex-scandals---new-york-city-elections---eliot-spitzer.

Chapter 4: Schopenhauer's Gloom

"So long as you do not know": *Johann Wolfgang von Goethe, "The Holy Longing," West-östlicher Divan* (or *West-Eastern Divan*), Book 4, 1814–19. Translation my own; German text: "Und so lang du das nicht hast, / Dieses: stirb und werde, / Bist du nur ein trüber Gast / Auf der dunklen Erde."

In this matter he even trumped Nietzsche: Schopenhauer had a darker outlook on and philosophy of life than Nietzsche because the former championed no invigorating response to what both would agree was life's intrinsic purposelessness. For an excellent treatment of this, see philosopher Grace Neal Dolson, "The Influence of Schopenhauer on Friedrich Nietzsche," *The Philosophical Review,* Duke University Press, Vol. 10, No. 3, May 1901, pp. 241–50. See especially pp. 247–48. Nietzsche's reference to being a "tragic optimist" is on p. 248. Available at https://www.jstor.org/stable/2176260?seq=1.

"Life is *a disappointment*": Arthur Schopenhauer, "On the Sufferings of the World," in *Studies in Pessimism, On Human Nature, Religion, etc.,* trans. T. Bailey Saunders, Digireads.com Publishing, Stillwell, Kansas, 2008, p. 6.

In one infamous episode: See Rick Lewis, "Brilliance and Gloom," *Philosophy* Now: *A Magazine of Ideas,* Issue 134, available at https://philosophynow.org/issues/134/Brilliance_and_Gloom.

"The sole thing that reconciles me": *ibid.,* pp. 10–11.

Part II: Yahweh in Our Relationships

"The striving for personal power": Alfred Adler, qtd. in Henry T. Stein, "Classical Adlerian Quotes: Power Addiction," Alfred Adler Institutes of San Francisco and Northwestern Washington;

originally in "The Psychology of Power," in *Gewalt und Gewaltlosogkeit: Handbuch des activen Pazifismus*, ed. Franz Kobler, Rotapfel-Verlag, Zurich, 1928, in AAAINW/ATP Archives.

Chapter 5: Was Freud Truly a "Godless Jew"?

"If God did not exist": Voltaire (François-Marie Arouet), 1774. On the origins of this aphorism, see "Voltaire and Religion," National Library of Russia, available at https://expositions. nlr.ru/eng/ex_rare/Voltaire_religion/, 2019–2022.

Freud's own, widely quoted description of himself as a "godless Jew": Freud's actual remark was "Incidentally, why did none of the pious create psychoanalysis? Why did one have to wait for a completely godless Jew?" This was in a letter to Oskar Pfister, October 9, 1918, in *Faith and Psychoanalysis: The Letters of Sigmund Freud and Oskar Pfister*, ed. Heinrich Meng and Ernst L. Freud, trans. Eric Mosbacher, Basic Books, New York, 1963, p. 63. Also cited in Peter Gay, *A Godless Jew: Freud, Atheism, and the Making of Psychoanalysis*, Yale University Press, New Haven and London, in association with Hebrew Union College Press, Cincinnati, 1987, p. 37. The translation of the above remark is a combination of Mosbacher's and Gay's.

"talked virtually without a pause for thirteen hours": C. G. Jung, *Memories, Dreams, Reflections* (hereafter referred to as *Memories*), ed. Aniela Jaffé, trans. Richard and Clara Winston, Vintage Books, Random House, New York, 1965, p. 149.

"I rejoice every day in *your* riches": letter of Jung to Freud, June 4, 1907, *The Freud/Jung Letters: The Correspondence between Sigmund Freud and C. G. Jung* (hereafter referred to as *Letters*), ed. William McGuire, trans. Ralph Manheim and R. F. C. Hull, Princeton University Press, Bollingen Series XCIV, Princeton, NJ, 1974, 1979, p. 56.

he regarded him as a father figure: See letter of Jung to Freud, *Letters*, February 20, 1908, in, p. 122.

"first man of real importance": Jung, *Memories*, p. 149.

In a letter later in the same year: letter of Jung to Freud, October 28, 1907, *Letters*, p. 95.

"[Jung] will save us": cited in Per Magnus Johansson and Elisabeth Punzi, "Jewishness and Psychoanalysis—the Relationship to Identity, Trauma and Exile. An Interview Study," *Jewish Culture & History*, Vol. 20, Issue 2, 2019, pp. 140–52. Also available at https://www.tandfonline.com/doi/full/10.1080/1462169X.2019.1574429.

It has been well documented that Freud was fascinated by Moses: See B. Goodnick, "Sigmund Freud and the Countenance of Moses," in *The Israel Journal of Psychiatry and Related Sciences*, Vol. 32, Issue 2, 1995, pp. 120–33.

"I now feel that I must avenge": letter of Freud to Jung, March 1, 1911, *Letters*, p. 400.

"indispensable for a proper understanding of mythology": letter of Jung to Freud, *Letters*, May 8, 1911, *Letters*, p. 421.

"knowledge that has been intuitively projected": letter of Jung to Freud, *Letters*, June 12, 1911, p. 427.

Later, Freud would explore the possibilities of parapsychology: He wrote about this at length, including "Psychoanalysis and Telepathy" (1921), "Dreams and Telepathy" (1922), both in *Beyond the Pleasure Principle, Group Psychology and Other Works*, Vol. 18 of *The Standard Edition of the Complete Psychological Works of Sigmund Freud*, ed. James Strachey, Hogarth Press, London, 1920–22, and "Dreams and Occultism" (1933), in *New Introductory Lectures on Psychoanalysis and Other Works*, Vol.

22 of *The Standard Edition of the Complete Psychological Works of Sigmund Freud*, ed. James Strachey, Hogarth Press, London, 1932–36. "Dreams and Telepathy" is also available in Sigmund Freud, *Studies in Parapsychology*, Collier Books, New York, 1971. See also Thomas Rabeyron and Renard Evrard, "Historical and Contemporary Perspectives on Occultism in the Freud-Ferenczi Correspondence," *Research in Psychoanalysis*, Vol. 13, Issue 1, January 2012, pp. 97–111; also available at https://www.cairn.info/revue-recherches-en-psychanalyse-2012-1-page-98.htm. Especially revealing is an interview Freud gave the journalist Cornelius Tabori, published in *My Occult Diary*, Rider & Co., 1951, pp. 218–19. He here suggests that in an occurrence of telepathy, the unconscious operates as a transmitter and receiver between two people, much like a telephone or radio (an outdated view at present but a provocative one nonetheless). It is a sad irony and loss that this development came too late for Freud and Jung to reconcile their differences. It would have been interesting to hear these giants dialoguing with each other about the extraordinary capacities of the human mind.

"Of course I have opinions which are not yours": letter of Jung to Freud, *Letters*, March 3, 1912, p. 491.

admitting he is defensive: letter of Freud to Jung, *Letters*, p. 492.

"The indestructible foundation of our personal relationship": *ibid.*, pp. 492–93. Freud uses the psychoanalytic term "affective cathexis," meaning formally a constellation of affect. However, it is implicitly clear that he is speaking of his affection toward Jung.

focusing in his next letter on others in their professional community: letter of Jung to Freud, *Letters*, March 10, 1912, pp. 493–94.

"The parallel with Adler is a bitter pill": letter of Jung to Freud, *Letters*, June 8, 1912, p. 509.

"there is no reason to suppose": letter of Freud to Jung, *Letters*, June 13, 1912, p. 510.

Freud was distressed by the "defections": Ernest Jones, in *Letters*, p. 514.

"his relations with Jung were beginning to be strained": *ibid.*

Sándor Ferenczi too would become Freud's scapegoat: See *The Correspondence of Sigmund Freud and Sándor Ferenczi*, Vol. 3: 1920–1933, ed. Ernst Falzeder and Eva Brabant, trans. Peter T. Hoffer, Belknap Press/Harvard University Press, Cambridge, MA, 1993.

In one exchange Freud accused Jung: letter of Freud to Jung, *Letters*, December 16, 1912, p. 534. The so-called slip was in the letter of Jung to Freud, *Letters*, December 11–14, 1912, p. 533.

This clearly triggered Jung: letter of Jung to Freud, *Letters*, December 18, 1912, pp. 534–35.

Freud responded with dignity and substance: letters of Freud to Jung, *Letters*, December 22, 1912, pp. 536–37 and January 3, 1913, pp. 538–39.

The final dissolution of all relations was in sight: letter of Freud to Jung, *Letters*, January 3, 1912, p. 539. It may be of interest to note one truly final interaction that took place in 1938 when Jung offered Freud financial assistance for the latter's escape from Vienna due to the Nazi occupation of Austria. Jung's views on the limitations of Freud's psychology might not have changed, but his humanity toward the man had evidently softened and matured. I am grateful to Beverley Zabriskie for directing me to the following source material on this matter: V. Walter Odajnyk writes that "Jung and Franz Riklin Sr., who had known Freud in earlier days, dispatched Riklin's son to Vienna with 10,000 dollars to help finance Freud's escape to England. Franz Riklin Jr. reported that Freud was adamant in declining the money, insisting repeatedly, 'I refuse to be beholden to my enemies'" (V. Walter Odajnyk, *Archetype and Character: Power, Eros, Spirit, and Matter Personality Types*, Palgrave Macmillan, Houndsmill, Basingstoke, Hampshire, United Kingdom and New York, 2012; Odajnyk cites Peter Gay, *Freud: A Life for Our Time*, W. W. Norton, New York, 1988, 2006, p. 779 and Robert

S. McCully, "Letters: Remarks on the Last Contact between Freud & Jung," *Quadrant: Journal for the C. G. Jung Foundation for Analytical Psychology*, 20:1, 1987, pp. 73–74).

"I can still recall vividly how Freud said to me": Jung, *Memories*, pp. 150–51.

"One thing was clear": *ibid.*, p. 151.

"There was one characteristic": *ibid.*, pp. 152, 153.

"It is a fearful thing": *D. H. Lawrence,* "The Hands of God," in *Last Poems*, ed. R. Aldington and G. Orioli, Viking Press, New York, 1933. Lawrence is here reflecting upon Heb. 10:31: "It is a fearful thing to fall into the hands of the living God" (KJV).

Chapter 6: The Marriage of Marilyn Monroe and Joe DiMaggio

"The most exciting attractions": Andy Warhol, The Philosophy of Andy Warhol (From A to B and Back Again), Houghton Mifflin Harcourt, New York, 1975, p. 44.

his staunch refusal to comply with the demands: In particular the committee wanted Miller to identify communist sympathizers in the entertainment industry, in which nearly three hundred actors and others were blacklisted or prevented from working. For the most significant portion of Miller's testimony, see "Excerpts from Arthur Miller's Testimony Before the House Un-American Activities Committee," *American Masters*, PBS, April 8, 2020, available at https://www.pbs.org/wnet/americanmasters/excerpts-from-arthur-millers-testimony-before-the-house-un-american-activities-committee/14006/.

"I think probably he changed my life": Marilyn Monroe in "You Start With Yourself, *Marilyn Monroe Video Archives*, March 17, 2017. Available at https://www.youtube.com/watch?v=w74jxMEwlhg.

"secret feeling that I'm really a fake": *ibid.*

"He carried with him the aura of a prophet": Elia Kazan, *Elia Kazan: A Life,* Knopf, New York, 1988. Available also on "Lee Strasberg," *Wikipedia*, under section on "Kazan as student."

Monroe wrote in her memoir, *My Story*: Marilyn Monroe with Ben Hecht, Rowman and Littlefield, Lanham, MD, 2007.

"They had one big thing in common": "Marilyn Monroe and Joe DiMaggio—Love, Marriage, Divorce," *Marilyn Monroe Video Archives*, November 3, 2014. Available at https://www.youtube.com/watch?v=fzguiNhVd1Q.

"I'll always remember": *ibid.*

To promote interest in the film: "Marilyn Monroe Marries Joe DiMaggio/This Day in History/January 14, 1954," *History Channel*, available at https://www.history.com/this-day-in-history/marilyn-monroe-marries-joe-dimaggio.

They argued about this in the days that followed: "Marilyn Monroe and Joe DiMaggio—Love, Marriage, Divorce," *op. cit.*

DiMaggio arranged for roses to be delivered: There are various versions of this arrangement. The one here is by Joseph Durso, "Joe DiMaggio, Yankee Clipper, Dies at 84," *The New York Times*, March 9, 1999, and the Associated Press, reprinted in *Wilmington Morning Star*, October 1, 1982.

"Where love reigns": C. G. Jung, "On the Psychology of the Unconscious" (1943), *Two Essays on Analytical Psychology*, Vol. 7 of *The Collected Works of C. G. Jung*, trans. R. F. C. Hull, Princeton University Press, Bollingen Series XX, Princeton, NJ, 1966, par. 78.

"The shadow side of Aphrodite": Arlene Diane Landau, *Tragic Beauty: The Dark Side of Venus*

Aphrodite and the Loss and Regeneration of Soul, Chiron Publications, Asheville, NC, 2019, cover description.

This at least is the viewpoint of the documentary, *Reframed: Marilyn Monroe*: dir. Karen McGann, CNN, January 16 and 23, 2022.

"the shock of her body's motion sped through me": Arthur Miller, qtd. in Lindsay Soladz, "Marilyn and Miller: Star-crossed Misfits," *The Ringer*, March 19, 2018, available at https://www. theringer.com/movies/2018/3/19/17136620/marilyn-and-miller-star-crossed-misfits.

Biographer Charles Casillo writes: Charles Casillo, *Marilyn Monroe: The Private Life of a Public Icon*, St. Martin's Press, New York, 2018.

"so many of the things that made Marilyn 'Marilyn'": Karina Longworth, qtd. in Soladz, *op. cit.*

Our archetypal complexes often have some connection with early trauma: See Donald Kalsched, *The Inner World of Trauma: Archetypal Defenses of the Personal Spirit*, Routledge, New York, 1996.

a critical father who would tell him he was "good for nothing": "Childhood," *The Official Site of Joe DiMaggio*, available at https://www.joedimaggio.com/the-man/childhood/, January 26, 2022.

"When we got together in the bedroom": Joe DiMaggio, qtd. in Rock Positano and John Positano, *Dinner With DiMaggio: Memories of an American Hero*, Simon & Schuster, New York, 2017.

According to a number of biographers: See Richard Ben Cramer, *Joe DiMaggio: The Hero's Life*, Touchstone/Simon & Schuster, New York, 2001 and Buzz Bissinger, "For Love of DiMaggio," *Vanity Fair*, September 2000, available at https://www.vanityfair.com/news/2000/09/dimaggio-200009.

"more defined than likes": Bissinger.

He had an estranged relationship with a son: "Joe DiMaggio Jr. Dies," *The Washington Post*, available at https://www.washingtonpost.com/archive/local/1999/08/09/joe-dimaggio-jr-dies/c5b89b19-ce6c-44a8-8b4c-814f163f1d9e/.

Obsessed with money, DiMaggio was alleged to have ties with the Mafia: see Cramer.

"I don't trust anyone": Joe DiMaggio, qtd. by Morris Engelberg in Bissinger.

"core of hollowness to his life": Bissinger.

His few friends were expected to obey his rules: Engelberg in Bissinger.

"I still am lost": Marilyn Monroe, qtd. in Christina Ng, "Letters From a 'Lost' Marilyn Monroe, Angry John Lennon to Be Auctioned," available at abcnews.go.com., March 30, 2013.

"there is absolutely nothing there": Marilyn Monroe, qtd. in Sam Kashner, "Marilyn and Her Monsters," *Vanity Fair*, October 5, 2010, November 2010 issue, available at https://www.vanityfair. com/culture/2010/11/marilyn-monroe-201011.

As Freud said, neurosis is the "result of a kind of ignorance": Sigmund Freud, *A General Introduction to Psycho-Analysis* (1915–17), in *The Major Works of Sigmund Freud*, Vol. 54 of *Great Books of the Western World*, *Encyclopaedia Britannica*, trans. Joan Riviere, editor in chief Mortimer J. Adler, Chicago, 1994, p. 560.

Chapter 7: The Breakup of the Beatles

"Now Yahweh came down to see the city": Gen. 11: 5–9, translation my own, combining NJPS, JB, and NOAB.

Paul would later describe this film: Paul McCartney, in *The Compleat Beatles*, dir. Patrick Montgomery, MGM, 1982.

George would refer to this period: George Harrison, in *Making "Let It Be,"* Apple Films, SOB Presentation, 2002.

Their producer George Martin explained: George Martin, in *The Compleat Beatles, op. cit.*

even quitting the band for a few days: *The Beatles: Get Back*, dir. Peter Jackson, Apple Corps Ltd., Wingnut Films, Disney Platform Productions, 2021.

On the surface, exchanges like the following: exchange between Paul McCartney and George Harrison, in *Let It Be* (film), dir. Michael Lindsay-Hogg, Apple Films, United Artists, 1970. All direct quotations from the Beatles and George Martin have been edited so that the vernacular does not distract from reading them. In no case has an edit altered the speaker's intended meaning.

It was to this that George was speaking when he later said: George Harrison, in *Making "Let It Be," op. cit.*

"The whole pressure of": John Lennon, *Making "Let It Be," ibid.*

what psychoanalysts, among others, understand as an intersubjective field: See Werner Bohleber, "The Concept of Intersubjectivity in Psychoanalysis: Taking Critical Stock," *International Journal of Psychoanalysis,"* Vol. 94, 2013, pp. 799–823. Also available at https://www.researchgate.net/publication/255705277_The_concept_of_intersubjectivity_in_psychoanalysis_Taking_critical_stock. Philosophers and sociologists have also written about the basic principle of intersubjectivity.

Lucien Lévy-Bruhl's related concept of this: See Lucien Lévy-Bruhl, How Natives Think, trans. Lilian A. Clare, Routledge/Taylor & Francis Group, New York, 1926, 2018. For Jung's understanding of this concept, see C. G. Jung, "Archaic Man" (1931), in *Civilization in Transition*, Vol. 10 of *The Collected Works of C. G. Jung*, trans. R. F. C. Hull, Princeton University Press, Bollingen Series XX, Princeton, NJ, 1978.

"I quit the band": Ringo Starr, in *George Harrison: Living in the Material World*, Part I, dir. Martin Scorsese, Grove Street Productions, HBO, 2011.

"It's interesting to see how people behave nicely": George Harrison, in *Making "Let It Be," op. cit.*

"Billy Preston was a great help": George Martin, *ibid.*

Paul later admitted was his "little dig at John and Yoko": Paul McCartney, in Joan Goodman, "Playboy Interview: Paul and Linda McCartney," *Playboy*, December 1984. Also available at http://beatlesinterviews.org/db1984.pmpb.beatles.html.

And as one of their final songs almost prophetically anticipated: McCartney said that "Carry That Weight" on *Abbey Road* was about the Beatles' business difficulties and the atmosphere at Apple at the time of that recording. See Barry Miles, *Paul McCartney: Many Years From Now*, Henry Holt and Co., New York, 1997, pp. 557–58. Also cited in "Carry That Weight," *Wikipedia*.

Their concluding message, also gentle and glorious: "The End," on *Abbey Road* (1969).

Chapter 8: The Rolling Stones' Relationship to Yahweh

"One of my views about people": Salman Rushdie, in Brendan Bernhard, "Mr. Rushdie's Planet," *LA Weekly*, Los Angeles, September 7–13, 2001, p. 34.

"The immediate problem was that Mick had developed": Keith Richards, *Life*, with James Fox, Little, Brown and Co., New York, Mindless Records, 2010, pp. 453–54.

"'Where's my drummer?' No answer": Keith Richards, *ibid.*, pp. 460–61.

"Thou shalt have no other gods in the band before me": The first of the Ten Commandments is "Thou shalt have no other gods before me" (Exod. 20:3).

Yahweh gunning for Moses one night in the desert wilderness: Exod. 4:24–26

"Once you release that acid": Keith Richards, *ibid.*, p. 453.

the noble magnanimity and trustworthiness by which Emerson defines "friendship": Ralph Waldo Emerson, "Friendship," in *The Collected Works of Ralph Waldo Emerson*, Vol. II, Essays: First Series, *ed.* Joseph Slater, Alfred R. Ferguson, *and* Jean Ferguson Carr, Harvard University Press, Cambridge, Massachusetts, 1980.

Richards apologized to him for publicly exposing it: See http://www.rollingstone.com/music/news/keith-richards-apologizes-to-mick-jagger-20120315, March 15, 2012, and https://www.youtube.com/watch?v=cCYbxcrB5H8.

"didn't know what kind of people they were dealing with": Stefan Ponek, on *Gimme Shelter* DVD, dir. Albert and David Maysles, Maysles Films, Cinema 5 (USA), 20th Century Fox (UK), 1970.

"something very funny happens when we start that number": Mick Jagger, on *Gimme Shelter* DVD, *ibid.* The song itself, "Sympathy for the Devil," written by Mick Jagger and Keith Richards, is available on *Beggars Banquet*, 1968; also on *The Rolling Stones, Singles Collection: The London Years*, 1989 (the lyrics are on p. 64 of the accompanying book) and *Forty Licks*, 2002.

performed to the stirring, syncopated rhythm of a samba: This is Jagger's own description in Jann Wenner, "Jagger Remembers," *Rolling Stone*, December 14, 1995. Also available at http://www.rollingstone.com/music/news/mick-jagger-remembers-20120725?page=2.

"was just one of many songs": Bill Wyman, interviewed on the podcast Raised on Radio, November 15, 1990, available at https://www.youtube.com/watch?v=8CNNf9DU7Tk.

An FBI agent's disclosure in 2008: reported on BBC Radio Four, March 3, 2008, and cited in Richard Eden, "Hells Angels Plotted to Kill Mick Jagger," *The Telegraph*, March 2, 2008. The latter is available at http://www.telegraph.co.uk/news/uknews/1580456/Hells-Angels-plotted-to-kill-Mick-Jagger.html.

An album with a title like *Their Satanic Majesties Request*: Rolling Stones, *Their Satanic Majesties Request*, ABKCO Music, London Records, 1967; ABKCO Music, Decca Records, 1967.

We should remember here that the Hebrew Bible depicts: In pre-Christian times, Satan was seen not as singularly diabolical but rather as an angel or servant of God. He was an "adversary"—or *ha-satan* in ancient Hebrew—on Yahweh's behalf. The Israelites knew *explicitly* that Yahweh and Satan were different sides of the same God, as illustrated in the two versions of the census story. The version in 2 Sam. 24:1–15 states that Yahweh commands David to take a census, whereas in the version in 1 Chron. 21:1 and 21:14, Satan incites him to take it. The end result, however, is the same: God sends a pestilence against Israel, killing seventy thousand of her people. There was an earlier occasion when Yahweh ordered a census (Exod. 30:12–14), and it did not have this result. It is unclear what Yahweh/Satan was angry about in this instance. Mike Aquilina explains some possibilities in his article "How the Bible Reveals the Tensions and Intentions Behind the Census," *Angelus*, March 26, 2020. Available at https://angelusnews.com/faith/how-the-bible-reveals-the-tensions-and-intentions-behind-the-census/. In any case, this episode suggests that Abraham Lincoln may have been mistaken in his "Meditation on the Divine Will," asserting that "God cannot be *for* and *against* the same thing at the same time."

as the New Testament proclaims, the prince or ruler of this world: Jn. 12:31, 14:30. The KJV uses the term "prince" while the RSV uses "ruler."

No one will ever turn Jagger into a saint: Mick Jagger and Keith Richards, "Saint of Me," *Bridges to Babylon,* Virgin Records B.V., 1997.

Dionysus, the Greek god of fertility, wine, ecstasy, and ritually induced madness: For an excellent treatment of the expression of Dionysian impulses in modern times, see Rafael Lopez-Pedraza, *Dionysus in Exile: On the Repression of the Body and Emotion,* Chiron Publications, Wilmette, Illinois, 2000, pp. 38–43, in which the author discusses bullfighting, flamenco, jazz, and carnivals such as Mardi Gras. The book as a whole is worthy of attention.

Ecstasy is the only thing they desire: Mick Jagger and Keith Richards, "Slipping Away," *Steel Wheels,* Rolling Stones Records, Promotone BV, Columbia Records, 1989.

"Heaven," also fittingly named, is their crowning paean: Mick Jagger and Keith Richards, "Heaven," *Tatoo You,* Colgems-EMI Music, Virgin Benelux B.V., 1981.

Part III: Yahweh in Our Midst

"Evil is an imitation of God": Lance Morrow, *Evil: An Investigation,* Basic Books/Perseus Books, New York, 2003, pp. 37, 235.

Chapter 9: The Bully and the Prince

"We hurt those to whom we need to make our power": Friedrich Nietzsche, *The Gay Science,* ed. Bernard Williams, trans. Josefine Nauckhoff, *Cambridge Texts in the History of Philosophy,* Cambridge University Press, New York, 2008, Section 13, p. 38. In the actual text, the word "hurt" is in italics to emphasize a comparison to benefiting others. I've removed these italics because we have no context for this comparison here.

"Nothing human is alien to me": Terentius, *Heauton Timoroumenos* (The Self-Tormentor), Act I, Scene I, 163 BCE; cited in Kwame Anthony Appiah, *Cosmopolitanism: Ethics in a World of Strangers,* W. W. Norton, New York, 2006, p. 111.

"Alfred and Brice apparently told everyone": Elliot Rodger, *My Twisted World: The Story of Elliot Rodger,* available at http://abclocal.go.com/three/kabc/kabc/My-Twisted-World.pdf.

"It was only when I first moved to Santa Barbara": *ibid.*

some authorities claim that Harris was more often a perpetrator: See Dave Cullen, *Columbine,* Twelve/Hachette Book Group, New York, 2009.

he wrote "Ich bin Got"—"I am God"—in his school planner: Peter Langman, "Keeping Kids Safe: Columbine, Bullying, and the Mind of Eric Harris," *Psychology Today,* available at http://www.psychologytoday.com/blog/keeping-kids-safe/200905/columbine-bullying-and-the-mind-eric-harris.

it is no accident that its frustration and absence in *The Lord of the Flies*: William Golding, *Lord of the Flies,* Perigee/Berkley/Penguin, New York, 1954.

Beelzebub, who in the Hebrew Bible was a Philistine god . . . and in the New Testament was identified as the devil: II Kings 1:2–3, 6, 16, NJPS; Matthew 10:25, 12:24, Mark 3:22, Luke 11:15, 18–19, KJV. All translations refer to him in the Hebrew Bible or Old Testament as Baal-zebub, connecting him, some scholars believe, to the Philistine god Baal. RSV and other translations refer to him in the New Testament as Beelzebul.

As Robert Bly points out: See Robert Bly, *Iron John: A Book About Men,* Da Capo Press/Perseus Books Group, Cambridge, Massachusetts, 2004.

In Mario Puzo's book and Francis Ford Coppola's film *The Godfather*: Mario Puzo, *The Godfather* (1969), Signet/New American Library/Penguin Group, New York, 1978. *The Godfather*, dir. Francis Ford Coppola, Alfran Productions, Paramount Pictures, 1972.

Even Michael Corleone's execution of his own brother in *The Godfather II*: *The Godfather II*, dir. Francis Ford Coppola, Coppola Company, Paramount Pictures, 1974.

***The Godfather III* poignantly shows:** *The Godfather III*, dir. Francis Ford Coppola, Zoetrope Studio, Paramount Pictures, 1990.

"I certainly was *very* confident that I'd never be caught": Lance Armstrong, in *The Armstrong Lie*, dir. Alex Gibney, Kennedy/Marshall Productions, Jigsaw Productions, Matt Tolmach Productions, Sony Picture Classics, 2013.

On *Larry King Live*, he boasted: *Larry King Live*, CNN, August 25, 2005. Available at http://transcripts.cnn.com/TRANSCRIPTS/0508/25/lkl.01.html.)

In a sworn deposition: Lance Armstrong, in *The Armstrong Lie*, op. cit.

"Why couldn't it just be 'proof,' that allegations must be followed up by proof?": David Walsh, in *Lance Armstrong: Stop at Nothing*, Showcase, dir. Alex Holmes, November 8, 2014.

When Betsy Andreu . . . accused Armstrong of doping: Betsy Andreu, cited in Kristen Jordan Shamus, "The Longest Ride: Betsy Andreu Says Faith Fueled Her Fight Against Doping Lies and Lance Armstrong," *Detroit Free Press*, February 2, 2014. Available at http://archive.freep.com/article/20140202/COL26/302020035/Betsy-Andreu-Lance-Armstrong-doping.

In his interview with Oprah Winfrey: Lance Armstrong, on *Oprah's Next Chapter*, OWN (Oprah Winfrey Network), January 17 and 18, 2012.

"I'm a fighter. I grew up as a fighter": Lance Armstrong, in *The Armstrong Lie*, op. cit.

"This is not a story about doping": Daniel Coyle, in The Armstrong Lie, op. cit. Coyle's book on this subject is *Lance Armstrong's War: One Man's Battle Against Fate, Fame, Love, Death, Scandal, and a Few Other Rivals on the Road to the Tour de France*, HarperCollins, New York, 2005.

the thorny question of Machiavelli's intentions and whether he was an advocate or teacher of evil: There are diverse arguments about this. For a few of them, see Jean-Jacques Rousseau, *Of the Social Contract, Or Principles of Political Right* (widely known as *The Social Contract*) (Hackett, Indianapolis, Indiana, 1987), in which Rousseau argues that *The Prince* is a satire; Isaiah Berlin, "The Originality of Machiavelli," in *Against the Current: Essays in the History of Ideas* (Princeton University Press, Princeton, New Jersey, 2013); and Leo Strauss, *Thoughts on Machiavelli* (University of Chicago Press, Chicago, 1978).

"For although the act condemn the doer, the end may justify him": Niccolò Machiavelli, Chapter 9 in Book I, *Discourses on the First Decade of Titus Livius* (widely known as *Discourses on Livy*), ed. Jim Manis, trans. Ninian Hill Thomson, The Electronic Classics Series, Pennsylvania State University, Hazleton, Pennsylvania, 2007–12, p. 46. Available at http://www2.hn.psu.edu/faculty/jmanis/machiavelli/machiavelli-discourses-titus-livius.pdf.

Yahweh was not interested in the kingdoms or statehood of the Israelites: On Yahweh not favoring the establishment of human kingship, see 1 Samuel 8:4–9 and 1 Samuel 10:17–25.

Harold Bloom points out that Machiavelli's prince: Harold Bloom, *Jesus and Yahweh*, op. cit., p. 159. Bloom is probably referring to these passages in *The Prince*: "[The question arises] whether it is better to be loved more than feared, or feared more than loved. The reply is, that one ought to be both feared and loved, but as it is difficult for the two to go together, it is much safer to be feared than loved, if one of the two is to be wanting." And *why* does fear rule over love? Because "men love at their own free will, but fear at the will of the prince. . . . [A] wise prince must rely on what is in his power and not what is in the power of others" (Niccolò Machiavelli, *The Prince*, trans. Luigi Ricci and E. R. P. Vincent, Mentor, Penguin Group, New York, 1952, pp. 89–90, 91).

"**[When innovators] depend on their own strength**": Niccolò Machiavelli, *The Prince*, Introduction by Christian Gauss, Mentor, Penguin Group, New York, 1952, p. 50.

"**[In] taking a state the conqueror must arrange**": *ibid.*, p. 62.

"**[A prince should] have no other aim or thought**": *ibid.*, p. 81. I have changed the spelling of "organization" from the British version to the American.

"**A man who wishes to make a profession of goodness**": *ibid.*, p. 84.

"**Nothing causes a prince to be so much esteemed**": *ibid.*, p. 110.

"**though during the 1968 campaign**": Hard evidence for this was disclosed by the Nixon Library in the notes of Bob Haldeman. See *LBJ: Triumph and Tragedy*, "Part IV: Final Days," dir. Pat Kondelis, CNN, February 21, 2022. Interviewed in this documentary, Jim Jones, special assistant to President Johnson, argued that about twenty-five thousand American soldiers lost their lives and tens of thousands more were maimed and wounded because Nixon's interference in the peace negotiations prolonged America's involvement in the war until 1975.

"**Nixon had a terrible inferiority complex**": James Shenton, "Richard Nixon and Watergate," *History of the United States*, *The Great Courses on Tape*, Teaching Company, Lecture 65, 1996. Also available at https://jamestillich.wordpress.com/2013/10/09/watergate-richard-nixons-political-suicide/#_ftn3.

to a "constant grimness," in the words of columnist George Will: George F. Will, "Brave But Melancholy: Nixon Lost What He Loved Most: Grimness Colored Victories," *The Ledger*, April 26, 1994, p. 9A. Available at https://news.google.com/newspapers?nid=1346&dat=19940426&id=_UdIAAAAIBAJ&sjid=bPwDAAAAIBAJ&pg=6781,3911024&hl=en. The spelling in the text is "a constant griminess," but it is evident that this is a misprint.

"**Sometime, hopefully, there will be a historian**": John Ehrlichman, in *Nixon by Nixon: In His Own Words*, HBO, September 29, 2014.

William Saxbe, Nixon's attorney general, described Ehrlichman: cited on *NBC Nightly News with Brian Williams*, August 25, 2010.

"**Memo to Haldeman**": Richard Nixon, memo to Haldeman, March 10, 1970; qtd. on *CBS Evening News with Scott Pelley*, July 21, 2011.

In his campaign for a congressional seat: *American Experience: Nixon*, dir. David Espar, PBS, 1990. Also available at http://www.pbs.org/wgbh/americanexperience/features/general-article/nixon-early/.

Hoover provided him with FBI reports: See Tim Weiner, *Enemies: A History of the FBI*, Random House, New York, 2012.

"**The Jews are born spies**": Richard Nixon, in *Nixon by Nixon, op. cit.*

"**Remember that any intellectual**": Richard Nixon, in Kenneth J. Hughes, Jr., "How Paranoid Was Nixon?," George Mason University's History News Network, August 12, 2007. Also available at http://historynewsnetwork.org/article/41698.

"**The guys from the best families**": *ibid.*

"**If they're from any Eastern schools**": *ibid.*

Nixon referred to Daniel Ellsberg, Leslie Gelb, and Morton Halperin: *ibid.*

It was him that a sobbing Nixon: Bob Woodward and Carl Bernstein, *The Final Days*, Simon & Schuster, New York, 1973, p. 423.

Likewise, Nixon filled his White House with other Jewish appointees: See Jonathan Rosenbloom, "What the Newest Nixon-Kissinger Tape Reveals," http://www.torah.org/features/firstperson/Nixon-Kissinger.html. Other Jewish appointees included Leonard Garment, chief counsel; Herbert Stein, chief economic advisor; William Safire, chief speechwriter; and Murray Chotiner, campaign manager.

"Never forget, the establishment is the enemy": Richard Nixon, in *Nixon by Nixon, op. cit.*

"We're up against an enemy, a conspiracy": *ibid.*

"I want the Brookings Institute safe cleared out": *ibid.*

"very aggressive, abrasive and obnoxious personalities" . . . by "an inferiority syndrome": Richard Nixon, https://www.youtube.com/watch?v=uD593z4kzXU.

what historian Richard Hofstadter describes as the paranoid style and anti-intellectualism: Richard Hofstadter, *The Paranoid Style in American Politics*, Vintage Books/Random House, New York, 2008 and *Anti-Intellectualism in American Life*, Vintage Books/Random House, New York, 1973.

"That's going to be fun": Richard Nixon, in *Nixon by Nixon, op. cit.*

"After the election": Richard Nixon, qtd. in "How Nixon Gave Ted Kennedy Bodyguards—to Spy on His Life," *The Guardian*, August 28, 2009. Available at http://www.theguardian.com/world/2009/aug/28/ted-kennedy-nixon-secret-service.

"I could only hope": *ibid.*

"long national nightmare": Gerald Ford, speech after taking the oath of office, August 9, 1974. Available at https://www.youtube.com/watch?v=LySpUpI9k1s.

Figures like . . . Trump use Machiavellian methods to gain control over others: In *Fear: Trump in the White House*, Bob Woodward's opening epigraph quotes Trump as follows: "Real power is—I don't even want to use the word—fear" (Simon & Schuster, New York, 2018).

Leonard Cohen said something thought-provoking: Asked in an interview about the inspiration for his song "The Traitor," he said it is about "failing or betraying some mission you were mandated to fulfill and being unable to fulfill it and then coming to understand that the real mandate was not to fulfill it but to stand guiltless in the predicament in which you found yourself." Taken from the film *Leonard Cohen: I'm Your Man*, dir. Lian Lunsun, Lions Gate Entertainment, 2005. Dylan makes a similar observation about failure in his song "Love Minus Zero/No Limit," on the album *Bringing It All Back Home* (1965).

"Always give your best": Richard Nixon, farewell speech to the White House staff, August 9, 1974, available at https://www.youtube.com/watch?v=32GaowQnGRw.

Chapter 10: Legalists, Fundamentalists, and Moral Perfectionists

"Religion can be the enemy of God": Bono, in *Bono: In Conversation with Michka Assayas*, Berkley Publishing Group/Penguin Publishing Group, New York, 2006, p. 223.

Psychologist Abraham Maslow observed that the original religious or "peak" experience: See Abraham H. Maslow, "The 'Core-Religious,' or 'Transcendent,' Experience," Chapter 3 in *Religions, Values, and Peak-Experiences*, Penguin Books, New York, 1976.

"It's wrong to criticize leaders of the Church": Dallin H. Oaks, in "The Mormons," Part II, *Frontline: American Experience*, PBS, Helen Whitney Productions, April 2007.

"So long as man remains free": Fyodor Dostoevsky, *The Brothers Karamazov*, trans. Constance

Garnet, edited and with a foreword by Manuel Komroff, a Signet Book, New American Library, New York, 1957, pp. 234, 237.

"This cleavage between the mystics and the legalists": Abraham Maslow, *op. cit.*, pp. 485–89. After the word "legalists," Maslow follows with "if I may call them that," which I have omitted in this quotation.

"All things truly wicked": Ernest Hemingway, *A Moveable Feast*, Book-of-the-Month Club, New York, 1993, p. 210.

His articulate *Defense* shows the care he took: Meister Eckhart, *Defense*, in *Meister Eckhart: A Modern Translation*, trans. Raymond B. Blakney, Harper & Row, New York, 1941, pp. 258–305.

"bloodhounds of error": Raymond B. Blakney, Introduction to *Meister Eckhart: A Modern Translation, ibid.*, p. xxiii.

"However fundamental to Judaism and Christianity": Bradley A. TePaske, *Sexuality and the Religious Imagination*, Spring Journal Books, New Orleans, Louisiana, 2008, p. 30.

Their grievance was that he wanted to return their order: On the Primitive Rule of the Order of the Blessed Virgin Mary of Mount Carmel, see http://www.ocd.pcn.net/reg_en.htm and http://ldysinger.stjohnsem.edu/@texts2/1208_carmelites/01_carm-intr.htm.

pillars of cloud and fire: Exod. 13: 21–22.

Ezekiel's extraordinary vision of him on his chariot-throne: See Ezek. 1:1–2:2.

the Incarnation and the Trinity, both of which, as Jung has shown: See "A Psychological Approach to the Dogma of the Trinity" (1948), "Transformation Symbolism in the Mass" (1954), and "Answer to Job" (1952), all in *Psychology and Religion: West and East*, Vol. 11 of *The Collected Works of C. G. Jung*, trans. R. F. C. Hull, Princeton University Press, Bollingen Series XX, Princeton, NJ, 1973.

"I am the Truth": Mansur al-Hallaj, qtd. in Paul Halsall, *Internet Medieval Source Book: Mansur al-Hallaj: Sayings* (New York: Fordham University, July 1988). Available at http://www.fordham.edu/halsall/source/all-hallaj-quotations.asp.

"Would that contemporary Islam could turn to their religious genius": J. Marvin Spiegelman, "On Behalf of the Mystical Fool: Jung on the Religious Situation," a review of the book with the same title, by John P. Dourley, *Psychological Perspectives: A Quarterly Journal of Jungian Thought*, Vol. 54, Issue 1, 2011, p. 112.

This is why theologian Paul Tillich saw faith and existential doubt as two poles: See Paul Tillich, *Faith and Doubt*, George Washington University, Washington, DC, 1962.

"When man has thus projected": Erich Fromm, *Psychoanalysis and Religion*, Bantam Books, New York, 1972, pp. 49–50. Two commas were added to the passage.

"The virtues are states of the soul": Moses Maimonides, Chapter 3 in *Eight Chapters*; also qtd. in Kenneth Seeskin, "Maimonides," in *Stanford Encyclopedia of Philosophy*, http://plato.stanford.edu/entries/maimonides/, 2010.

"there is no possibility of an excess or a deficiency": Moses Maimonides, *Guide for the Perplexed*, 2.28; also qtd. in Kenneth Seeskin, "Maimonides," in *Stanford Encyclopedia of Philosophy*, http://plato.stanford.edu/entries/maimonides/, 2010.

"So don't overdo goodness and don't act the wise man to excess": Eccles. 7:16, 20, NJPS. I have changed the spelling of "dumfounded" to the more common spelling.

He committed adultery and murder . . . but upon his repentance, and not without much retribution, Yahweh forgave him: This episode is described in 2 Sam. 11–12, and the retribution, forecast in 2 Sam. 12:11–12, continues through the following chapters until 2 Sam. 19.

"So as He is merciful, so should you be merciful": Talmud, tractate Shabbat 133b.

"The Lord spoke to Moses": Lev. 19:1–2, NJPS.

"You, therefore, must be perfect": Jesus, Matt. 5:48, RSV.

Yahweh's two commandments that one should not covet his neighbor's wife and commit adultery: Exod. 20:14, 13, NJPS. Repeated in Deut. 5:18, 17, NJPS, Lev. 18:20, NJPS.

Maimonides here interpreted the term "covet": Moses Maimonides, Talmud, Hilkhot Gezeila Va-aveida 1:11. See also Michael Leo Samuel, "Thou Shalt Not Covet: Can a Feeling be Legislated?," http://rabbimichaelsamuel.com/2010/02/thou-shalt-not-covet-can-a-feeling-be-legislated/.

"everyone who looks at a woman lustfully": Jesus, Matt. 5:28, RSV. I have combined the words "every one" into one word.

"Let him who is without sin": Jn. 8:7, RSV.

a barbarism that the Talmud soon enough also condemned: The Talmud's condemnation of stoning applies to burning, slaying (by the sword), and strangling, too, i.e., to any type of death penalty. Mishnah Makkot 1:10 states: "A Sanhedrin that puts a man to death once in seven years is called destructive. Rabbi Eliezer ben Azariah says: even once in seventy years. Rabbi Akiba and Rabbi Tarfon say: had we been in the Sanhedrin none would ever have been put to death. Rabban Simeon ben Gamaliel says: they would have multiplied shedders of blood in Israel."

The doctrine of original sin—a Christian (and especially Pauline) idea: The doctrine of original sin was formally introduced by Paul in Rom. 5:12–21 and 1 Cor. 15:22.

according to Augustine, in a state of "total depravity": See Augustine, Chapter 3 in Book XIII, *City of God*. Available at http://www.newadvent.org/fathers/120113.htm.

This notion tends to breed a contempt not only for humanity but also for the physical world: Of this contempt, Nietzsche writes: "Christianity was from the start essentially and thoroughly disgust and weariness with life, which only dressed itself up, only hid itself in, only decorated itself with the belief in an 'other' or 'better' life. The hatred of the 'world,' the curse against the emotions, the fear of beauty and sensuality, a world beyond created so that the world on this side might be more easily slandered, at bottom a longing for nothingness, for extinction, for rest, until the 'Sabbath of all Sabbaths'—all that, as well as the absolute desire of Christianity to value only moral worth, has always seemed to me the most dangerous and most eerie form of all possible manifestations of a 'Will to Destruction,' at least a sign of the deepest illness, weariness, bad temper, exhaustion, and impoverishment in living" (Friedrich Nietzsche, *The Birth of Tragedy*, trans. Ian C. Johnston, Blackmask Online, 1872, 2003, p. 5).

since when man fell, Paul tells us, all creation, too, became subject to decay: See Rom. 8:20–23.

"groaning in travail together until now": Rom. 8:22, RSV.

"I have come into this world to judge it": Jn. 9:39, International Standard Version.

"I came to cast fire upon the earth": Lk. 12:49, RSV.

"Christ becomes more formidable": Martin Luther, qtd. in Erik H. Erikson, *Young Man Luther: A Study in Psychoanalysis and History* (1958), W. W. Norton, New York, 1962, pp. 195, 71. Erikson cites Otto Scheel, *Dokumente zu Luthers Entwicklung*, J. C. B. Mohr, Tubingen, Germany, 1929, I, 20, Nos. 182, 406, 430.

"he was so meticulous": Erik H. Erikson, *ibid.*, pp. 155–56. Erikson cites Otto Scheel, *ibid.*, No. 487. See also Erikson, p. 163, where he cites Luther's acknowledgment that concupiscence is a leftover of original sin.

"One woman said that she beat herself": Robert E. Lerner, *The Heresy of the Free Spirit in the Later Middle Ages*, University of California Press, Berkeley, California, 1972, p. 114. Also qtd. in Bradley A. TePaske, *Sexuality and the Religious Imagination*, Spring Journal Books, New Orleans, Louisiana, 2008, p. 65.

both Martin Luther and John Calvin . . . were Yahwists: Luther's teaching on original sin is captured in the second article in Lutheranism's "Augsburg Confession": "It is also taught among us that since the fall of Adam all men who are born according to the course of nature are conceived and born in sin. That is, all men are full of evil lust and inclinations from their mothers' wombs and are unable by nature to have true fear of God and true faith in God. Moreover, this inborn sickness and hereditary sin is truly sin and condemns to the eternal wrath of God all those who are not born again through Baptism and the Holy Spirit" ("The Augsburg Confession [1530]," in Theodore G. Tappert, *The Book of Concord: The Confessions of the Evangelical Lutheran Church, Fortress Press, Philadelphia, 1959, p. 29)*. On Luther's personal struggle with sin, see Erik H. Erikson, *Young Man Luther, op. cit.*

Calvin arrived at a similar position on original sin as Luther did but by way of Augustine's notion of total depravity. Even after spiritual regeneration or rebirth, the inextricable evil in human nature is mixed with and distorts even our good deeds. See John Calvin, *The Institutes of the Christian Religion*, Vol. 2, Library of Christian Classics, trans. Ford Lewis Battles, ed. John T. McNeill, Westminster, Philadelphia, 1960, p. 251. See also William J. Bouwsma, *John Calvin: A Sixteenth-Century Portrait*, Oxford University Press, New York, Questia Online Library, 1989, p. 139, and Richard A. Muller, *Calvin and the Reformed Tradition*, Baker Academic, e-book edition, Grand Rapids, MI, 2012, p. 51.

In his American tale *The Scarlet Letter*: Nathaniel Hawthorne's *The Scarlet Letter, Bloom's Modern Critical Interpretations*, ed. Harold Bloom, Chelsea House Publishers, New York, 2007.

Even a Christian existential thinker like Søren Kierkegaard: See Erik H. Erikson, *Insight and Responsibility: Lectures on the Ethical Implications of Psychoanalytic Insight*, W. W. Norton, New York, 1972, p. 202, and *Young Man Luther, op. cit.*, p. 240. See also Simon D. Podmore's excellent article "Kierkegaard as Physician of the Soul: On Self-forgiveness and Despair," *Journal of Psychology and Theology*, Vol. 37, No. 3, 2009, pp. 174–85. Also available at http://www.thedivineconspiracy. org/Z5241K.pdf.

prompted Jung to describe his condition as a complicated intellectual neurosis: See James P. Driscoll, *The Unfolding God of Jung and Milton*, University Press of Kentucky, Lexington, Kentucky, 1993, pp. 211–12, n. 55. Driscoll cites C. G. Jung, letter to Arnold Kunzli, March 16, 1943, *C. G. Jung Letters*, Vol. 1, 1906–1950, eds. Gerhard Adler and Aniela Jaffé, trans. R. F. C. Hull, Princeton University Press, Bollingen Series XCV, Princeton, NJ, 1975, p. 332; and letter to Willi Bremi, December 26, 1953, Vol. 2, 1951–61, p. 145.

"Water that is too pure has no fish": *Ts'ai Ken T'an*, trans. William Scott Wilson, *The Roots of Wisdom: Faikontan*, Kodansha International, Tokyo, New York, 1985. This is a book of Taoist, Confucian, and Zen Buddhist homilies compiled during China's Ming dynasty, 1368–1644.

Chapter 11: The Sacrilege of Holy War

"Men never do evil so completely": Blaise Pascal, *Pensées,* trans. W. F. Trotter, E. P. Dutton, New York, 1958, quote No. 894 or 895 depending on the edition.

"Onward, Christian soldiers, marching as to war": "Onward, Christian Soldiers," Sabine Baring-Gould, in *Church Times,* 1865. The lyrics of this hymn are based on a passage in Paul's second letter to Timothy: "Share in suffering as a good soldier of Christ Jesus" (2 Timothy 2:3, RSV). However, the literal application of this imagery to actual war rests on Yahwistic underpinnings, since the connection of God with war finds its beginnings in the Abrahamic religions with Yahweh.

In the course of the eight main Crusades, three million died by conservative estimates: A range of scholarly estimates are provided by Matthew White at "Selected Death Tolls for Wars, Massacres and Atrocities Before the 20th Century," © 1999–2010; available at http://necrometrics. com/pre1700a.htm#Crusades. John M. Robertson estimates that as many as nine million died; see *A Short History of Christianity*, Watts & Co., London, 1902, p. 278. Available at https://archive.org/stream/ashorthistorych00unkngoog#page/n8/mode/2up.

thirty thousand Jews and Muslims were slaughtered in two days: *ibid.*

One witness reported: *ibid.*

The Fourth Crusade even involved an attack: *ibid.*

"a primitive backwater, isolated from other civilizations": *ibid.*

The rock band Arcade Fire makes a noble attempt: Arcade Fire (Win Butler, Regine Chassagne, Tim Kingsbury, Richard R. Parry, William Butler, and Jeremy Gara), "Windowsill," *Neon Bible*, Merge Records, lyrics © EMI Music Publishing, 2007.

journalist Joe Klein accurately assessed him as an "Old Testament tyrant": Joe Klein, "Number Four: Bashar Assad, the Lethal Tyrant," *Time*, December 23, 2013, p. 127.

the UN declared his actions a genocide: The UN's criteria of a genocide are set forth in UN Resolution 260, which adopts the guidelines of the 1948 International Convention on the Prevention and Punishment of the Crime of Genocide.

"Alawites practice a unique but little known form of Islam": Primoz Manfreda, "The Difference Between Alawites and Sunnis in Syria: Why Is There Sunni-Alawite Tension in Syria?," *About News*. Available at http://middleeast.about.com/od/syria/tp/The-Difference-Between-Alawites-And-Sunnis-In-Syria.htm. I have pluralized the word "century."

an estimated 7.5 million people died in the Thirty Years' War: http://necrometrics.com/pre1700a.htm#30YrW, No. 33. A variety of sources are provided here. See also *Encyclopaedia Britannica* at http://www.britannica.com/EBchecked/topic/195896/history-of-Europe/58335/Demographics#ref=ref310375; http://web.archive.org/web/20080504165414/http://www.czech.cz/en/czech-republic/history/all-about-czech-history/the-thirty-years-war/.

"You are part of Antichrist": Oliver Cromwell, Declaration to the Irish Catholic Clergy, 1650. Available at http://www.sparknotes.com/biography/cromwell/section6.rhtml.

The rabbinic sage largely responsible for this shift was Yohanan Ben Zakkai: Rabbinic scholar Adin Steinsaltz writes: "After the destruction of the Temple, [Yohanan Ben Zakkai] faced the challenge of establishing a new center for the people and helping them adjust to the new circumstances whereby religious ardor had to be diverted to another focal point now that the Temple had ceased to exist. Yohanan Ben Zakkai issued ten important and urgently needed ordinances in order to adapt Jewish life and *halakhah* [the practice of the Law] to the new reality and perpetuate the memory of the Temple until such time as it could be rebuilt. The very fact that Jews were able to nurture and develop their national and cultural life in the 2,000 years that followed attests to the success of his endeavors" (*The Essential Talmud*, Basic Books, New York, 1976, p. 27).

"both the Great Revolt of 66 CE": Reuven Firestone, "Holy War: A Jewish Problem, Too," *MyJewishLearning*, available at http://www.myjewishlearning.com/beliefs/Issues/War_and_Peace/Combat_and_Conflict/Holy_War.shtml?p=2. I have capitalized the *g* in "Great."

the Revolt Against Heraclius from 613–14 CE. . . . With the Persians' permission, the Jews effectively controlled the city for the next five years: see "Jewish Revolt Against Heraclius," Project Gutenberg Self-Publishing Press, available at http://self.gutenberg.org/articles/jewish_revolt_against_heraclius, and Lambert M. Surhone, Mariam T. Tennoe, and Susan F. Henssonow, *Jewish Revolt Against Heraclius*, Betascript Publishing/International Book Market Service, Beau Bassin-Rose Hill, Mauritius, 2010.

The Bible also tells us that Abraham had two sons: Gen. 16.

Hagar—an Egyptian slave who was Sarah's maid: Gen. 16:1.

Yahweh told Abraham to not be distressed: Gen. 21:12–13.

both sons will be the founders of great nations: Abraham's role as a founder of nations is also implied by his name, which in ancient Hebrew means "father of a host of nations."

An angel later repeated the same about Ishmael to Hagar: Gen. 21:17–18.

"shall be a wild ass of a man": Genesis 16:12, combined translation from NJPS and the Jerusalem Bible.

"He would be a wild man": Ismail ibn Kathir, qtd. in Reuven Firestone, *Journeys in Holy Lands: The Evolution of the Abraham-Ishmael Legends in Islamic Exegesis,*: SUNY Press, Albany, New York, 1990, p. 42. Firestone is quoting from Ibn Kathir's "The Birth of Ishmael from Hagar."

Amir claimed he was acting in accordance with Jewish law. . . . He believed Rabin's policies endangered his fellow Jews: See Steven Opager, "A History of Violence in Religions," in *Encyclopedia of Murder and Violent Crime*, ed. Eric Hickey, Sage Publications, Thousand Oaks, California, 2003, p. 220.

to be conducted by composer David Woodard: Susan Carpenter, "In Concert at a Killer's Death," *Los Angeles Times*, May 9, 2001. Available at http://articles.latimes.com/2001/may/09/news/cl-60944.

his final meal consisted of two pints: Dina Spector, "Famous Last Meals: What Notorious Criminals Ate Before They Were Executed," *Business Insider*, October 22, 2011. Available at http://www.businessinsider.com/famous-last-meal-2011-10#timothy-mcveigh-two-pints-of-mint-chocolate-chip-ice-cream-1.

Two kinds were originally distinguished: For an overview of the lesser jihad, see T. David Curp, "War Without End: A Brief History of the Muslim Conquests," *Crisis Magazine*, November 1, 2005. Available at http://www.crisismagazine.com/2005/war-without-end-a-brief-history-of-the-muslim-conquests.

"Fighting and conquering negativity in your heart is the real jihad": Shah Rukh Khan, qtd. in *Daily News & Analysis,* Mumbai, India, November 15, 2001.

"In Islam's first centuries": T. David Curp, *op. cit.*

"a battle for the sake of God": qtd. in Reza Aslan, *Beyond Fundamentalism*, Random House, New York, 2010, p. 4. Originally published in a slightly different form as *How to Win a Cosmic War*, Random House, New York, 2009.

"They were engaged": Reza Aslan, *ibid.*, p. 5.

"Those who are educated": Ömer Taşpinar, "You Can't Understand Why People Join ISIS Without Understanding Relative Deprivation," *TheWorldPost*, a partnership of the Huffington Post and Berggruen Institute, March 25, 2015, available at http://www.huffingtonpost.com/amer-tapaenar-/isis-relative-deprivation_b_6912460.html.

a short and recent "history of rage and retribution": Bobby Ghosh, "Flashpoint: Death in Benghazi," *Time*, September 24, 2012, p. 31.

"People find their selfhood": Salman Rushdie, *The Charlie Rose Show*, PBS, September 18, 2012.

more than five thousand mesmerizing speeches promising his followers: Amanda Macias, "How Hitler's Populist Rhetoric Contributed to His Rise to Power," *Business Insider*, May 13, 2015, available at https://www.businessinsider.com/why-hitler-was-such-a-successful-orator-2015-5.

"What we must fight for": Adolf Hitler, "A Reckoning," Vol. 1 of *Mein Kampf*, Chapter 8, "The Beginning of My Political Activity," trans. Ralph Manheim, Houghton Mifflin, Boston, 1971, p. 71. Also available at https://mondopolitico.com/library/meinkampf/v1c8.htm. I have capitalized "Fatherland" and "Creator," as have some other translations.

As theologian Charles Henkey, among others, have said: personal communication, Loyola of Montreal, Montreal, 1973.

telling them they were being "resettled" in labor camps and getting showers to rid themselves of lice: See "Deportations to Killing Centers," *Holocaust Encyclopedia*, United States Holocaust Memorial Museum, Washington, DC, available at https://encyclopedia.ushmm.org/content/en/article/deportations-to-killing-centers; "At the Killing Centers," *ibid.*, available at https://encyclopedia.ushmm.org/content/en/article/at-the-killing-centers.

some seventy-five million people, by one estimate: "Casualties of World War II," Chapter 28 in *History of Western Civilization II*, ER Services, available at https://courses.lumenlearning.com/suny-hccc-worldhistory2/chapter/casualties-of-world-war-ii/.

"If the crusaders, seized by a common enthusiasm": qtd. in James H. Moorhead, "Preaching the Holy War (Bible in America)," *Christian History Institute*, available at https://christianhistoryinstitute.org/magazine/article/preaching-the-holy-war-ch138.

"The stage is set": Woodrow Wilson, speech accompanying submission of the Treaty of Versailles to the US Senate, July 10, 1919. This quotation is also inscribed on Wilson's tombstone in Washington National Cathedral in Washington, DC.

For a variety of reasons: See Richard Striner, *Woodrow Wilson and World War One: A Burden Too Great to Bear*, Rowman & Littlefield, Lanham, MD, 2014, pp. 219–20.

scientific thinking vs. anti-scientific thinking: See Richard Hofstadter, *Anti-Intellectualism in American Life*, Vintage Books/Random House, New York, 1973.

Yahweh Sabaoth—one of Yahweh's various biblical names: The name "Yahweh Sabaoth" or "Lord of Hosts" appears well over two hundred times in the Hebrew Bible or Old Testament, mostly in the prophetic books. It first appears in 1 Sam. 1:3. It also appears at least twice in the New Testament: Rom. 9:29 and Jas. 5:4.

Chapter 12: The Embers of Western and Islamic Imperialism

"Emotional neglect lays the groundwork": bell hooks, *The Will to Change: Men, Masculinity, and Love*, Atria Books/Simon & Schuster, New York, © 2004 by Gloria Watkins, p. 51.

In New England, for instance, colonists believing that one of their own . . . sold them into slavery in Bermuda: Keith Evans, *American and Latin-American Indians: A Brief and Informative Guide—and Much More*, Xlibris, Bloomington, IN, 2000, p. 122.

The film *Even the Rain* unabashedly shows: *Even the Rain*, dir. Icíar Bollaín, Morena Films, Alebrije Cine y Video, Mandarin Cinema, 2010.

The renowned Spanish theologian Juan Ginés de Sepúlveda argued: Eduardo Galeano, *Open*

Veins of Latin America: Five Centuries of the Pillage of a Continent, trans. Cedric Belfrage, Foreword by Isabel Allende, Monthly Review Press, New York, 1997, p. 41.

"The Spaniards in Mexico and Peru": Bertrand Russell, *Why I Am Not a Christian and Other Essays on Religion and Related Subjects,* George Allen & Unwin/Touchstone/Simon & Schuster, New York, 1957, p. 35.

In spite of Pope Paul III's declaration . . . even Enlightenment thinkers like Voltaire, Montesquieu, and Hume: Eduardo Galeano, *Open Veins of Latin America, op. cit.,* p. 41.

one of the worst in terms of cruelty and war crimes on the part of the United States: See Howard Zinn, *A People's History of the United States,* HarperCollins, New York, 1990, pp. 307–8. Chapter 12, "The Empire and the People," provides a brief but excellent treatment of the subject of American imperialism. Zinn cites the Philadelphia *Ledger* for the following quotes: "God damn the U.S. for its vile conduct in the Philippine Isles" (William James). "We have pacified some thousands of the islanders and buried them; destroyed their fields; burned their villages, and turned their widows and orphans out-of-doors; furnished heartbreak by exile to some dozens of disagreeable patriots; subjugated the remaining ten millions by Benevolent Assimilation, which is the pious new name of the musket; we have acquired property in the three hundred concubines and other slaves of our business partner, the Sultan of Sulu, and hoisted our protecting flag over that swag. And so, by these Providences of God—and the phrase is the government's, not mine—we are a World Power" (Mark Twain). See also Richard E. Welch, Jr., "American Atrocities in the Philippines: The Indictment and the Response," *Pacific Historical Review,* University of California Press, Vol. 43, No. 2, May 1974, pp. 233–53; available at https://en.wikipedia.org/wiki/Philippine–American_War.

"There was nothing left for us to do": William McKinley, based on an account of what he told a group of ministers who visited the White House; qtd. in Zinn, *ibid.,* pp. 305–6.

"When he wants a new market": George Bernard Shaw, *The Man of Destiny* (1898), in *Plays Pleasant,* Penguin Books, London, New York, 1946, p. 205. Shaw is here speaking in the character of Napoleon.

Although Chief Justice John Marshall ruled: Jon Meacham, *American Lion: Andrew Jackson in the White House,* Random House, New York, 2008, p. 152.

Because some four thousand of the sixteen thousand Cherokees who made this journey died: *ibid.,* p. 318. On the historical events and legal decisions leading to the Trail of Tears, see http://www.georgiaencyclopedia.org/articles/government-politics/worcester-v-georgia-1832.

However, Jackson—a militant, imperial Yahwist if ever there was one: Jon Meacham offers an insightful portrait of Jackson's Yahwism that has larger implications as well: "In the saga of the Jackson presidency, one marked by both democratic triumphs and racist tragedies, we can see the American character in formation and in action. To understand him and his time helps us to understand America's perennially competing impulses. Jackson's life and work—and the nation he protected and served—were shaped by the struggle between grace and rage, generosity and violence, justice and cruelty" (Meacham, *op. cit.,* p. xx). Is this not also the struggle of Yahweh? John C. Calhoun said of Jackson: "Infatuated man! Blinded by ambition—intoxicated by flattery and vanity! Who, that is the least acquainted with the human heart; who, that is conversant with the page of history, does not see, under all this, the workings of a dark, lawless, and insatiable ambition . . . ?" (qtd. in Meacham, p. 288). Jonathan Chait, too, is most critical of Jackson: "Andrew Jackson, still introduced to schoolchildren as the hero of the common man, was a white supremacist with a fanatical hatred for any government role in economic development—a kind of 19th-century Ron Paul, but with a genocidal militaristic foreign policy" (Jonathan Chait, "History Will Be Very Kind," *New York Magazine*, January 12, 2014. Also available at http://nymag.com/daily/intelligencer/2015/01/obamas-legacy-chait.html).

"a riddle wrapped in a mystery inside an enigma": Winston Churchill, BBC broadcast, London, October 1, 1939. Available at http://www.churchill-society-london.org.uk/RusnEnig.html.

What did President Vladimir Putin want when: poll taken by the All-Russian Center for Public Opinion Research and reported by *USA Today*, March 19, 2014. Available at http://www.usatoday.com/story/news/world/2014/03/18/crimea-ukraine-putin-russia/6564263/.

restore Russia's place in the ranks of great powers: Michael Crowley and Simon Shuster, "What Putin Wants/Czars in His Eyes/'This is War,'" *Time*, May 19, 2014, p. 33. I have changed the Russian transliteration of "Kiev" to the Ukrainian and more currently used "Kyiv." See also Michael Hirsh, "Putin's Thousand-Year War: *Foreign Policy*, March 12, 2022, available at https://foreignpolicy.com/2022/03/12/putins-thousand-year-war/.

on the grounds, as he falsely claimed, of ending a genocide by a Ukrainian Nazi regime: In a speech on February 23, 2022, Putin claimed, "The purpose of this operation is to protect people who, for eight years now, have been facing humiliation and genocide perpetrated by the Kyiv regime. To this end, we will seek to demilitarize and denazify Ukraine, as well as bring to trial those who perpetrated numerous bloody crimes against civilians, including against citizens of the Russian Federation." Qtd. in Ewelina U. Ochab, "Is Putin Committing Genocide in Ukraine?," *Forbes*, April 4, 2022, available at https://www.forbes.com/sites/ewelinaochab/2022/04/04/is-putin-committing-genocide-in-ukraine/?sh=1974e9e5557b. I have changed the Russian transliteration of "Kiev" to the Ukrainian and more currently used "Kyiv."

what a number of Western leaders have observed: Bill Clinton, George W. Bush, Robert M. Gates, and John Bolton are among a few of them. See "'One Cold Dude: US Presidents on Putin," *The Times of India*, April 15, 2021, available at https://timesofindia.indiatimes.com/world/us/one-cold-dude-us-presidents-on-putin/articleshow/83539477.cms; "John Bolton Says Putin Isn't Unstable—He's a 'Cold, Hard, Calculating Man,' " Marita Vlachou, *Huffpost*, March 7, 2022 (in turn qtd. from *BBC News*).

"For 400 years, from the mid-9th century": William W. Cooper and Piyu Yue, *Challenges of the Muslim World: Present, Future and Past*, Emerald Group Publishing, Bingley, United Kingdom, 2008, p. 215.

"The Mohammedan conquest of India": Will Durant, *The Story of Civilization: Our Oriental Heritage*, Vol. 1, Simon & Schuster, New York, 1935, p. 459.

As many as a million were enslaved: See Robert C. Davis, *Christian Slaves, Muslim Masters*, Palgrave Macmillan, Basingstoke, United Kingdom/New York, 2003.

"Show me just what Muhammad brought": Manuel II Palaiologos, from a widely qtd. dialogue believed to have occurred in 1391 between Manuel II and a Persian scholar, and recorded in Dialogue 7 in a book by Manuel II, *Twenty-six Dialogues with a Persian*. In modern times, Churchill more or less expressed the same view: "Individual Moslems may show splendid qualities, but the influence of the religion paralyzes the social development of those who follow it. No stronger retrograde force exists in the world. Far from being moribund, Mohammedanism is a militant and proselytizing faith. It has already spread throughout Central Africa, raising fearless warriors at every step, and were it not that Christianity is sheltered in the strong arms of science, the science against which it (Islam) has vainly struggled, the civilization of modern Europe might fall, as fell the civilization of ancient

Rome" (Winston Spencer Churchill, *The River War*, Longmans, Green & Co., London, 1899, Vol. II, pp. 248–50).

When Pope Benedict XVI . . . repeated these words in a speech: This speech is known as the Regensburg Lecture. It was delivered on September 12, 2006, at the University of Regensburg, Germany, where Ratzinger had previously served as a professor of theology. The actual title of the lecture was "Faith, Reason and the University—Memories and Reflections." It is considered an important papal statement on world affairs. See Raymond J. de Souza, "Regensburg Revisited: Faith, Reason and the Islamic State," *National Catholic Register*, March 22, 2015; available at http://www. ncregister.com/daily-news/regensburg-revisited-faith-reason-and-the-islamic-state.

Riots broke out in the Middle East. . . . "Jesus is the slave of Allah": See "The Pope and Islam: Is There Anything that Pope Benedict XVI Would Like to Discuss?," *New Yorker*, April 2, 2007; available at http://www.newyorker.com/magazine/2007/04/02/the-pope-and-islam.

A Catholic priest and nun were murdered: See "Iraq Priest 'Killed Over Pope Speech," *Aljazeera*, October 12, 2006, available at http://www.aljazeera.com/archive/2006/10/2008410112440673544. html, and David Gibson, "Pope Benedict XVI's Regensburg Lecture on Islam Gets a Second Look in the Wake of Islamic State," *Huffington Post*, September 11, 2014, available at http://www. huffingtonpost.com/2014/09/11/pope-benedict-xvi-islam_n_5800440.html.

"Muslims around the world unintentionally confirmed": Stephen Andrew Missick, *The Hammer of God: The Stories of Judas Maccabeus and Charles Martel*, Xulon Press, Maitland, FL, 2010, p. 213.

"in the sense of a state ruled by the church or by priests": Bernard Lewis, *What Went Wrong?: Western Impact and Middle Eastern Response*, Oxford University Press, New York, 2002, p. 114.

"in the Muslim conception, God is the true sovereign of the community": *ibid.*, p. 113.

"The first and in many ways the most profound difference": *ibid.*, pp. 100–101.

"absence of a native secularism in Islam": *ibid.*, p. 100.

"Render to Caesar the things": Mk. 12:17, KJV. Lewis quotes Matt. 22:21 on p. 97 of *What Went Wrong?*

Augustine further clarified the differences: See Augustine, *City of God*. Available at http:// www.newadvent.org/fathers/120113.htm.

"Muslim scholars argue that the Qur'an advocates": Ibrahim B. Syed, "Rise and Fall of Muslims," Islamic Research Foundation International, © 1988–2012. Available at http://www.irfi. org/articles/articles_201_250/rise_and_fall_of_muslims.htm.

And this, as Lewis would say, is what went wrong with Islam: Bernard Lewis, *What Went Wrong?, op. cit.*

Such an attitude, Arnold Toynbee warns: See Arnold Toynbee, *A Study of History*, ed. Arnold Toynbee and Jane Caplan, Portland House, New York, 1988, especially Part III, "The Growths of Civilizations," Part IV, "The Breakdowns of Civilizations," and Part V, "The Disintegrations of Civilizations," pp. 127–318.

apocalyptic fever fires the ideology of both its ayatollahs and nonclerical leaders: See Bernard Lewis, "Islam and the West: A Conversation with Bernard Lewis," Pew Forum on Religion & Public Life, Pew Research Center, Washington, DC, April 27, 2006. Available at http://www. pewforum.org/2006/04/27/islam-and-the-west-a-conversation-with-bernard-lewis/.

"all bets are off": Benjamin Netanyahu, *The Charlie Rose Show*, PBS, October 1, 2013.

Wahhabism or Salafism . . . still has a strong presence in these states: "Wahhabi–Islamic

Movement," *Encyclopaedia Britannica*, available at https://www.britannica.com/topic/Wahhabi; "Analysis–Wahhabism," *Frontline*, PBS, available at https://www.pbs.org/wgbh/pages/frontline/shows/saudi/analyses/wahhabism.html.

as Lewis and others have described this phenomenon: See Bernard Lewis, "The Roots of Muslim Rage: Why So Many Muslims Deeply Resent the West, and Why Their Bitterness Will Not Easily Be Mollified," *The Atlantic*, September 1, 1990; available at http://www.theatlantic.com/magazine/archive/1990/09/the-roots-of-muslim-rage/304643/. See also Samuel P. Huntington, *The Clash of Civilizations and the Remaking of World Order*, Touchstone/Simon & Schuster, New York, 1997; *The Clash of Civilizations?: The Debate*, ed. Samuel P. Huntington, Simon & Schuster, New York, 1996; and Basil Mathews, *Young Islam on Trek: A Study in the Clash of Civilizations*, Friendship Press, New York, 1926. The term was coined by Mathews.

our own "war against terror": Harold Bloom, *op. cit.*, p. 157.

gruesome photographs and videos of torture and prisoner abuse: See http://www.disclose.tv/action/viewvideo/168485/Iraq_Abu_Ghraib_Prison_Torture_Uncensored_Pictures_and_Video_Footage/.

"War belongs to our souls": James Hillman, *A Terrible Love of War*, Penguin Press, New York, 2004, p. 214.

"In the case of [Muslim extremists], their radical Islamist dream": Thomas Singer, "Cultural Complexes and Archetypal Defenses of the Group Spirit," in *Terror, Violence and the Impulse to Destroy: Perspectives from Analytical Psychology*, John Beebe, ed., Papers from the 2002 North American Conference of Jungian Analysts and Candidates, Daimon Verlag, Einsedeln, Switzerland, 2003, p. 203.

what Benjamin Barber calls "McWorld": Benjamin R. Barber, "Jihad vs. McWorld," *The Atlantic*, March 1, 1992, available at http://www.theatlantic.com/magazine/archive/1992/03/jihad-vs-mcworld/303882/.

"The basic issue goes back to the late eighteenth century": Itamar Rabinovich, *The Charlie Rose Show*, PBS, March 21, 2013.

Part IV: God Bless Yahweh

"And I will betroth thee unto Me forever": Hos. 2:21–22. This passage may be found in any translation of the Hebrew Bible. In the Old Testament, it corresponds to Hos. 2:19–20, any translation. However, the translation I use here is from the *Prayer Book: Abridged for Jews in the Armed Forces of the United States*, National Jewish Welfare Board, New York, 1943, p. 130. I have combined the words "for ever" into one word. These verses are regularly recited as part of the ritual practice of putting on the *tefillin* or phylacteries every morning (except Sabbath and major holy days) as prescribed in Exod. 13:9, 13:16 and Deut. 6:8, 11:18, any translation.

Chapter 13: The Calling of Winston Churchill

"Centuries ago words were written": Winston Churchill, first broadcast as prime minister, May 19, 1940, on record at the Churchill Centre and Museum at the Churchill War Rooms, London. Churchill adopted the quotation from 1 Maccabees 3:58–60. The four Books of the Maccabees, also spelled as "Machabbes," are not in the Hebrew Bible, though the first two of these books are part of canonical scripture in the Septuagint and the Vulgate and are in the Protestant Apocrypha. Churchill somewhat edited the text.

"The Enemy Within," an episode from the original *Star Trek* series: "The Enemy Within," *Star Trek*, dir. Leo Penn, written by Richard Matheson, created and produced by Gene Roddenberry, airdate October 6, 1966, © 1999 Paramount Pictures.

On one occasion at age 13, he was playing with toy soldiers: cited in C. Brian Kelly and Ingrid Smyer, *Best Little Stories from the Life and Times of Winston Churchill*, Cumberland House Publishing, Nashville, Tennessee, 2008, p. 36.

"god of storm and frenzy": C. G. Jung, "Wotan" (1936), in *Civilization in Transition*, Vol. 10 of *The Collected Works of C. G. Jung*, trans. R. F. C. Hull, Princeton University Press, Bollingen Series XX, Princeton, NJ, 1978, par. 375.

what he called "Christian civilization" and "Christian ethics": See Jonathan Sandys and Wallace Henley, "Preserving 'a Certain Way of Life'," Chapter 7 in *God and Churchill: How the Great Leader's Sense of Divine Destiny Changed His Troubled World and Offers Hope for Ours*, Foreword by James Baker III, Tyndale Momentum/Tyndale House Publishers, Carol Stream, IL, 2015, pp. 115–32. This entire volume is an excellent treatment of Churchill's religious orientation and inner calling.

For him, both of these explicitly included their Jewish foundation: See Steven F. Hayward, "Was Churchill a Zionist?," *The Weekly Standard*, June 16, 2008, available at American Enterprise Institute, https://www.aei.org/articles/was-churchill-a-zionist/.

"one of the greatest of human beings": Winston Churchill, qtd. in Sandys and Henley, pp. 119–20.

he didn't believe in the divinity of Jesus and rarely went to church: Christopher Gehrz, "Winston Churchill Fought for 'Christian Civilization,' but He Rarely Went to Church," *Christianity Today*, January 21, 2021. Available at https://www.christianitytoday.com/ct/2021/january-web-only/winston-churchill-fought-for-christian-civilization-but-he-.html. This is a book review of Gary Scott Smith's Duty and Destiny: The Life and Faith of Winston Churchill.

he espoused Jesus's Sermon on the Mount as "the last word in ethics": qtd. in Andrew Roberts, *Finest Hour*, no. 163, "Churchill Proceedings—Winston Churchill and Religion—A Comfortable Relationship with the Almighty," International Churchill Society, p. 52, available at https://winstonchurchill.org/publications/finest-hour/finest-hour-163/churchill-proceedings-winston-churchill-and-religion-a-comfortable-relationship-with-the-almighty/. Roberts in turn cites John Colville (Churchill's private secretary), *Fringes of Power*, Hodder & Stoughton, London, 1983, p. 648.

"We sang 'Onward, Christian Soldiers' indeed": Winston Churchill, in Ace Collins, *Stories Behind the Hymns That Inspire America*, Zondervan, Grand Rapids, Michigan, 2003, pp. 153–54.

"I felt as if I were walking with destiny": Winston Churchill, *The Second World War, Volume I: The Gathering Storm*, Houghton Mifflin, New York, 1948, p. 601.

"This country will be subjected": qtd. in Jonathan Sandys and Wallace Henley, *op. cit.*, pp. 3, 4. Original source is Winston S. Churchill, "Finest Hour, Man of the Millennium," *Finest Hour*, no. 104, Autumn 1999, pp. 12–15. I substituted the British spelling of "defences" with the American spelling of "defenses."

"God-haunted man": *ibid.*, p. xxx. Quote actually in Wallace Henley's part of the Introduction.

"I go the way that Providence dictates for me": Adolf Hitler, speech of March 14, 1936, Munich. Leaning toward pantheism, Hitler appeared to have viewed Providence as a natural force and as a kind of Aristotelian first principle or original cause of things. This would be in sync with the Wotanism he was unconsciously in service to, as Wotan was a nature god—that is, an aspect of nature. On Hitler's view of God, see Richard Weikart, *Hitler's Religion: The Twisted Beliefs that Drove the Third Reich*, Regnery History/Salem Media Group, Washington, DC, 2016. This book was also reviewed by Donald A. Yerxa in *Reading Religion*, available at https://readingreligion.org/9781621575009/, June 6, 2017.

"For everything there is a season": Ecclesiastes 3:1, American Standard Version.

Chapter 14: The Solomonic Wisdom of Abraham Lincoln

"But I will ask you": John Hay, *Addresses of John Hay*, Century Co., New York, 1906, p. 239. This passage is based on a fragment by Lincoln that Hay found in Lincoln's desk. Written after discouraging days of personal sorrow and military defeats, some of the other thoughts in it appear in Lincoln's second inaugural address (March 4, 1865), whose sublime words Hay accurately said "sound like a new chapter of Hebrew prophecy."

"a matter of but little practical importance": James Buchanan, qtd. in Frank Freidel, *The Presidents of the United States of America*, with contributing author Hugh S. Sidey, Foreword by Bill Clinton, White House Historical Association with the cooperation of the National Geographic Society, Washington, DC, 1964, 1994, p. 36.

"I acknowledge no master but the law": James Buchanan, qtd. in Philip Shriver Klein, *President James Buchanan: A Biography*, Pennsylvania State University Press, University Park, Pennsylvania, 1962, p. 305.

He admitted that if he could pursue a course: Lincoln's specific words were "If I could save the Union without freeing any slave, I would do it; and if I could save it by freeing all the slaves I would do it; and if I could save it by freeing some and leaving others alone, I would also do that" (response in August 1862 to Horace Greeley's editorial in the *New-York Tribune* demanding emancipation; qtd. in Howard Zinn, *A People's History of the United States, op. cit.*, p. 186).

A nation "conceived in liberty": Abraham Lincoln, Gettysburg Address, November 19, 1863.

"last best hope of earth": Abraham Lincoln, Second Annual Message to Congress, December 1, 1862. The entire sentence is "We shall nobly save, or meanly lose, the last best hope of earth."

He was here influenced by the popular writings of the War Department solicitor William Whiting: See William Whiting, *The War Powers of the President and the Legislative Powers of Congress in Relation to Rebellion, Treason, and Slavery*, Boston, 1862; 10th edition, with large additions, 1863; 43rd edition, 1871.

"And all Israel heard": I Kings 3:28, RSV.

Edward Edinger comments that this capacity: Edward Edinger, in "An American Jungian: Edward F. Edinger in Conversation with Lawrence Jaffe," Part 2: "The Psyche in Culture," produced and directed by Dianne D. Cordic. This is a videotaped interview that is available from the C. G. Jung Bookstore and Max & Lore Zeller Library of the C. G. Jung Institute of Los Angeles.

"a good many bloody struggles with the mosquitoes": Abraham Lincoln, speech before the US Congress, 1848, qtd. in James M. McPherson, "Lincoln as Commander in Chief," *Smithsonian* magazine, 2009, at http://www.smithsonianmag.com/history-archaeology/Commander-in-Chief. html#.

Yet as president, he became a sophisticated military strategist: On Lincoln's military sophistication, Herman Hattaway writes: "Lincoln grasped that individual battles were unlikely to be decisive and that the means of victory lay in occupying the enemy's territory and breaking the lines of communication. Early he explained that his 'general idea of the war' was that 'we have the greater numbers, and the enemy has the greater facility of concentrating forces upon the points of collision; that we must fail unless we can find some way of making our advantage an overmatch for his; and that this can be done by menacing him with superior forces at different points, at the same time; so that we can safely attack one, or both, if he makes no change, and if he weakens one to strengthen the other, forebear to attack the strengthened one, but seize, and hold the weakened one, gaining so much.' Modern students of military history have termed this 'the principle of simultaneous advance.' It became a decisive factor in the Union strategy" (Herman Hattaway, "Lincoln's Presidential Example in Dealing with the Military," *Journal of the Abraham Lincoln Association*, Vol. 7, Issue 1, 1985; available at http://hdl.handle.net/2027/spo.2629860.0007.104).

Lincoln said, "I can't spare this man—he fights": Abraham Lincoln, qtd. in Frank Freidel, *op. cit.*, p. 43.

"dripped from him": William Herndon, in Philip B. Kunhardt III, Peter W. Kunhardt, and Peter W. Kunhardt, Jr., *Looking for Lincoln: The Making of an American Icon,* Alfred A. Knopf, New York, 2008, p. 96.

He even called for national days of repentance, which, as historian Garry Wills points out: Garry Wills, cited in *Life,* Collector's Edition: "Celebrating Our Heroes," 1997, Time, Inc., "Hall of Heroes," p. 31.

With his policy of malice toward none and charity for all: Lincoln's actual words in his second inaugural address were "With malice toward none, with charity for all, with firmness in the right as God gives us to see the right, let us strive on to finish the work we are in, to bind up the nation's wounds, to care for him who shall have borne the battle and for his widow and his orphan, to do all which may achieve and cherish a just and lasting peace among ourselves and with all nations" (March 4, 1865).

"Despite interviewing dozens of Lincoln's associates": David Von Drehle, "Lincoln to the Rescue: What the Master Politician Can Teach the Presidential Hopefuls of 2012," in *Time,* November 5, 2012, p. 32.

As author Bruce Feiler has shown, another biblical figure: Bruce Feiler, *America's Prophet: Moses and the American Story,* William Morrow/HarperCollins, New York, 2009, pp. 157–75.

"the Moses of my people": Elizabeth Keckly, qtd.in Philip B. Kunhardt III et al., *op. cit.*, p. 131.

a style emanating what Max Weber described as charismatic authority: Max Weber, *Economy and Society: An Outline of Interpretive Sociology,* Vol. 1., ed. Guenther Roth and Claus Wittich, University of California Press, Berkeley, California, 1978, p. 215.

"I am the president of the United States of America, clothed with immense power": Abraham Lincoln, qtd. in Doris Kearns Goodwin, *Team of Rivals: The Political Genius of Abraham Lincoln,* Simon & Schuster, New York, 2005, p. 687. Goodwin quotes John B. Alley, *Reminiscences of Abraham Lincoln,* ed. Rice, 1886 edition, pp. 585–86.

"a solemn vow before God . . . crown the result": qtd. by Lincoln's secretary of the Navy, in Bruce Feiler, *op. cit.,* p. 162.

His secretary of the Navy described this vow as Lincoln's covenant with God: *ibid.*

As Michael Burlingame suggests: Michael Burlingame, "Surrogate Father Abraham," Chapter 4 in *The Inner World of Abraham Lincoln,* University of Illinois Press, Urbana and Chicago, 1994, pp. 73–91.

"The more the light the deeper the shadow": Johann Wolfgang von Goethe, *Goetz Von Berlichingen with the Iron Hand: A Drama in Five Acts*, Carey, Lea & Blanchard, Philadelphia, 1837, Act I, p. 38. Available at https://books.google.com/books?id=b9CTv4LsKTAC&pg=PR3&source=g bs_toc_r&cad=3#v=onepage&q&f=false. I have changed the sentence; this translation has it as "The more light, the deeper shadow."

If people are about as happy . . . as Lincoln reportedly said: The actual quote is "Folks are usually about as happy as they make up their minds to be." It was first attributed to Lincoln by Frank Crane about fifty years after his death. For a history of the use of this quotation, see http://quoteinvestigator.com/2012/10/20/happy-minds/.

a better angel of our nature, as Lincoln would say: Lincoln's phrase "the better angels of our nature" is from his first inaugural address, March 4, 1861.

"[Lincoln] could be a devious and supple politician": Mario M. Cuomo, *Why Lincoln Matters*, Harcourt, New York, 2004, pp. 24, 26.

Chapter 15: Bob Dylan's Apocalyptic Sensibility

"If we understand the image of the 'Apocalypse'": Edward F. Edinger, *Archetype of the Apocalypse: Divine Vengeance, Terrorism, and the End of the World*, ed. George R. Elder, Open Court, Chicago and La Salle, IL, 1999, pp. 13–14. I have replaced the word "archetype" with "psychic force."

"Dylan has sold out to God": Allen Ginsberg, cited in Sean Wilentz, "Bob Dylan, the Beat Generation, and Allen Ginsberg's America," in The New Yorker, August 16, 2010. Also available at http://www.newyorker.com/online/blogs/newsdesk/2010/08/sean-wilentz-bob-dylan-in-america.html.

his simple yet resonant "Father of Night": This song is on *New Morning* (1970). On "Father of Night" as an interpretation of the Jewish prayer, the Amidah, see *Bob Dylan: The Complete Guide*, an e-book by the Wikemedia Foundation, http://books.google.com/books?id=KwPm3_ge28wC&d q=father+of+night+amidah+bob+dylan&source=gbs_navlinks_s, p. 122.

"I believe in giving credit where credit's due": Bob Johnston, in the documentary *No Direction Home*, dir. Martin Scorsese, Apple, *American Masters*, PBS, 2005, disc 2.

"Not Dark Yet": This song is on *Time Out of Mind* (1997).

"Death Is Not the End": This song is on *Down in the Groove* (1988).

"Things Have Changed": This song is on *The Essential Bob Dylan* (2000). Also available on *Wonder Boys: Music From The Motion Picture*.

"Señor (Tales of Yankee Power)": This song is on *Street Legal* (1978).

Although there appear cloaked references to . . . the Roman Empire: See, for example, Rev. 17:1–2, which refers to a "great harlot who is seated upon many waters, with whom the kings of the earth have committed fornication, and with the wine of whose fornication the dwellers on earth have become drunk" (RSV).

"Go and pour out on the earth": Rev. 16:1, RSV.

Catholic theologians especially distinguish: See Paul Thigpen, "After Death, Two Judgments," *Simply Catholic*, available at https://www.simplycatholic.com/after-death-two-judgments/.

Maimonides pictured it: David Wolpe summarizes Maimonides's view of what will happen at the end of days: "It will not be a time of revenge or cruelty or even supernatural wonders. 'You must not imagine that the messiah must prove his messianism by signs and miracles, doing something unexpected, bringing the dead to life, or similar things.' Rather, nations will dwell together in harmony. People will settle quarrels without malice or injury. All will seek and achieve a knowledge of their Creator as far as possible by human understanding. And Maimonides caps his image of the end time with a quote from the prophet: 'For the earth shall be full with the knowledge of the Lord as the waters cover the sea' (Isa. 11:9)" ("The End Time in Judaism," *Huffington Post*, July 17, 2011, http://www.huffingtonpost.com/rabbi-david-wolpe/end-times-judaism_b_863313.html). A similar passage is Ezek. 39:29: "I will never again hide My face from them, for I will pour out My spirit upon the House of Israel—declares the Lord" (NJPS).

"And many of those who sleep": Dan. 12:2, RSV.

Though on the whole, this awakening will be most joyful: See, for example, Ps. 96:11–13.

"artists and writers going back at least to the Renaissance": These include Bosch, Dürer, Dante, Shakespeare, Milton, Boccaccio, Spenser, and Goethe. More recently, the Apocalypse motif surfaces in the work of Melville, Conrad, Yeats, and Eliot, and it is no stranger to other contemporary authors like Doris Lessing, P. D. James, and Cormac McCarthy. It pervades the science fiction of Arthur C. Clarke, Isaac Asimov, and Philip K. Dick, and is also a favorite among filmmakers, including Ingmar Bergman and Francis Ford Coppola.

Edward Edinger's warning: personal communication, 1995.

Edinger informs us that the Apocalypse motif: *Archetype of the Apocalypse*, *op. cit.*, pp. 5, 10, 12–13, 20, 25–26, 48–49, 52, 58, 75, 98, 108, 119, 127, 139, 143–144, 151, 159, 161, 171, 173–74.

"Ballad of a Thin Man": This song is on *Highway 61 Revisited* (1965).

"Desolation Row": *ibid.*

"One More Cup of Coffee": This song is on the album *Desire* (1976).

"Where Are You Tonight? (Journey Through Dark Heat)": This song is on *Street Legal* (1978).

"When the Night Comes Falling From the Sky": This song is on *Empire Burlesque* (1985).

"Tryin' to Get to Heaven": This song is on *Time Out of Mind* (1997).

"Ain't Talkin' ": This song is on *Modern Times* (2006).

"Watching the River Flow": This song is on *Bob Dylan's Greatest Hits, Vol. II* (1971).

"I Shall Be Released": *ibid.*

"Trust Yourself": This song is on *Empire Burlesque* (1985).

"Every Grain of Sand": This song is on *Shot of Love* (1981).

Dylan himself believes that he has been transfigured: Bob Dylan, in Mikal Gilmore, "Bob Dylan: The Rolling Stone Interview," *Rolling Stone*, New York, Issue 1166, September 27, 2012, pp. 46–47.

"I truly had a born-again experience": Bob Dylan, qtd. in Yo Zushi, "Bob Dylan and His Vengeful, Conservative God," *New Statesman*, November 9, 2017. Available at https://www.newstatesman.com/culture/music-theatre/2017/11/bob-dylan-and-his-vengeful-conservative-god.

"Are you ready for the judgment?": Bob Dylan, qtd. in Richard Williams, "Bob Dylan's Controversial Born-again Phase Explored in New Film," *The Guardian*, March 16, 2018. Available at https://www.theguardian.com/music/2018/mar/16/fire-and-brimstone-new-compilation-resurrects-bob-dylans-born-again-phase.

"Precious Angel": This song is on *Slow Train Coming* (1979). Lyrics available also in Bob Dylan, *Lyrics, 1962–1985*, Alfred A. Knopf, New York, 1994, p. 426.

His first of three evangelical albums: *Slow Train Coming* (1979). The other two albums are *Saved* (1980) and *Shot of Love* (1981).

a painful time in his life by all accounts: See, for example, Clinton Heylin, *Bob Dylan: Behind the Shades Revisited*, HarperEntertainment/HarperCollins, New York, 1991, 2001 and "Shelter from the Storm—the Inside Story of Bob Dylan's Blood on the Tracks," *Uncut*, November 15, 2013, available at https://www.uncut.co.uk/features/shelter-from-the-storm-the-inside-story-of-bob-dylan-s-blood-on-the-tracks-15656/. Naturally, Dylan himself attests to his suffering during this period in the three albums preceding *Slow Train Coming*: *Blood on the Tracks* (1975), *Desire* (1976), and *Street-Legal* (1978).

as songwriter Alvin Muckley put it: personal communication, 1985.

"Each man struggles within himself": Bob Dylan, in Barbara Kerr, interview in four parts in *Toronto Sun*, March 26–29, 1978. Also available at https://en.wikipedia.org/wiki/Where_Are_You_Tonight%3F_(Journey_Through_Dark_Heat).

"The coming of the Antichrist": C. G. Jung, *Aion: Researches into the Phenomenology of the Self* (1950), Vol. 9, Part II of *The Collected Works of C. G. Jung*, trans. R. F. C. Hull, Princeton University Press, Bollingen Series XX, Princeton, NJ, 1968, par. 77.

Chapter 16: How to Live with Our Yahweh Complex

"The possession of complexes does not": C. G. Jung, "Psychotherapy and a Philosophy of Life" (1943), *The Practice of Psychotherapy*, Vol. 16 of *The Collected Works of C. G. Jung*, trans. R. F. C. Hull, Princeton University Press, Bollingen Series XX, Princeton, NJ, 1966, par. 179.

"How to Dismantle an Atomic Bomb is an odd title": Bono, u2.com, specifically, https://www.u2.com/music/albums/4068.

"an unwanted figure of authority": Bono, qtd. in James Ward, "U2 Star Bono Reveals His Father's Agonised Last Words to Him as He Lay Dying from Cancer," *Mirror*, April 12, 2015. Available at https://www.mirror.co.uk/news/world-news/u2-star-bono-reveals-fathers-5507030.

Even his last words were angry ones: See "Bono Reveals Dad's Dying Words," *The Sun*, December 7, 2001, available at https://www.atu2.com/news/bono-reveals-dads-dying-words.html. His last words were "Are you all fuckin' mad. This place is a prison and I want to go home." "And I guess he did," Bono said.

"[When he died] his demise set me off on a journey": Bono, qtd. in Kim Washburn, *Breaking Through by Grace: The Bono Story*, Zonderkidz, Grand Rapids, MI, 2010.

"The hardest thing is facing yourself": John Lennon, in *Rolling Stone*, interview for issue of December 5, 1980. Reported on *NBC Nightly News with Brian Williams*, December 5, 2010.

Freud's famous observation that depression is anger turned inward: See Sigmund Freud, "Mourning and Melancholia," Vol. 14 of *The Standard Edition of the Complete Psychological Works of Sigmund Freud*, ed. James Strachey, Hogarth Press, London, 1914–16, pp. 243-58. Freud does not express this observation in such succinct terms, but the essay clearly conveys it.

"a complex can be really overcome": C. G. Jung, *The Archetypes and the Collective Unconscious*, Vol. 9, Part I of *The Collected Works of C. G. Jung*, trans. R. F. C. Hull, Princeton University Press, Bollingen Series XX, Princeton, NJ, 1977, par. 184.

Ronald Fairbairn calls this feature the internal saboteur: See W. Ronald D. Fairbairn, *An Object-Relations Theory of the Personality*, Basic Books, New York, 1954 and David P. Celani, *Fairbairn's Object Relations Theory in the Clinical Setting*, Columbia University Press, New York, 2010.

"The unconscious mind sees correctly": C. G. Jung, *Answer to Job* (1952), in *Psychology and Religion: West and East*, Vol. 11 of *The Collected Works of C. G. Jung*, trans. R. F. C. Hull, Princeton

University Press, Bollingen Series XX, Princeton, NJ, 1973, par. 608. Also available as a separate volume published by Princeton University Press, Bollingen Paperback Editions, Princeton, NJ, 1973.

what psychoanalyst Ernst Kris calls a regression in the service of the ego: See Danielle Knafo, "Revisiting Ernst Kris's Concept of Regression in the Service of the Ego in Art," in *Psychoanalytic Psychology, Vol. 19, No.* 1, 2002, pp. 24–49. Available at https://www.researchgate. net/publication/232505708_Revisiting_Ernst_Kris%27s_concept_of_Regression_in_the_service_ of_the_ego_in_art

"a genuine attempt to get at something necessary": C. G. Jung, "Some Aspects of Modern Psychotherapy (1929), in *The Practice of Psychotherapy: Essays on the Psychology of the Transference and Other Subjects*, Vol. 16 of *The Collected Works of C. G. Jung*, trans. R. F. C. Hull, Pantheon Books, Bollingen Series XX, 2nd edition (1966), Princeton, NJ, 1973, par. 55.

"I finally fell asleep": Barack Obama, *Dreams from My Father: A Story of Race and Inheritance*, Three Rivers Press, New York, 1995, 2004, pp. 371–72.

Jung in particular concluded that the unconscious has the ability to defy the law of cause and effect: This ability makes possible the universally reported occurrence of precognitive dreams and similar paranormal phenomena. If Obama's dream was indeed such an occurrence, he would not have been the first political leader to have experienced one. Curiously, both Churchill and Lincoln also did. On one occasion during World War II, Churchill obeyed an intuitive impulse to sit opposite to the side where he usually sat in his chauffeur-driven car. A bomb fell near his car that night, and were he sitting in his usual place, he would most probably have been killed (see Jack Fishman and W. H. Allen, *My Darling Clementine*, Pan Books, London, 1964, p. 136). Lincoln had a different response to his experience of dreaming—a few days before his assassination—that he entered the East Room of the White House and saw a throng of people grieving beside a coffin. Asking one of the soldiers guarding it, "Who is dead in the White House?" he was told, "The president. He was killed by an assassin" (see Ward Hill Lamon, *Reflections of Abraham Lincoln: 1847–1865*, ed. Dorothy Lamon, A. C. McClurg and Co., 1895). Lincoln dismissed the dream, assuming it was about someone other than him. Apparently, he interpreted the dream too literally. See Michael Gellert, "Untapped Possibilities," Chapter 3 in *Modern Mysticism: Jung, Zen and the Still Good Hand of God*, Nicolas-Hays, York Beach, ME, 1991, 1994, pp. 49–92. This chapter sets forth a theory of parapsychological phenomena and includes Churchill and Lincoln's experiences, among others.

"Moses said, 'Show me your glory'": Exod. 33:18–23, JB. Spelling and quotation marks have be changed from British style to American style.

The *Shiur Komah*, a text written probably in the second century CE: Literally, "shiur komah" means "the measure of the body," i.e., the body of God. This is a text from the Hekhalot or Gnostic literature of the pre-Kabbalistic Merkabah mystics. See Gershom Scholem, "*Shiur Komah*: The Mystical Shape of the Godhead," Chapter 1 in *On the Mystical Shape of the Godhead: Basic Concepts in the Kabbalah*, Schocken Books, New York, 1976, 1991, pp. 15–55; "Shi'ur Komah," *Encyclopedia. com*, available at https://www.encyclopedia.com/religion/encyclopedias-almanacs-transcripts-and-maps/shiur-komah.

Yahweh's "back *parts*" were exposed, implying also his buttocks: Exod. 33:23, KJV.

"A leopard lies in wait by their towns": Jer. 5:6, NJPS.

The leopard and other wildcats often . . . are shamanic or totem animals: See John Lockley, *Leopard Warrior: A Journey into the African Teachings of Ancestry, Instincts, and Dreams*, Sounds True, Boulder, CO, 2017.

In Dylan's "Highway 61 Revisited," Abraham is warned: This song is on the album with the same title, *Highway 61 Revisited* (1965). Indeed, what would Yahweh have done if Abraham had chosen to *not* sacrifice Isaac? With this question often in mind, the story of Abraham and Isaac has been visited by thinkers and artists in both Judaism (in which it is known as the "Akeida") and Christianity, including Buber, Heschel, Soloveitchik, Kook, Luther, Kant, Kierkegaard, Rembrandt, Titian, and Caravaggio.

"The fear of the Lord is the beginning of wisdom": Ps. 111:10, KJV. Also repeated in Prov. 9:10 and elsewhere.

the Swedish filmmaker Ingmar Bergman said: See "An Introduction to Ingmar Bergman," dir. and executive producer Lewis Freedman, Public Broadcast Laboratory Series, 1968.

"I form the light, and create darkness": Isa. 45:7, KJV.

"The only trustworthy thing in the universe": Edward F. Edinger, *Ego and Self: The Old Testament Prophets—From Isaiah to Malachi*, trans. and ed. J. Gary Sparks, Inner City Books, Toronto, 2000, p. 146. I have capitalized the *h* in "How."

Buddhist teacher Michele McDonald's technique of RAIN: See https://tricycle.org/magazine/rain/.

the "nourishing art of mindful inquiry": See https://learn.tricycle.org/courses/rain.

"This thing of darkness": William Shakespeare, *The Tempest,* Act V, Scene I.

"We cannot change anything until we accept it": C. G. Jung, *Modern Man in Search of a Soul*," Psychology Press, East Sussex, UK, 2001, p. 240.

"Radical Acceptance is the willingness": Tara Brach, *Radical Acceptance: Embracing Your Life With the Heart of a Buddha*, Bantam Dell/Random House, New York, 2003, p. 4.

"Be careful in your choice of hypnotists": Sidney Jourard, cited in Ann Faraday, *Dream Power: The Use of Dreams in Everyday Life,* Pan Books, London, p. vi.

"The Rainmaker": in C. G. Jung, *Mysterium Coniunctionis: An Inquiry into the Separation and Synthesis of Psychic Opposites in Alchemy* (1955–56), Vol. 14 of *The Collected Works of C. G. Jung*, trans. by R. F. C. Hull, Princeton University Press, Bollingen Series XX, Princeton, NJ, 1963, 1970, pp. 419–20, fn. 211. Slight modifications have been made for reading purposes.

"The sage manages affairs without action": Lao Tzu, *Tao Te Ching*, *A Source Book in Chinese Philosophy*, ed. and trans. Wing-tsit Chan, Princeton University Press, Princeton, NJ, 1972, Chapter 2, p. 140. See also Chapter 37, p. 158 and Chapter 63, p. 169.

"Any judgment of another person": Marshall B. Rosenberg, *Nonviolent Communication: A Language of Compassion,* PuddleDancer Press, Encinitas, CA, 2002, pp. 141, 142.

can be found in Rosenberg's book, *Nonviolent Communication: A Language of Life*: PuddleDancer Press, 3rd edition, Encinitas, CA, 2015.

"Knowing your darkness": C. G. Jung, letter to Kendig B. Cully, September 25, 1931, *C. G. Jung Letters*, Vol. 1, 1906–1950, eds. Gerhard Adler and Aniela Jaffé, trans. R. F. C. Hull, Princeton University Press, Bollingen Series XCV: 2, Princeton, NJ, 1973, pp. 236–37.

"An inflated consciousness": C. G. Jung, *Psychology and Alchemy*, Vol. 12 of *The Collected Works of C. G. Jung,* trans. R. F. C. Hull, Bollingen Series XX, Princeton University Press, Princeton, NJ, 1968, par. 563.

"The life and strength of our authority": Winston Churchill, qtd. in Jonathan Sandys and Wallace Henley, *God and Churchill: How the Great Leader's Sense of Divine Destiny Changed His Troubled World and Offers Hope for Ours*, Foreword by James Baker III, Tyndale Momentum/Tyndale

House Publishers, Carol Stream, IL, 2015, p. 124. Original source is Richard M. Langworth, ed., *Churchill by Himself: The Definitive Collection of Quotations*, Public Affairs, New York, 2008, p. 76. Churchill made this statement in 1903.

"In a resolute struggle": *The I Ching or Book of Changes*, the Richard Wilhelm Translation rendered into English by Cary F. Baynes, Foreword by C. G. Jung, Princeton University Press, Bollingen Series XIX, Princeton, NJ, 1976, pp. 166–67. The particular hexagram Wilhelm is commenting upon is 43, *Kuai*/Break-through (Resoluteness). A comma has been added after "reasons."

"hatred is a form of subjective involvement": *ibid.*, p. 130. The particular hexagram Wilhelm is commenting upon is 33, *Tun*/Retreat).

"Sleep Like a Baby Tonight": U2, on the album *Songs of Innocence*, Island Records, 2014.

"Hell is empty": William Shakespeare, "I Boarded the King's Ship" soliloquy spoken by Ariel in *The Tempest*, Act 1, Scene 2. Older versions include "Hell is empty, / And all the devils are here" and "Hell is empty, and / All the devils are here."

"When misfortune has spent itself": *I Ching*, p. 96. The particular hexagram Wilhelm is commenting upon is 23, *Po*/Splitting Apart.

"Integration of the unconscious": C. G. Jung, *Symbols of Transformation: An Analysis of the Prelude to a Case of Schizophrenia,* Vol. 5 of *The Collected Works of C. G. Jung*, trans. R. F. C. Hull, Bollingen Series XX, Princeton University Press, Princeton, NJ, 1967, par. 672.

There is a learning theory: On "Four Stages of Competence," *Wikipedia* states the following in the history section: "Management trainer Martin M. Broadwell described the model as 'the four levels of teaching' in February 1969. Paul R. Curtiss and Phillip W. Warren mentioned the model in their 1973 book *The Dynamics of Life Skills Coaching*. The model was used at Gordon Training International by its employee Noel Burch in the 1970s; there it was called the 'four stages for learning any new skill.' Later the model was frequently attributed to Abraham Maslow, incorrectly since the model does not appear in his major works." Further bibliographic information in *Wikipedia* is provided in the reference section.

Epilogue: Globalization and the Yahweh Complex

"When faced with a totally new situation": Marshall McLuhan and Quentin Fiore, *The Medium is the Massage: An Inventory of Effects*, Bantam Books, New York, 1967, pp. 74–75.

unlike Krishna in his tutelage of Arjuna: See the *Bhagavad Gita*, any translation.

Marshall McLuhan . . . coined this term in 1962: McLuhan's first use of the term "global village" in Marshall McLuhan, *The Gutenberg Galaxy: The Making of Typographic Man*, University of Toronto Press, 1962, 1968, p. 31.

"grand and global alliance": John F. Kennedy, Inaugural Address, January 20, 1961, pars. 23, 22. Available at: http://www.bartleby.com/124/pres56.html.

a human population of 9.7 billion by 2050: United Nations, Department of Economic and Social Affairs, June 17, 2019. See https://www.un.org/development/desa/en/news/population/world-population-prospects-2019.html.

"city on a hill": This term was coined by Jesus: "You are the light of the world. A city set on a hill cannot be hid" (Matt. 5:14, RSV). This idea, however, originates with Ezekiel in the sixth century BCE when he gave Jerusalem a new name that would coincide with the construction of the Second Temple: "The name of the city from that day on shall be 'The Lord Is There'" (Ezek. 48:35, NJPS).

Then in the fifth century CE, St. Augustine championed his idea of the "city of God," a beacon of light in contrast to the dark, sinful, and godless "city of man" that typically exists everywhere and that he modeled upon Babylon (see Aurelius Augustine, *The City of God*, Vols. I and II, trans. Marcus Dods, T. & T. Clark, Edinburgh, 1871). It is to be noted that the Book of Revelation's notion of a "New Jerusalem" differs from the above ideas, as it is connected with Armageddon and the Second Coming. It is an eschatological idea, whereas the city of God, in Augustine's words, "sojourns on earth" (Chapter 17 in Book XIX, Vol. II, pp. 326, 327), meaning that it is a possibility available to us here and now.

Appendix I: A List of the Main Features of the Yahweh Complex

"**We are still as much possessed by autonomous psychic contents**": C. G. Jung, "Commentary on 'The Secret of the Golden Flower' " (1957), *Alchemical Studies*, Vol. 13 of *The Collected Works of C. G. Jung*, trans. R. F. C. Hull, Princeton University Press, Bollingen Series XX, Princeton, NJ, 1970, par. 54.

Appendix II: A Partial List of Apocalyptic Songs in Rock 'n' Roll

"**Let the end of the world be inside you**": widely attributed to Eckhart Tolle.

"**Those songs are me going out of my head**": "Ryan Adams–'Hotel Chelsea Nights,'" qtd. in *Don't Forget the Songs 365–Lyrical Explorations from This Writer on the Storms*, October 14, 2012, available at https://dontforgetthesongs365.wordpress.com/2012/10/14/ryan-adams-hotel-chelsea-nights/.

this song is about finding God and "concentrating on the afterlife you would hope for": Chris Cornell, qtd. in blazek, "'The Story Behind: 'Like a Stone,'" Steemit, available at https://steemit.com/music/@blazek/the-story-behind-like-a-stone-by-audioslave.

McCartney stated that it is about the rise and fall of the Roman Empire: See Barry Miles, *Paul McCartney: Many Years From Now*, Henry Holt and Co., New York, 1997.

Late for the Sky, **1974, a concept album described in** *Rolling Stone*: "Late for the Sky," Stephen Holden, *Rolling Stone*, November 7, 1974.

a "bicentennial statement using California as a microcosm": Andrew Vaughan, *The Eagles FAQ: All That's Left to Know About Classic Rock's Superstars*, Backbeat Books, Milwaukee, WI, 2015.

Taupin claims it's about his alienation due to urban life: See Paul Gambazzini, *A Conversation with Elton John and Bernie Taupin*, Flash Books, New York, 1975.

Lennon's screaming in the song . . . has been attributed to his treatment of primal therapy: See Wilfrid Mellers, *Twilight of the Gods: The Music of the Beatles*, Schirmer Books, New York, 1973, pp. 163–65.

"**[It] isn't mine anymore**": Trent Reznor, qtd. in Geoff Rickly, "Geoff Rickly Interviews Trent Reznor," *Alternative Press*, June 26, 2004, available at http://www.theninhotline.net/archives/articles/manager/display_article.php?id=11

"**a reflection of our complex world**": Patti Smith, qtd. in "Patti Smith to Release Banga on June 5," *Cision*, PR News Wire, April 1, 2012, available at https://www.prnewswire.com/news-releases/patti-smith-to-release-banga-on-june-5-145476345.html.

Springsteen described this song as a hymn and as one of his best: *The Howard Stern Interview: Bruce Springsteen*, HBO, November 27, 2022.

Springsteen described this song as a prayer: *ibid*.

told from the perspective of Mary as a mother distressed losing her son: See J-P Mauro, "Bruce Springsteen Sings of Mary's Loss in 'Jesus Was an Only Son," *Aleteia*, June 4, 2018, available at https://aleteia.org/2018/06/04/bruce-springsteen-sings-of-marys-loss-in-jesus-was-an-only-son/.

Devils & Dust, 2005, probably a concept album about the Iraq War: See Amanda London, "Bruce Springsteen's 'Devils & Dust' Lyrics Meaning," *Song Meanings and Facts*, August 11, 2020, available at https://www.songmeaningsandfacts.com/bruce-springsteens-devils-dust-lyrics-meaning/.

a concept album whose title refers to the chair of the psychotherapist: See Paul Lester, "Songs From The Big Chair," *AlbumLinerNotes.com*, available at http://albumlinernotes.com/Songs_From_The_Big_Chair.html.

"I Still Haven't Found What I'm Looking For": Bono described this song as "an anthem of doubt more than faith." Qtd. in "U2's Fifty Greatest Songs," Christopher R. Weingarten et al., *Rolling Stone*, November 30, 2019, song #2. Available at https://www.rollingstone.com/music/music-lists/u2-band-greatest-songs-bono-the-edge-205104/40-201620/.

Index

CPSIA information can be obtained
at www.ICGtesting.com
Printed in the USA
JSHW080455080723
44217JS00001B/6